Essentials of Immigration Law

AILA TITLES OF INTEREST

AILA'S OCCUPATIONAL GUIDEBOOKS

Immigration Options for Physicians

*Immigration Options for Nurses
& Allied Health Care Professionals*

Immigration Options for Religious Workers

Immigration Options for Academics and Researchers

Immigration Options for Investors and Entrepreneurs

STATUTES, REGULATIONS, AGENCY MATERIALS & CASE LAW

Immigration & Nationality Act (INA)

Immigration Regulations (CFR)

*Agency Interpretations of Immigration Policy
(Cables, Memos, and Liaison Minutes)*

AILA's Immigration Case Summaries

CORE CURRICULUM

Selected Fundamentals of Immigration Law

Immigration Law for Paralegals*

*AILA's Guide to Technology and Legal Research
for the Immigration Lawyer*

CD PRODUCTS & TOOLBOX SERIES

AILALink CD-ROM

The AILA Immigration Practice Toolbox

The AILA Litigation Toolbox

Client Brochures (10 Titles)

FOR YOUR CLIENTS

Client Brochures (10 Titles)

*U.S. Tax Guides for Foreign Persons and Those
Who Pay Them, 3 volumes (H-1Bs, L-1s, J-1s)**

TREATISES & PRIMERS

Kurzban's Immigration Law Sourcebook
by Ira J. Kurzban

Professionals: A Matter of Degree
by Martin J. Lawler

AILA's Asylum Primer
by Regina Germain

*Immigration Consequences
of Criminal Activity*
by Mary E. Kramer

Essentials of Removal and Relief
by Joseph A. Vail

Essentials of Immigration Law
by Richard A. Boswell

OTHER TITLES

David Stanton Manual on Labor Certification

*AILA's Global Immigration Guide: A Country-by-
Country Survey*

Immigration & Nationality Law Handbook

*The Visa Processing Guide and Consular
Posts Handbook*

Ethics in a Brave New World

*Immigration Practice Under NAFTA
and Other Free Trade Agreements*

GOVERNMENT REPRINTS

BIA Practice Manual

Immigration Judge Benchbook (Print or CD)

Citizenship Laws of the World

EB-5 Manual

Tables of Contents and other information about these publications can be
found at ***www.ailapubs.com***. Orders may be placed at that site or by
calling 1-800-982-2839.

*An AILA-distributed title

Essentials *of* Immigration Law

Richard A. Boswell

Edited by
Stephanie L. Browning

AMERICAN IMMIGRATION LAWYERS ASSOCIATION
918 F Street NW, Washington, DC 20004 ◆ (202) 216-2400 ◆ *www.aila.org*

This publication is designed to provide accurate and
authoritative information in regard to the subject matter
covered. It is distributed with the understanding that the
publisher is not engaged in rendering legal, accounting, or
other professional service. If legal advice or other expert
assistance is required, the services of a competent professional
should be sought.

*—from a Declaration of Principles jointly adopted by a Committee of the
American Bar Association and a Committee of Publishers*

Printed in the United States of America

ISBN 1-57370-166-1
Stock No. 81-66

To Karen

Summary of Contents

DETAILED TABLE OF CONTENTS

PREFACE

As this book comes closer to being finalized, the debate continues to rage over immigration "reform." For those of us who have spent most of our lives studying immigration law, this debate has been a regular ritual. This year, the "debate" has left many scars. Immigrants are cast by some as the source of all of our greatest fears and failures. On the other hand, for the first time in recent memory, the immigrant not only has acquired a face but a distinctive voice. It is only with the human face of immigration will there be hope that the laws ultimately enacted will be, in fact, just and equitable.

One of the fundamental flaws of our system is the judicially sanctioned notion that there are barely any limits to the congressional power over immigration legislation. It is reinforced by our legal system's reluctance to incorporate international human rights principles as part of our domestic jurisprudence. This leaves us with a situation in which the courts countenance congressional enactments unheard of in any other area of the law.

In the more than 25 years of teaching immigration law in law schools and lecturing on the subject before a variety of audiences, I have been struck by several things. Whether the audience consists of law students, lawyers new to the field, or non-lawyers, they all find themselves in a mental collision between what is expected and what is real. The consequence of this confusion makes it difficult to fully grasp the subject of immigration law. The study of this immigration maze takes one on a labyrinthine journey that often defies all notions of logic or reason.

As I tell my students, the law—and especially immigration law—has a tremendous impact on the lives of human beings. Every rule, every interpretation, every decision to take on or prosecute a case will have a lasting human impact, and that is especially true in immigration law. Therefore, the need to get it right, to do justice is so profoundly important—for, as to paraphrase Justice Louis D. Brandeis, to deport a person is to take away from them all that makes life worth living.

I have endeavored in this book to distill immigration law into its most essential elements and principles. While I have done this to make the subject easily understandable for those who are new to the field, I hope that it also can be a tool for those with much broader knowledge. At the same time, this book is not meant to answer every question but to provide the reader with the basics, to shine the light a little bit brighter to help you get through the labyrinth—a labyrinth described by Justice Irving Kaufman as bearing resemblance to King Minos' ancient Crete. A quick route to finding one's way through this labyrinth are other books published by AILA, most notably *Kurzban's Immigration Law Sourcebook*.

I would be remiss if I did not mention Dale Schwartz as one of the inspirations for doing this book, and to Randy Auerbach who has been there to make it all happen. I am indebted to the watchful eye of so many people who have looked over various drafts and sections of this book. My students, who, over a number of years have been subjected to various versions and have given me helpful suggestions, deserve special thanks. Special thanks are reserved to the library staff at University of California, Hastings—Grace Takatani and Julie Horst, who do not realize how much they helped to locate those hard to find sources. My warmest thanks and appreciation go to Anna Gallagher, Jerome Ingber, Nancy Lawrence, Amy Novick, Michael Olivas, and Jose Pertierra. This book could not have been completed without the *tour de force* of editors from AILA—Stephanie L. Browning, Tatia L. Gordon-Troy, and Silvia S. Wang. Their unlimited patience and wise counsel have greatly improved this project. Finally, to Karen Musalo my life partner, best friend, and inspiration, without whom none of this could have happened. All this being said, I assume full responsibility for any errors that might have found their way into this book.

Richard A. Boswell
June 2006

People often ask me if I can recommend a single comprehensive yet readable book about immigration law. Until now, my answer has been 'no.' But that's changed with the publication of the *Essentials of Immigration Law* by Professor Richard Boswell. This book is ideal for law students, paralegals, law clerks, and laypersons. The word 'essential' in the title is most appropriate, because the book covers everything that one needs to know about this dynamic and complex field of law. Professor Boswell's book is now that one comprehensive yet readable book about immigration law. I recommend it with pleasure.

—*Alberto Manuel Benitez, Professor of Clinical Law and Director, Immigration Clinic, The George Washington University School of Law*

Professor Richard Boswell has written a thoughtful and extremely useful text on the essentials of immigration and refugee law. Drawing from his own excellent scholarship and that of others, he has put together a primer that covers all the bases in this fascinating and important field of study and practice. It is well organized, carefully constructed, and very detailed. I expect to use this often: for convenience, for reference, and for teaching short courses ....

—*Michael A. Olivas, William B. Bates Distinguished Chair in Law, University of Houston Law Center*

Essentials of Immigration Law is geared toward attorneys who are new to the practice of immigration law. The book provides a brief overview of the entire body of immigration law, and does it in a format that is easy to read and comprehend.

—*Nancy M. Lawrence, professorial lecturer and adjunct professor at The George Washington University and American University*

The author, Richard Boswell, takes a remarkably complex area of the law—which many have compared to the even more complicated area of U.S. tax law—and makes it interesting and understandable to the reader. This book is an excellent resource for law students studying immigration law. This text is also 'must have' for lawyers and non-lawyers alike, who are not familiar with U.S. immigration laws but need a handy tool to refer to with questions on this area of the law. The author's many years of both practical and teaching experience come together in this work to produce a much needed resource for all those interested in the immigration and nationality laws and history of the United States.

—*Anna Marie Gallagher, attorney and author,* Immigration Law Service, 2d, *a Thomson-West immigration law treatise*

ABOUT AILA

The American Immigration Lawyers Association (AILA) is a national bar association of nearly 10,000 attorneys who practice immigration law and/or work as teaching professionals. AILA member attorneys represent tens of thousands of U.S. families who have applied for permanent residence for their spouses, children, and other close relatives for lawful entry and residence in the United States. AILA members also represent thousands of U.S. businesses and industries who sponsor highly skilled foreign workers seeking to enter the United States on a temporary or permanent basis. In addition, AILA members represent foreign students, entertainers, athletes, and asylum-seekers, often on a pro bono basis. Founded in 1946, AILA is a nonpartisan, not-for-profit organization that provides its members with continuing legal education, publications, information, professional services, and expertise through its 35 chapters and over 50 national committees. AILA is an affiliated organization of the American Bar Association and is represented in the ABA House of Delegates.

American Immigration Lawyers Association
918 F Street, NW
Washington, DC 20004
Tel: (202) 216-2400
Fax: (202) 783-7853
www.aila.org

CHAPTER 1
The Administration and Development of Immigration Law and Immigrants' Rights Under the Constitution

History repeats itself.
That's one of the things wrong with history.
—Clarence Darrow

THE STUDY OF IMMIGRATION LAW

Mastering the subject matter of immigration law is more difficult than other areas of law. Many immigration provisions created by Congress are inconsistent—be they provisions to allow non–American citizens to enter the United States or provisions to effect their removal.[1] Immigration law is a patchwork of promulgations and represents a tide-like shift between restrictiveness and openness toward immigrants. For instance, Congress, on numerous occasions, has created measures designed to restrict immigration only to follow those with other provisions attempting to alleviate a perceived hardship created by the previous enactment.

Furthermore, Congress has delegated broad and, arguably, unchecked discretion to myriad government agencies to enforce the immigration statutes. The involvement of multiple agencies exacerbates the "patchwork" feel of immigration law, as this decentralization creates further inconsistencies in the implementing regulations.

---

[1] Immigration laws are codified at 8 USC §§1101–1524, primarily the Immigration and Nationality Act of 1952 (INA), Pub. L. No. 82-414, §§101 *et seq.*, as amended. Immigration lawyers usually cite to the INA section rather than the U.S. Code. References in this book, for the most part, cite to both the U.S. Code and the INA. Also, an INA-USC conversion table is provided in the appendix materials.

1

AGENCIES INVOLVED IN THE
ADMINISTRATION OF THE IMMIGRATION LAWS

Focusing on procedure is key to understanding immigration law. However, to understand procedure, one must look at the government agencies that share responsibilities for administering the laws—it is a dizzying distribution of duties among the departments.

Some immigration functions were consolidated with the passage of the Homeland Security Act in 2002,[2] which ensured that most decisions would be made by officers of the Department of Homeland Security (DHS). DHS includes U.S. Citizenship and Immigration Services (USCIS), U.S. Customs and Border Protection (CBP), and U.S. Immigration and Customs Enforcement (ICE).[3] USCIS is responsible for adjudicating immigration benefits such as change and extension of visas; granting Green Cards; naturalization; and asylee/refugee matters. Housed within USCIS is its own appellate body for reviewing visa decisions—the Administrative Appeals Office (AAO).[4] CBP is responsible for all matters relating to the inspection of persons and goods arriving at the border. ICE is responsible for investigating violations of the immigration laws, and enforcing the departure of non–American citizens who are not authorized to be in the United States.[5]

The Department of State (DOS) retains some decision-making authority over visas. When a person applies for a visa, he or she does so before an American consul overseas who is under the authority of the Secretary of State. While the consular officer has the authority to issue the visa, the rules governing the requirements for the visa are promulgated and interpreted by DHS. Prior to the Homeland Security Act, these decisions, when involving overseas visa applicants, were within the exclusive jurisdiction of the consular officer. A Memorandum of Understanding between DHS and DOS attempts to clarify the shared authority

---

[2] Pub. L. No. 107-296, 116 Stat. 2135 (2002).

[3] Following the reorganization, the agency was originally called the Bureau of Immigration and Customs Enforcement (BICE). The name was changed to ICE in September 2003. *See* "BCIS, Other DHS Agencies Plan Name Changes to Replace 'Bureau' with 'U.S.,'" 80 *Interpreter Releases* 1244 (2003).

[4] In some cases, an application will be decided initially by an officer within the Department of Labor (DOL), and any administrative review will be before a special unit within DOL (Board of Alien Labor Certification Appeals—BALCA), not the AAO.

[5] In addition, ICE's Office of Federal Protective Service is responsible for the protection of federal facilities.

in current cases.[6] When a person who has been issued a visa arrives at the border, he or she goes through an inspection process that is totally within the control of DHS officers (usually, a border or customs inspector within CBP).[7]

Most decisions involving removal and appeals are determined within the Executive Office for Immigration Review (EOIR)—the immigration courts. The immigration court system is directed by the Attorney General as part of the Department of Justice (DOJ). EOIR was created in 1983, and although both it and the former Immigration and Naturalization Service (INS) were overseen by DOJ, EOIR was its own separate unit. An alien might appear before an immigration judge (IJ) if he or she either is apprehended by CBP upon entry at the border, or by ICE while inside the country. Any appeal from a decision of the IJ will go to the Board of Immigration Appeals (BIA), which is also part of EOIR and under the jurisdiction of the Attorney General.

Also within DOJ is the Office of Special Counsel, which is responsible for immigration-related employment discrimination. Antidiscrimination claims and cases involving sanctions imposed on employers who illegally hire foreign workers are heard by special administrative law judges within the DOJ's Office of the Chief Administrative Hearing Officer (OCAHO).[8]

Decisions involving the U.S. labor market and workforce issues are made by certifying officers of the Department of Labor (DOL), with adverse decisions subject to administrative review by the Board of Alien Labor Certification Appeals (BALCA).

Finally, a limited set of decisions regarding unaccompanied minors in removal proceedings are made by the Office of Refugee and Resettlement, under the auspices of the Department of Health and Human Services (HHS).[9]

---

[6] 68 Fed. Reg. 56517–19 (Sept. 30, 2003).

[7] Prior to the Homeland Security Act, the customs inspectors were part of the Treasury Department.

[8] *See* 8 USC §1324b, INA §274B.

[9] *See* ORR at *www.acf.hhs.gov/programs/orr.*

A BRIEF HISTORY OF IMMIGRATION

From the Revolution to the Civil War

Up to 1790, there were no direct legal restrictions on immigration. However, during much of this so-called "open door" period, many immigrants encountered difficulties in colonial America.[10] The first federal restrictions on immigration were enacted when Congress passed the Naturalization Act of 1790,[11] which established requirements for citizenship—limiting it to "free white persons"—and further established a two-year waiting period for naturalization (later changed to five years in 1795).[12]

During the early 1800s, a large number of Catholics began immigrating to the United States as a result of economic and political problems in their native lands. Stemming from this, a nativist movement began to develop in the 1830s that advocated immigration restrictions to prevent further arrivals of Catholics. The nativist movement of the 1830s resurfaced in the late 1840s and developed into a political party called the Know-Nothing Party. Adherents in the western United States added an anti-Chinese sentiment to the anti-Catholic rhetoric. Even though these anti-immigrant attitudes did not materialize into federal legislation, many discriminatory local regulations and statutes were enacted.[13]

During the mid-19th century, political unrest and economic difficulties in China caused the large-scale immigration of Chinese to America. Their numbers steadily increased, not only due to the poor state of the Chinese economy, but also to the widespread discovery of gold in California.[14] The economic growth no doubt created a demand for workers from wherever they might come.

---

[10] Gerald Neuman explores the extensive state laws that attempted to restrict the admission of noncitizens. *See* G. Neuman, "The Lost Century of American Immigration Law (1776-1875)," 93 *Colum. L. Rev.* 1833, 1841–44 (1993).

[11] *See* Naturalization Act of 1790, 1 Stat. 103 (1790) (repealed 70A Stat. 644 (1956)). The 1790 Naturalization Act was enacted because the Constitution did not define the word "citizen."

[12] In addition to limiting citizenship to "free white persons," the 1790 Act provided the first uniform system for naturalization and the conferral of citizenship. *See* I. Haney-López, *White by Law: The Legal Construction of Race* 42–46 (1996).

[13] One example was a San Francisco ordinance regulating public laundries and enforced primarily against Chinese-Americans. The regulation was eventually found to be unconstitutional in *Yick Wo v. Hopkins*, 118 U.S. 356 (1886).

[14] See U.S. Commission on Civil Rights, The Tarnished Golden Door: Civil Rights Issues in Immigration (1980) (hereinafter Tarnished Golden Door).

During this century, the Supreme Court handed down some significant decisions regarding immigration and citizenship. In 1849, in *The Passenger Cases*,[15] the U.S. Supreme Court held that the federal power over matters involving foreign commerce was superior to that of the states; specifically, the Court held that a state's imposition of a tax upon noncitizens was unconstitutional. Moreover, the Court held that it was the power of the federal government, not the states, to regulate immigration.

In 1856, during the political battle over slavery, the Supreme Court held that citizenship was not necessarily determined by a person's birth in the United States.[16] In 1868, following the Civil War, the 14th Amendment to the Constitution was ratified, establishing for the first time that "[a]ll persons born or naturalized in the United States and subject to the jurisdiction . . ." were citizens of the United States and were to be accorded "equal protection" of the laws.[17]

Post–Civil War

The post–Civil War era (until the end of the 19th century) witnessed the beginning of federal enactments designed to control the admission of noncitizens in a more systematic way, and, thus, has been described as the "first restrictionist period." The first restrictions provided for the exclusion of convicts and prostitutes.[18] Additional restrictions enacted in 1882 imposed a head tax on "aliens" and provided for the exclusion of "idiots, lunatics," those with various criminal convictions, and persons likely to become a public charge.[19] Many of these restrictions were enacted as a result of racial tensions stemming from the influx of Asians coming to the United States. In 1882, Congress passed the Chinese Exclusion Act[20] (providing for the exclusion of persons from China), which was upheld in 1889 as constitutional, and was enforced for more than 60 years until it was repealed in 1943.[21] Following the Chinese Exclusion Act, additional measures were enacted that controlled the admission of

---

[15] *Smith v. Turner*, 48 U.S. (7 How.) 283 (1849).

[16] *Dred Scott v. Sandford*, 60 U.S. 393 (1856).

[17] *See U.S. Const.*, amend. XIV.

[18] Act of March 3, 1875, 18 Stat. 477.

[19] Act of August 3, 1882, 22 Stat. 214.

[20] 22 Stat. 59, ch. 126 (1882), amended by the Act of July 5, 1884, 23 Stat. 115, ch. 220 (1884).

[21] *See Chae Chan Ping v. United States* (*The Chinese Exclusion Case*), 130 U.S. 581 (1889).

foreign workers by limiting their status to contract laborers: a person's admission would be prohibited if his or her employment would depress the labor market. The Chinese Exclusion Act was strengthened in 1885 and 1887 by the addition of deportation provisions for persons who entered the United States in violation of the contract labor laws.[22]

In 1891, laws were enacted that provided for the inspection and exclusion of persons for reasons of health, crimes, poverty, and polygamy.

Restrictionism—Turn of the Century

From 1900 to 1920, more than 20 million new immigrants came to the United States; this period of immigration was spurred by the increased demand for labor during America's growth in the Industrial Revolution.[23] However, a wide range of immigration restrictions[24] were legislated as a result of such a large number of people immigrating to the United States, as well as to specific incidents, such as the assassination of President William McKinley.[25] These restrictions resulted in the establishment of the Dillingham Commission, which was charged with the task of studying immigration policy. The Dillingham Commission's report, produced in 1911, generated support for restrictive immigration measures leading to legislation enacted in 1917.[26]

In 1917, Congress, over the veto of President Woodrow Wilson, imposed even stricter controls on foreign immigration.[27] Such restric-

---

[22] Act of Feb. 26, 1885, 23 Stat. 332; Act of Feb. 23, 1887, 24 Stat. 414.

[23] This was a period in which the largest number of immigrants came to this country.

[24] Provisions enacted included the exclusion of epileptics, professional beggars, and anarchists. *See* Immigration Act of March 3, 1903, ch. 1012, §2, 32 Stat. 1213, 1214, repealed by Immigration Act of February 5, 1917, ch. 29, §38, 39 Stat. 874, 897. Other provisions included the exclusion of unaccompanied "feeble minded children," persons with tuberculosis, and others whose physical and mental problems might adversely affect their ability to earn a living. *See* Immigration Act of February 20, 1907, ch. 1138, §43, 34 Stat. 898, 899, repealed by Immigration Act of February 5, 1917, ch. 29, §38, 39 Stat. 874, 897.

[25] The assassination of President McKinley in 1902 by Leon Czolgosz, a native born U.S. citizen and self-proclaimed anarchist, catalyzed legislation barring the admission of anarchists and others on ideological grounds. *See* E. Hutchinson, *Legislative History of American Immigration Policy* 423 (1981).

[26] *See* C. Gordon, S. Mailman & S. Yale-Loehr, *Immigration Law and Procedure* §2.02(2) (rev. ed. 2006).

[27] *See* Immigration Act of 1917, Pub. L. No. 64-301, 39 Stat. 874, ch. 29. The 1917 law described those to be kept from admission as persons from the geographic area (with the exception of persons from Japan and the Philippines) stretching from Afghanistan to the Pacific Ocean. Japanese were allowed to come to the United States under what was known as the "Gentleman's Agreement," in which the Japanese government agreed to restrict the issuance of passports to a limited number of its workers. Later, in 1934, after providing independence to the Philippines, legislation was passed that restricted Filipino migration to 50 persons per
continued

tions included laws that created the "Asiatic Barred Zone"—designed to exclude Asians from the United States. The enactments also imposed a literacy requirement. Two years earlier, U.S. leaders had made an unsuccessful effort to exclude all persons of African ancestry.[28]

In an effort to further curtail immigration, Congress, relying on the 1917 restrictions, passed a temporary quota law in 1921.[29] The quota limited the number of persons who could immigrate to 3 percent of that nationality group that had lived in the United States since 1910. (The total annual immigration quota in 1910 was set at 350,000.) At that time, a person from the Western Hemisphere was exempt from the quota if the country of his or her nationality was an independent nation and the applicant had lived in the United States for at least one year. The clear purpose of the 1910 national origin quota was to "confine immigration as much as possible to western and northern European stock."[30]

In 1924, Congress confirmed the 1917 restrictions via the National Origins Quota Act.[31] This act lowered the annual quota of immigrants allowed into the United States to 150,000, and the nationality-based limit was set at 2 percent of the members of that nationality already represented in the United States, according to the 1890 census.[32]

The 1924 act coupled with the Great Depression was extremely effective in curtailing immigration to the United States. In addition, during this period, immigration authorities began deporting Mexican-Americans. Nearly a half-million Mexican-Americans, including U.S. citizens, were deported under a program called the "repatriation campaign."[33]

There was not a great deal of legislation between the time of the National Origins Quota Act of 1924 and the Immigration and Nationality Act of 1952 (discussed *infra*). However, the Alien Registration Act of 1940, otherwise known as the Smith Act, was enacted to increase

---

year. *See* Tydings-McDuffie Act of 1934, Pub. L. No. 73-127, 48 Stat. 459, ch. 84 (1934).

[28] *Tarnished Golden Door, supra* note 14, at 9.

[29] *See* Pub. L. No. 42-5, ch. 8, 42 Stat. 5 (1921).

[30] *Tarnished Golden Door, supra* note 14, at 8.

[31] Pub. L. No. 43-139, 43 Stat. 153 (1924). The 1924 Act made permanent the quotas that had been imposed in 1921. When one looks at current immigration law, one sees its roots in these earlier quotas.

[32] *Id.*

[33] *See Tarnished Golden Door, supra* note 14, at 10 n.51.

governmental powers to protect the country from subversives and criminals.[34] Further enhancing the government's ability to deal with subversives was the enactment of the Internal Security Act of 1950.[35] With the exception of specific post–World War II legislation, most of the immigration laws enacted after the deportation of Mexican-Americans as part of the "repatriation campaign" primarily dealt with issues of security and reflected fears of political instability.

Despite the primarily restrictive laws following World War II, laws were enacted that permitted the admission of nearly 700,000 immigrants, mostly from Europe, including refugees and spouses, children, and fiancées of U.S. servicemen.[36] The United States admitted all of these people without regard to the immigration quotas that had been previously established. While these numbers stand out in contrast to the earlier restrictionist immigration policies, these admissions did not come easily, as evidenced by the significant efforts made by President Dwight D. Eisenhower to secure the admission of Hungarian refugees following the revolt in that country in 1956.[37]

The McCarran-Walter Act of 1952 and Its Aftermath

The comprehensive immigration legislation that forms the core of contemporary immigration law was the McCarran-Walter Act of 1952,[38] otherwise known as the Immigration and Nationality Act of 1952 (INA). It set the framework and structure for modern immigration law by performing the following:

- retaining the 1924 national origins quota, yet establishing a visa allotment preference system based on family relationships and skills necessary to the economy;[39]
- launching an entry procedure;

---

[34] Pub. L. No. 76-670, 54 Stat. 670 (1940). The law was found by the Supreme Court to be applicable retroactively. *Harisiades v. Shaughnessy*, 342 U.S. 580, 593–96 (1952).

[35] Pub. L. No. 81-831, 64 Stat. 987 (1950).

[36] *See* Displaced Persons Act, Pub. L. No. 80-774, 62 Stat. 1009 (1948), as amended by Pub. L. No. 81-555, 64 Stat. 219 (1950). *See also* Fiancées Act, Pub. L. No. 79-471, 60 Stat. 339 (1946); War Brides Act of Dec. 28, 1945, Pub. L. No. 271, 59 Stat. 659.

[37] *See The Hungarian Revolt, October 23–November 4, 1956* (R. Lettis & W. Morris, eds., Scribner 1960).

[38] Pub. L. No. 82-414, 66 Stat. 163 (1952).

[39] Today, these are known as family-based and employment-based preferences (discussed in detail, *infra*, Chapter 5).

- enumerating a list of excludable and deportable individuals; and
- instituting a system of relief from deportation based on familial relationships with U.S. citizens and permanent residents.

The legislation came about as a result of extensive and controversial congressional hearings, and was passed by a large majority over President Harry S. Truman's veto.

Following the enactment of the INA, President Truman established the Perlman Commission on immigration and naturalization. It led to numerous far-reaching proposals for reform, most of which have never been enacted, yet have been revived in current debates on immigration law and policy.[40] The period between 1952 and 1964 (prior to 1965's INA amendments) saw piecemeal legislation that dealt with specific issues, like refugees,[41] registry,[42] judicial review,[43] grounds for inadmissibility and deportation,[44] and relief.[45]

---

[40] *See* Exec. Order No. 10392, 3 CFR §896 (1952). For example, the Perlman Commission recommended the creation of a statutory board of immigration appeals in 1953, and, in 1983, the Attorney General established a separate Board of Immigration Appeals by executive regulation. It also recommended the establishment of a board of visa appeals, which has never been created. The Commission's recommendation that all visa functions be put into a single federal agency was not done, even in the far-reaching Homeland Security Act of 2002.

[41] *See* Refugee Relief Act of 1953, 67 Stat. 400, which was designed to deal with the large numbers of refugees fleeing communist Eastern Europe; 1957 Refugee Escapee Act, Act of Sept. 11, 1957, Pub. L. No. 85-316, §15(c)(1), 71 Stat. 639 (in addition to helping refugees, the 1957 Refugee Escapee Act expanded immigration benefits for adopted and orphaned children and those born out of wedlock to citizens and residents, and expanded waivers of inadmissibility for certain relatives of citizens and residents).

[42] Act of Aug 8, 1958, Pub. L. No. 85-616, 72 Stat. 546 (liberalizing a provision authorizing the granting of residency to certain persons who had been continuously in the United States since June 28, 1940, through "registry").

[43] Act of Sept. 26, 1961, Pub. L. No. 87-301, §5, 75 Stat. 650, 651 (enacting a statute on judicial review permitting the review of deportation orders in the federal appeals courts on petition for review, and limiting the review of exclusion orders to habeas corpus).

[44] Act of July 18, 1956, 70 Stat. 555 (establishing bar to admission and ground of deportability for possession of narcotics).

[45] Act of Sept. 3, 1954, 68 Stat. 1145 (creating exemption from inadmissibility for a petty offense); Act of Oct. 24, 1962, Pub. L. No. 87-885, 76 Stat. 1247 (amendments to the relief of suspension of deportation, creating two categories of persons eligible for relief—criminals and other "bad actors" and all other persons).

1960s Reform—Immigration Act of 1965

In July 1963, President John F. Kennedy proposed reforms that would eliminate the national origin quotas. The proposed legislation sought to remove spouses, minor children, and parents of U.S. citizens and permanent residents from quota restrictions. In place of the National Origins Quota Act of 1924, President Kennedy proposed an immigration system based on skills needed in the United States, family ties to U.S. citizens, and the issuance of immigrant visas based on "priority of registration." President Kennedy's proposals also contemplated the need for flexibility, allowing for adjustment in the numbers of immigrants admitted in a given timeframe, as well as a transition period to deal with the changes that an increased influx of immigrants would have on the rest of the population. With regard to immigrants coming to the United States based on their work skills, the proposal included a preference for immigrants with special skills, and also allowed for some immigrants with lesser skills.

What was ultimately enacted from the broad proposals made by President Kennedy came only after his assassination in the form of legislation signed into law by President Lyndon B. Johnson in 1965, and accomplished the following:

- elimination of the national origins quota system effective June 30, 1968;
- creation of a category of immediate relatives;
- removal of the restrictions relating to persons from Asia and prohibition of discrimination based on race, sex, nationality, place of birth, or residence;
- establishment of an annual quota system outside of the Western Hemisphere of 170,000 and the prohibition of more than 20,000 persons from any single foreign state;
- restriction of Western Hemisphere migration after June 30, 1968, to 120,000;
- reformulation of the preference system based on family relationships and skills in allocating immigrant visas;
- restrictions on Western Hemisphere migration based on skills unless the Secretary of Labor had certified that there were no qualified and available workers, and the employment of the person would not adversely affect the wages and working conditions of U.S. workers at the place where the immigrant intended to work; and

- establishment of a Select Commission on Western Hemisphere Immigration to study and make recommendations by January 1968.[46]

Worldwide Quota, the Refugee Act, and the Select Commission (Late 1970s–Early 1980s)

In 1978, the Eastern and Western Hemisphere separate quotas were eliminated and a new worldwide quota of 290,000 was established. In addition, Congress created the Select Commission on Immigration and Refugee Policy, a commission that would later make major proposals leading to reforms in the 1980s. One of the provisions of the Act of October 5, 1978, was for the adjustment of status of refugees who had been "paroled"[47] into the country prior to September 30, 1980.[48] Numerous other laws were enacted in this same year—from the modification of the U.S. Code to conform with Supreme Court decisions on expatriation, to the prohibition of the admission and the requirement of the expulsion of persons who participated in persecution in association with the Nazi government of Germany during World War II.[49]

In 1980, Congress enacted a comprehensive reform of the laws dealing with the protection of persons fleeing persecution. The Refugee Act of 1980 provided a system for the admission of overseas refugees as well as the adjudication of asylum claims for those at the border or within the United States.[50] Until this act, refugees had been admitted on an ad hoc basis by the Attorney General's power to parole persons into the United States. Refugees had previously been "conditionally" admitted under what was known as the "Seventh Preference" category. The 1980 Refugee Act established a system where the President, in consultation with Congress, would set the numbers of refugees to be admitted from overseas in any given year.[51]

---

[46] Immigration Act of 1965, Pub. L. No. 89-236, 79 Stat. 911.

[47] Parole is a device that allows for a person's physical admission, yet that person is to be treated in a legal sense as if he or she was still at the border seeking admission. *See* 8 USC §1182(d)(5), INA §212(d)(5).

[48] Act of Oct. 5, 1978, Pub. L. No. 95-412, 92 Stat. 907.

[49] *See* Act of Oct. 10, 1978, Pub. L. No. 95-432, 92 Stat. 1046; Holtzman Amendment, Pub. L. No. 95-549, 92 Stat. 2065.

[50] *See* Refugee Act of 1980, Pub. L. No. 96-212, 94 Stat. 102.

[51] *See* B. Hing, *Detention to Deportation: Rethinking the Removal of Cambodian Refugees* 891, 928 (2005).

Other changes in the 1980 legislation included a reduction in the annual immigration quota from 290,000 to 270,000; the restriction of the use of parole in dealing with refugee crises; the removal of ideological limitations on the protection of refugees (previously, only persons fleeing Communism or persons from certain countries in the Middle East could receive protection); and the prohibition against returning a person to a country where his or her life or freedom would be threatened.[52]

In the following year, the Select Commission issued a report of significant recommendations, including: (1) the imposition of sanctions on employers who knowingly hired undocumented noncitizens coupled with a legalization program for persons who had been in the United States illegally before January 1, 1980; (2) an increase in the annual immigration quota from 270,000 to 350,000, with additional increases in the first five years; (3) creation of additional immigration preferences, allowing permanent resident adults to petition for their parents and allowing grandparents and sons and daughters of U.S. citizens to immigrate outside of the quota system; (4) the establishment of a statutory immigration court; and (5) the separation of the enforcement and service functions of the Immigration and Naturalization Service (INS).

The Select Commission had been appointed by President Jimmy Carter and issued its report as the administration of President Ronald Reagan took office.[53] In response to the Select Commission's report, President Reagan established a Task Force that recommended: (1) civil sanctions for employers who knowingly hired undocumented persons; (2) a limited temporary status that could become a permanent residence after 10 years for persons in the United States prior to January 1, 1980; (3) an increase to 310,000 of the annual immigration quota, with Canada and Mexico each granted 40,000 with whatever one did not use to be transferred to the other; (4) expedited exclusion hearings and establishment of special asylum officers, not IJs, to hear asylum claims; and (5) statutory provisions allowing for the interdiction of vessels on the high seas.[54]

---

[52] For an excellent exploration of this legislation, see D. Anker & M. Posner, "The Forty Year Crisis: A Legislative History of the Refugee Act of 1980," 19 *San Diego L. Rev.* 9 (1981).

[53] *See* U.S. Immigration Policy and the National Interest: Staff Report of the Select Commission on Immigration and Refugee Policy (1981).

[54] White House and Dept. of Justice Press Release of July 3, 1981, 58 *Interpreter Releases* 379 (1981).

Enforcement: IRCA and IMFA (Late 1980s)

The reform debate of the 1970s and the work of the Select Commission and Presidential Task Force culminated in a series of laws that attempted to impose still greater controls on immigration. In 1986, two important laws were enacted—the Immigration Reform and Control Act of 1986 IRCA)[55] and the Immigration Marriage Fraud Amendments of 1986 (IMFA).[56] (There also were other enactments that added to the already complex set of laws in this area.[57])

IRCA, also known as the Simpson-Mazzoli or the Simpson-Rodino-Mazzoli bills, provided a blanket amnesty for agricultural workers[58] and others who had been in the United States since 1982. The amnesty provisions granted temporary residence to those who qualified, with the promise of permanent residence after 18 months. At the same time that the law granted legal status, it also set up a system for imposing sanctions on employers who hired persons who did not have permission to work. This created, for the first time, a universal procedure for all persons in the United States—including citizens—to follow in order to work.[59] IRCA also made other changes to the immigration laws, such as the creation of a pilot program for waiver of the visa requirement for persons from certain countries, new restrictions on adjustment of status for certain persons, and the establishment of an office within DOJ to protect against discrimination as a result of the employer sanction provisions of the law.

IMFA established a two-step process for persons seeking status based on marriage, so that a person initially would receive conditional resident status that could be converted to permanent status after two years.[60] IMFA placed a two-year bar on obtaining permanent residency through a marriage

---

[55] Pub. L. No. 99-603, 100 Stat. 3359 (1986).

[56] Pub. L. No. 99-639, 100 Stat. 3537 (1986).

[57] *See, e.g.*, Immigration and Naturalization Amendments of 1986, Pub. L. No. 99-653, 100 Stat. 3655.

[58] The agricultural amnesty program was more generous and easier to qualify for than the amnesty for those present in the United States since 1982.

[59] IRCA requires employers to verify both identity and employment eligibility of every individual hired and to maintain records of the verification. USCIS requires employers to use Form I-9, Employment Eligibility Verification, to comply with the verification requirements. The verification process applies to U.S. citizens (American born or foreign born) and to noncitizens.

[60] Pub. L. No. 99-639, 100 Stat. 3537 (1986).

entered into while the person was in exclusion or deportation proceedings and a five-year bar on a permanent resident's petitioning for a new spouse where he or she had obtained status based on an earlier marriage.[61]

Liberal Reform (Early 1990s)

The period leading up to and including the passage of IRCA had been marked by much legislative activity in the immigration arena. The first major legislation of the 1990s to be passed was the Immigration Act of 1990[62] (IMMACT90)—the first time since the McCarran-Walter Act that Congress attempted to restructure the immigration laws. Where IRCA primarily was an enforcement bill, IMMACT90 focused on channels for legal immigration. Based on the themes of family unity and employment creation, IMMACT90 set worldwide immigration at 700,000. Of the total, 465,000 visas were reserved for family-based immigrant visas, and 140,000 for employment-based immigrant visas, with 65,000 for a new category—diversity visas (a lottery for immigration from underrepresented countries).[63] IMMACT90 established an "employment creation" category by allocating up to 10,000 visas for immigrants who set up businesses in the United States with a capital investment of at least $1 million—or $500,000 if made in a rural or high unemployment area. The law also increased from 5,000 to 10,000 per year the number of asylees who could become permanent residents.[64] IMMACT90 created a new category of O and P visas for persons in the sciences, arts, business, and athletics.[65] IMMACT90 also created Temporary Protected Status, a form of temporary safe haven that had previously only been available in the exercise of the immigration authority's exercise of prosecutorial discretion.[66] Although mainly a liberalization bill, IMMACT90 added two new grounds of aggravated felonies—crimes of violence and money laundering crimes.

---

[61] The five-year bar could be waived upon a showing that the previous marriage had been *bona fide*. The two-year bar could not be waived.

[62] Pub. L. No. 101-649, 104 Stat. 4978 (1990).

[63] Each of these visa categories will be discussed further in Chapter 5.

[64] Distinguish this from overseas refugees for whom there is no quota regarding permanent residency following admission. As mentioned earlier, the number of refugee admissions is set by the President after consulting with Congress.

[65] These visas are discussed in more detail in Chapter 4.

[66] Temporary Protected Status or TPS is for people who would be in danger in their home countries as a result of armed conflict, natural disaster, or other extraordinary or temporary conditions. See 8 USC §1254a, INA §244.

The period from 1991 to 1994 was marked by a flurry of specialized legislation and technical amendments, some of which made significant changes to the law. For example, in 1991, Congress created a special immigration category for persons who served honorably in the U.S. Armed Forces.[67] As a result of the massacres at Tiananmen Square and continuing difficulties in China, laws in 1992 granted special adjustment of status to Chinese nationals from the People's Republic of China who had arrived in the United States by April 11, 1990.[68] Other legislation allowed up to 750 scientists and engineers from the former Soviet Union with expertise in nuclear, chemical, biological, or other high-technology fields to come as immigrants without having a specific job offer.[69] Other laws included broader crime control provisions, created a new nonimmigrant category for counterterrorism witnesses, and immigration relief for immigrant victims of family violence so they would not need their U.S. citizen or permanent resident spouse or parent to petition for them in order to remain in the United States.[70]

RESTRICTION—AEDPA AND IIRAIRA (END OF THE 20TH CENTURY)

From 1996 to the present, there have been more efforts at restricting immigrants' access to the courts and expanding the power to remove them. The early 1990s saw efforts in states like California to limit immigrant access to state education, health, and other programs. During this period, there was increasing suspicion of noncitizens. This was particularly so following the shooting outside CIA headquarters in Langley, Va., in January 1993,[71] and the bombing of the World Trade Center in February 1993.[72]

The first major effort to deal with terrorism was passed in 1996 with the Antiterrorism and Effective Death Penalty Act of 1996 (AEDPA)[73]

---

[67] Armed Forces Immigration Adjustment Act of 1991, Pub. L. No. 102-110, 105 Stat. 555.

[68] Chinese Student Protection Act of 1992, Pub. L. No. 102-404, 106 Stat. 1969.

[69] Soviet Scientist Immigration Act of 1992, Pub. L. No. 102-509, 106 Stat. 3316.

[70] Violent Crime Control and Law Enforcement Act of 1994, Pub. L. No. 103-322, 108 Stat. 1796.

[71] It was reported that a 28-year-old Pakistani living in Virginia opened fire on cars waiting to enter the grounds of the CIA headquarters in Langley. He killed two people, both employees of the agency, and wounded three others. He then fled to Pakistan, where he was captured in 1997. *See www.vpc.org/studies/wgun930125.htm* (last visited Mar. 16, 2006).

[72] "Trade Center Blast Fuels New Immigration Worries," *St. Louis Post Dispatch*, Mar. 14, 1993, at 1A.

[73] Pub. L. No. 104-132, 110 Stat. 1214 (AEDPA).

and later that year with the Illegal Immigration Reform and Immigrant Responsibility Act of 1996 (IIRAIRA).[74] These two acts have been criticized by scholars as some of the most far-reaching and draconian legislation enacted in nearly a century.[75] In AEDPA, Congress established a special deportation procedure for persons who were considered terrorists, an expedited exclusion process to remove certain persons arriving to the United States without the benefit of a hearing, and severely limited judicial review and habeas corpus relief. The statute also expanded the definition of terrorism for purposes of exclusion and deportation, and expedited the deportation procedures for a broad range of crimes.

Congress incorporated into IIRAIRA many of the AEDPA provisions and made even greater changes to the immigration laws. The most significant changes were broadening the definitions of "conviction" and "aggravated felony"; eliminating numerous forms of relief for aliens convicted on aggravated felonies; creating mandatory detention provisions for many aliens with criminal convictions; and limiting judicial review for certain removal orders and petition denials. Additionally, IIRAIRA reformulated the entire framework of removal of foreign nationals, by changing the legal mechanisms on which determination of the grounds of removal (inadmissibility/excludability and removability/deportability) were based.[76] After IIRAIRA, the prior procedures for excludability (a hearing by the government keeping out a foreign national) and deportability (a different hearing by the government to expel a foreign national after he or she already gained admittance) were combined into one "removal" proceeding and only a legal admission (the touchstone on which the grounds are evaluated) would allow a person to face the slightly less stringent deportability (compared to excludabililty/inadmissibility) grounds.

The Nicaraguan Adjustment and Central American Relief Act (NACARA),[77] enacted in 1997, allowed special adjustment of status for Nicaraguans and Cubans who had been in the United States since at

---

[74] Illegal Immigration Reform and Immigrant Responsibility Act of 1996, Division C of the Omnibus Appropriations Act of 1996 (H.R. 3610), Pub. L. No. 104-208, 110 Stat. 3009 (IIRAIRA).

[75] B. Hernandez-Truyol & K. Johns, "Global Rights, Local Wrongs, and Legal Fixes: An International Human Rights Critique of Immigration and Welfare 'Reform'," 71 *S. Cal. L. Rev.* 547, 550 (1998).

[76] A person facing excludability grounds had fewer substantive and procedural rights than someone facing the deportability grounds.

[77] Nicaraguan Adjustment and Central American Relief Act, Tit. II, Div. A, Pub. L. No. 105-100, 111 Stat. 2160 (1997).

least December 1995. It also allowed certain Salvadorans and Guatemalans who had been members of a class action challenging immigration policies as violating their due process, as well as certain Eastern Europeans, to take advantage of pre-IIRAIRA lower burden suspension of deportation relief.[78]

During the following year, Congress passed special adjustment of status legislation for Haitians[79] as a result of criticism for the favorable treatment accorded to Central Americans. At the same time, a law was enacted implementing the United Nations Convention Against Torture, and making certain violators of religious freedom inadmissible to the United States.[80]

Human Rights and Business Efficiency (2000)

In 2000, significant laws that dealt with human trafficking and victims of criminal violence were passed.[81] These laws created a new nonimmigrant T visa to protect trafficking victims and a U visa for those suffering substantial physical or mental abuse as a result of criminal activity. Furthermore, the Legal Immigration Family Equity Act (LIFE Act),[82] enacted in 2000, extended the expanded adjustment of status provisions enacted in 1997 and created a nonimmigrant V visa for spouses and children of permanent residents who, because of immigrant quota backlogs, had been forced to wait for more than four years to receive their status. It also established another nonimmigrant visa (K3) for spouses of U.S. citizens who sought admission while awaiting approval of their immediate relative petitions. The American Competitiveness in the 21st Century Act (AC21)[83] dealt with a number of issues relating to the admission of highly-skilled workers to the United States.

---

[78] The Central Americans were required to have been in the United States and have applied for asylum before April 1990, and the Eastern Europeans to have applied before December 3, 1990.

[79] Haitian Refugee Immigration Fairness Act of 1998, Pub. L. No. 105-277, Div. A, §101(h), Tit. IX, 112 Stat. 2681 (1998) (HRIFA).

[80] International Religious Freedom Act of 1998, Pub. L. No. 105-292, 112 Stat. 2787.

[81] Victims of Trafficking and Violence Protection Act of 2000, Pub. L. No. 106-386, 114 Stat. 1464.

[82] Pub. L. No. 106-553, 114 Stat. 2762; *see also* LIFE Act Amendments, Pub. L. No. 106-554, 114 Stat. 2763.

[83] Pub. L. No. 106-313, 114 Stat. 1251 (2000).

Security (Post-9/11)

Following the terrorists acts of September 11, 2001, Congress enacted the USA PATRIOT Act,[84] which contained numerous immigration provisions. The act tripled the number of border patrol agents and immigration inspectors. It required development of a system for verifying the identity of persons applying for a visa or entering the country, and permitted greater sharing of information between DOS and INS. It also required the Attorney General to develop biometric technology[85] for use at the border. The statute expanded the definition of terrorism to include endorsement of terrorist acts, and applied this definition retroactively. The PATRIOT Act authorized the detention of persons for seven days before deciding whether to charge them, and permitted indefinite detention after securing a removal order.[86]

In the following year, additional security-related immigration provisions were enacted as part of the Enhanced Border Security and Visa Entry Reform Act,[87] which established a number of procedures to improve law enforcement capabilities during the visa issuing and inspection processes. The Homeland Security Act of 2002[88] catalyzed the most significant bureaucratic overhaul in at least a half-century. This act abolished INS and moved most its functions to DHS, dividing its work into three components within DHS—USCIS, CBP, and ICE.

On May 11, 2005, President George W. Bush signed the REAL ID Act of 2005 under the broad umbrella of an antiterrorism measure.[89] REAL ID made broad judicial review and jurisdictional changes. Pursuant to new INA §242, judicial review of removal orders based on consti-

---

[84] Uniting and Strengthening America by Providing Appropriate Tools Required to Intercept and Obstruct Terrorism Act of 2001, Pub. L. No. 107-56, 115 Stat. 272. On March 9, 2006, President Bush signed into law the USA PATRIOT Improvement and Reauthorization Act of 2005, Pub. L. No. 109-177, 120 Stat. 192 (2006).

[85] Biometrics is defined as the science of identifying or authenticating the identity of a living person based on their unique physiological or behavioral characteristics. *See* R. Feldman, "Considerations on the Emerging Implementation of Biometric Technology," 25 *Hast. Communications & Entertainment L.J.* 653 n.1 (2003).

[86] Habeas corpus actions challenging detention survived the USA PATRIOT Act.

[87] Pub. L. No. 107-173, 116 Stat. 543 (2002).

[88] Pub. L. No. 107-296, Tit. IV, Subtitles C-F, 116 Stat. 2135 (2002); Homeland Security Act of 2002 Amendments Act, Pub. L. No. 108-7, 117 Stat. 11 (2003).

[89] Emergency Supplemental Appropriations Act for Defense, the Global War on Terror and Tsunami Relief, Pub. L. No. 109-13 (2005). The legislation was placed in Section 2, Division B, of the Appropriations Act.

tutional or question of law claims is now under direct jurisdiction of the federal appellate courts (formerly, the U.S. district courts had initial jurisdiction of such claims). Moreover, habeas corpus petitioning as a means of review for immigration court-based removal orders was eliminated. However, habeas corpus remains viable for district court review of detention issues and for review of expedited removal orders.

REAL ID also included numerous amendments to judicial review and asylum law. Among the provisions that attempt to raise the standard for asylum and restriction on removal is the requirement that an applicant show that the "central reason" for his or her persecution was or will be on account of one of the five stated grounds.[90] Other provisions allow IJs to require, even of credible asylum applicants, corroborating evidence establishing eligibility unless the applicant does not have the evidence or cannot reasonably obtain it. One of the few noncontroversial provisions was the removal of the 10,000 annual cap on asylees who may adjust to permanent residence status.[91]

IMMIGRANTS AND THE CONSTITUTION

The Constitution establishes citizenship for persons born within the United States who are subject to the jurisdiction of the United States.[92] For individuals not born in the United States, Congress determines who may be admitted and who can be expelled. One of the fundamental principles of immigration law is this plenary power doctrine, which was first articulated in 1889 by the U.S. Supreme Court in the *Chinese Exclusion Case*.[93] The appellant was a U.S. resident from China who had traveled abroad during the time that Congress had enacted the Chinese Exclusion Act of 1882, a statute prohibiting the admission of Chinese to the United States. The appellant argued that the denial of his readmission violated his rights as well as a treaty between the United States and China. The Court held that the *power to determine who could be admitted to the United States rested with Congress and the President*, and that the judicial branch was powerless to review it. The Court further held that this

---

[90] *Id.* at Division B, §101(a)(3). See Chapter 3 for a discussion of the five grounds.

[91] *Id.* at Division B, §101(g).

[92] The 14th Amendment provides that all persons born in the United States and subject to the jurisdiction of the United States are citizens.

[93] *Chae Chan Ping v. U.S.*, 130 U.S. 581 (1889).

power was inherent and essential to the sovereignty held by all nations.[94] Subsequent decisions by the Court extended the holding in the *Chinese Exclusion Case* permitting the retroactive application of the immigration laws,[95] the exclusion of noncitizen immediate relatives of U.S. citizens,[96] and even the long-term detention of noncitizens seeking admission to the United States.[97]

While Congress has broad powers to determine who may be admitted and who may acquire citizenship, this does not mean that noncitizens who seek admission, or who are within the United States have no rights. The legal rights of noncitizens depend on their immigration situation—is the person seeking admission, or physically within the United States, and is the government acting against them to prevent their admission?[98] There is no cognizable constitutional challenge where the immigration power is being asserted against someone seeking admission—this is the plenary power at its core.[99] Congress gives aliens rights via statutes, and the courts' power is, thus, limited to its interpretation of the relevant statute. In comparison, once an individual is admitted to the United States, constitutional rights such as equal protection are implicated. Congress's plenary power over immigration is challengeable when an immigration statute conflicts with a right enumerated or inherent in the Constitution. In addition, this plenary power is only accorded to Congress where it is asserting its authority to control immigration. Where the Congress or Executive branch are acting outside of their authority, and where the courts have jurisdiction, they may go beyond statutory interpretation and decide the actual validity of immigration laws vis-à-vis constitutional rights.

---

[94] *Id.* at 608–09.

[95] *See Knauff v. Shaughnessy*, 338 U.S. 537 (1950).

[96] *See Fiallo v. Bell*, 430 U.S. 787 (1977).

[97] Indefinite detention has long been permitted and was only recently found impermissible on statutory, not constitutional grounds. *See Clark v. Martinez*, 125 S. Ct. 716, 724 (2005). In *Clark*, the Court was following its prior holding in a case also decided on the basis of statutory interpretation. *See Zadvydas v. Davis*, 533 U.S. 678 (2001).

[98] *See Landon v. Plasencia*, 459 U.S. 21, 32 (1982) (lawful permanent resident returning from short trip abroad and placed in exclusion proceedings was entitled to due process under the Constitution); *Rafeedie v. INS*, 880 F.2d 506 (D.C. Cir. 1989).

[99] If the person is seeking an immigration benefit—the right to be admitted and remain in the United States—such a claim is a direct challenge to the nation's sovereignty and the plenary power doctrine.

Courts have further held that the power to control immigration is an incident of national sovereignty and does not rest with the states.[100] The Constitution also extends to Congress the plenary power to determine rules for naturalization, as well as for the acquisition of U.S. citizenship for the children of U.S. citizens born abroad.[101]

While Congress has broad powers to determine who may be admitted as nonimmigrants and immigrants, and who may acquire citizenship, this does not mean that noncitizens seeking admission to, or within, the United States have no rights. The Constitution provides that noncitizens within the United States may not be deprived of their liberty or property without due process of law.[102] It grants *all persons* within the United States certain levels of equal protection under the law;[103] even aliens facing criminal charges are afforded full Fifth Amendment protection.[104] Furthermore, the INA provides procedures and criteria to which the Executive branch is bound for determining which persons may be admitted.

In weighing a constitutional challenge to governmental action, a court, depending on the interests involved and who has acted, has applied a number of legal tests—including a rational basis, intermediate scrutiny, and a strict scrutiny test. Under a rational basis test, the classification must bear a fair and substantial relation to the purpose of the law and must be reasonable and not arbitrary. It is not difficult for the government to withstand a challenge to an immigration statute under the

---

[100] For example, in 1994, California voters enacted Proposition 187, which attempted to deter illegal immigration by among other things, denying public benefits and education to undocumented "aliens" in California. In 1995, a federal court judge ruled that substantial portions of the law were unconstitutional. *See LULAC v. Wilson*, 908 F. Supp 755 (C.D. Ca. 1995) (summary judgment motions), 997 F. Supp. 1244 (C.D. Ca. 1997) (modification of decision in light of Congress's enactment of the Personal Responsibility Act of 1996). The court in *LULAC* only upheld the provision denying access to post-secondary public education and criminalization of false documents.

[101] The naturalization power is found in *U.S. Const.*, art. I, §8, cl. 4. *See* discussion on naturalization in Chapter 7. The courts also have held that Congress has broad powers to set rules for the acquisition of citizenship abroad.

[102] *See Wong Wing v. U.S.*, 163 U.S. 228 (1896).

[103] The 14th Amendment provides that no "State [shall] deprive any person of life, liberty, or property, without due process of law; nor deny to any person within its jurisdiction the equal protection of the laws." *U.S. Const.*, amend. XIV, §1.

[104] *See Wong Wing*, 163 U.S. at 237–38. The Supreme Court has stated that "even aliens whose presence in this country is unlawful, have long been recognized as 'persons' guaranteed due process of law by the Fifth and Fourteenth Amendments." *See Plyler v. Doe*, 457 U.S. 202, 210 (1982).

rational basis test since it is not a rigorous one; a classification could be sustained where there was conceivably a reasonable justification for it.[105] In applying an intermediate level of scrutiny, the governmental objective must be an important one, and there must be a substantial relation between the classification and the governmental objective.[106] Where a classification based on race or national origin is implicated, the court will normally apply a strict scrutiny test.[107]

---

[105] *See, e.g., Fiallo v. Bell,* 430 U.S. 787 (1977); *Kleindeinst v. Mandel,* 408 U.S. 753, 769–70 (1972) (upholding denial of nonimmigrant visa holder who had been invited to speak in the United States on claim that the denial of the visa violated the First Amendment rights of the university professors who had invited the speaker).

[106] For example, a state's effort at restricting access by undocumented school children was found to be in violation of the Constitution using an intermediate scrutiny test. *Plyler v. Doe,* 457 U.S. 202. On the other hand, an immigration statute's gender-based classification that made it more difficult for a father to petition for his child who was born overseas survived intermediate scrutiny. *See Nguyen v. INS,* 533 U.S. 53, 60 (2001). The implication of the immigration power was sufficiently compelling to satisfy this lesser degree of scrutiny.

[107] *Yick Wo v. Hopkins,* 118 U.S. 356 (1886). In *Yick Wo,* the Court found that the petitioner, a citizen of China living in the United States, was denied equal protection guaranteed under the 14th Amendment when the city of San Francisco denied him a permit to operate a laundry, ostensibly because he was Chinese.

CHAPTER 2
Inadmissibility, Deportability, Waivers, and Relief from Removal

It is the spirit and not the form of law
that keeps justice alive.
—*Chief Justice Earl Warren*

OVERVIEW

The power to determine who is eligible for admission and who is permitted to remain in the United States is within Congress's authority and limited only by rules of statutory interpretation.[1] Who may enter or remain in a nation reflects, in part, how the nation sees itself; immigration rules represent what a nation will be in the future, and, hence, are the subject of much debate.[2] Participation in this debate requires a clear understanding of the existing admissibility and deportability categories and the provisions governing them. Admissibility refers to those persons who may be legally admitted to the country and deportability refers to those persons who, after admission or entry, may be removed. Even upon careful review, the reader will find it difficult to see a cohesive pattern in the statutes.

---

[1] As was noted earlier, the broad powers to control immigration law lie with the legislative and not the executive branch. Therefore, there are only two possible arguments that can be raised to challenge the action on the part of an immigration official—either Congress, in enacting the statute, was acting outside of its authority granted under the Constitution, or the agency was acting outside of the authority granted to it under the statute.

[2] One scholar has argued that the reason the United States has had great difficulty in developing a coherent immigration policy is because the choices in developing such a policy tug at the very moral fabric of the nation. *See* L. Fuchs, "Immigration Policy and the Rule of Law," 44 *U. Pitt. L. Rev.* 433, 433 (1983).

The law provides a long list of persons who are either prohibited from entering or are to be removed should their presence be discovered in the United States. The grounds of inadmissibility are laid out at Immigration and Nationality Act (INA)[3] §212(a), and the deportability grounds at INA §237. Each of the grounds was incorporated into the immigration laws as Congress thought of situations calling for the exclusion or removal of a particular group of people. At the same time that the law prohibits the admission and requires the removal of broad categories of persons, there are provisions allowing the waiver of these grounds of inadmissibility and deportability.[4]

The inadmissibility and deportability grounds can be described as falling into seven general categories: (1) health-related; (2) economic; (3) criminal; (4) security and foreign policy; (5) immigration violations; (6) quasi-criminal; and (7) miscellaneous. The deportability grounds nearly mirror the inadmissibility provisions and will be described under a separate section within each of the above six categories.[5] The descriptions later in this chapter give the statute more order and make it easier to understand. That section will explore the grounds of inadmissibility and deportability, as well as the criteria for obtaining waivers from those provisions.

APPLICATION OF THE INADMISSIBILITY AND DEPORTABILITY PROVISIONS

There is often a great deal of confusion between inadmissibility and deportability because of changes made to the immigration law by the Illegal Immigration Reform and Immigrant Responsibility Act of 1996 (IIRAIRA).[6] Current law provides for the "removal" of a wide range of individuals. In this context, removal means the ejection of a person from the United States. Included in the INA is a long list of "inadmissibility" and "deportability" provisions.[7] The deportability provisions are applied

---

[3] Immigration and Nationality Act of 1952, Pub. L. No. 82-414, 66 Stat. 163 (codified as amended at 8 USC §§1101 *et seq.*) (INA).

[4] In addition to the ameliorative forms of relief that may be available, immigration authorities have considerable prosecutorial and other discretionary authority to allow a person to be admitted notwithstanding his or her inadmissibility or to remain even though he or she is deportable. *See Reno v. American-Arab Anti-Discrimination Comm.*, 525 U.S. 471 (1999).

[5] The grounds also are summarized in Charts 1 and 2 at the end of this chapter.

[6] Illegal Immigration Reform and Immigrant Responsibility Act of 1996, Division C of the Omnibus Appropriations Act of 1996 (H.R. 3610), Pub. L. No. 104-208, 110 Stat. 3009 (IIRAIRA).

[7] *See* 8 USC §§1182 and 1227, INA §§212 and 237.

to a person who has been formally admitted to the United States and the inadmissibility grounds are applied to those who have not been legally admitted to the country (or who seek a new status that is the equivalent to a request for "admission). The procedure for ejecting or removing any person, irrespective of whether they have been legally admitted is termed a "removal" hearing. Prior to 1996, the immigration statute provided that questions involving the application of the inadmissibility and deportability provisions were, as a general rule, governed by whether a person had gained entry into the United States.[8] The proceedings for those seeking admission were called "exclusion hearings," and for those who had managed to enter, "deportation hearings." In exclusion hearings, the immigration judge (IJ) determined the applicability of the inadmissibility provisions. In deportation hearings, the IJ would determine the application of the deportability provisions.

With the enactment of IIRAIRA, a different framework was established, at least insofar as the hearing was concerned. Exclusion and deportation hearings are no longer separate and distinct, but are unified as one procedure—a "removal hearing"—for all persons, irrespective of whether the person seeks admission or the government tries to eject him or her following admission. Whether the inadmissibility or deportability provisions are applicable in a given situation will depend on whether an individual has been admitted to the United States or is seeking admission. A person who *has been admitted* faces the deportability grounds, and a person *seeking admission* must overcome the inadmissibility grounds.[9]

In addition to creating a unified procedure for removal, IIRAIRA limited a person's ability to avail him- or herself of constitutional protections by placing persons physically present in the United States in the posture of an applicant for admission.[10] The question of whether a person has made an entry or has been admitted is significant in terms

---

[8] In situations where a person is allowed to physically enter under parole, he or she would be confronted with having to overcome grounds of inadmissibility. Parole is discussed later in this chapter.

[9] The definition of admission is contained in the statute at 8 USC §1101(a)(13), INA §101(a)(13), and will be explored further in this section.

[10] As is explored in greater detail, *infra*, the statute also authorizes the application of expedited removal to certain persons who are unable to prove that they have been in the United States for a certain period of time. *See* 67 Fed. Reg. 68924 (2002); 69 Fed. Reg. 48877 (2004). Under 8 USC §1101(a)(13)(A), INA §101(a)(13)(A), a person not yet "admitted," by definition, remains an applicant for admission.

of constitutional protections. Persons coming into the United States were governed by INA §101(a)(13), which had constitutional protections adhering to them following their "entry." "Entry" has been replaced by "admission"; importantly, "entry" did not carry with it the legal hurdles of the current term "admission." Thus, the substitution of terms attempts to make unavailable certain protections that were previously available to some noncitizens.

Persons seeking admission may not avail themselves of protections of the Constitution. However, once a person is admitted into the United States, the person is considered a "person within the United States" subject to the Constitution, and is entitled to its various protections such as equal protection under the Fourteenth Amendment.[11] The Supreme Court has held on numerous occasions that the Due Process Clause is applicable to "all persons within the United States including aliens, whether their presence is unlawful, temporary or permanent."[12]

Placing a person already present in the United States in the posture of one seeking admission raises a constitutional question—does this person truly seek admission or does he or she fall under the deportability grounds, which are governed by the "person within the United States"-based constitutional protections? Congress, via the 1996 amendments,[13] distinguished between physical and legal presence and, since then, only legal "admission" triggers the constitutionally-subjected deportability grounds (which offer more protection against removal). Moreover, the statute contains provisions that place the burden of proof on the applicant or respondent to show by clear and convincing evidence that he or she is lawfully present based on a prior admission; otherwise, the person must prove that he or she is clearly and beyond a doubt entitled to ad-

---

[11] See Yick Wo v. Hopkins, 118 U.S. 356 (1886) (holding municipal regulation as violative of the Fourteenth Amendment's equal protection clause).

[12] See Zadvydas v. Davis, 533 U.S. 678, 693 (2001); Wing Wong v. U.S., 163 U.S. 228, 238 (1896) (finding the Fifth Amendment's due process clause applicable to the federal government); Hampton v. Wong, 426 U.S. 88, 103 (1976) ("When the Federal Government asserts an overriding national interest as justification for a discriminatory rule which would violate the Equal Protection Clause if adopted by a State, due process requires that there be a legitimate basis for presuming that the rule was actually intended to serve that interest.").

[13] The 1996 amendments are the combined ramifications of IIRAIRA and the Antiterrorism and Effective Death Penalty Act of 1996, Pub. L. No. 104-132, 110 Stat. 1214.

mission.[14] Prior to IIRAIRA, the government had the burden of proof in cases where a person was arrested *within* the United States.[15]

When are the inadmissibility provisions triggered? The issue of inadmissibility arises initially when a person appears before a U.S. consul overseas seeking permission to come to the United States—usually a request for an immigrant or nonimmigrant visa or a parole document (see discussion, *infra*).[16] It arises again when the person arrives at the port of entry (airport, sea port, or land port) seeking admission. At this point, the person is subject to "inspection," whereby a U.S. Customs and Border Protection (CBP) officer considers whether the person is admissible. There are a number of different outcomes to the inspection process— the person can be detained; returned quickly under "expedited removal"; granted "deferred inspection"; paroled; or admitted. Where the person arrives under the Visa Waiver Program, he or she can be summarily denied admission, paroled, or admitted.[17] As long as a person has not been formally admitted into the country, he or she remains subject to the inadmissibility grounds.

Moreover, the question of inadmissibility remains relevant, in certain circumstances, even if the person *initially* is admitted to the United States. For example, if the person later seeks lawful permanent resident (LPR) status, or leaves the United States and attempts to return, or is placed in removal proceedings because the government believes that he or she was inadmissible at the time of the last admission, the person must be prepared to establish admissibility.[18]

What immigration posture triggers deportability? If the person, after initial entry, remains in the United States, there is a presumption that his or her status is lawful, and the government will have the initial burden when challenging the person's status. That is, once admitted, a person can only be removed through the removal process upon a showing of

---

[14] 8 USC §§1229a(c)(2)(A) and (B); INA §§240(c)(2)(A) and (B).

[15] *See, e.g., Zhang v. Slattery*, 55 F.3d 732, 751 (2d Cir. 1995).

[16] *See* 8 USC §§1182(d)(5) and 1229b, INA §§212(d)(5) and 240A(b)(4)(A).

[17] A person who seeks admission under the Visa Waiver Program, who is found inadmissible, and who expresses a desire to apply for asylum will not be subject to expedited removal. *See Matter of Kanagasundram*, 22 I&N Dec. 963 (BIA 1999); 8 CFR §235.3(b)(10).

[18] As will be seen later, "inadmissibility at entry" is a burden that the government must meet since it actually is a deportability provision. The charge means that the government believes that at the time of the person's last admission, the person, in fact, should not have been admitted.

deportability, which has the opposite burden of proof compared to in-admissibility and offers more constitutional protections. This rule is ap-plicable unless on a previous visit to the United States, the person was ordered removed and he or she somehow managed to re-enter the United States.[19] Such an individual does not qualify as "admitted," and such a person may be removed even without the benefit of a full re-moval hearing;[20] this process is called reinstatement of removal.

Returning Lawful Permanent Residents

Pursuant to the 1996 amendments, a person who is a returning LPR will not be treated as if he or she is seeking a new admission if: (1) the per-son has not abandoned the permanent residency; (2) the person's ab-sence did not exceed 180 days; (3) he or she was not engaged in illegal activity following departure; (4) his or her departure was not while under removal or extradition proceedings; and (5) the person is not inadmissi-ble under one of the criminal grounds of inadmissibility, unless he or she was granted a waiver or cancellation relief.[21]

Prior to the 1996 amendments, some returning permanent residents were protected from the inadmissibility provision under the Supreme Court decision, *Rosenberg v. Fleuti*,[22] where the Court held that the grounds of inadmissibility were inapplicable to an LPR who was return-ing from an "innocent casual and brief" trip abroad.[23] The *Fleuti* or re-entry doctrine, as it became known, protected LPRs from being sub-jected to the inadmissibility provisions that were different from the pro-visions for deportability.[24]

---

[19] The statute provides that where a person was previously removed and re-entered illegally, the original removal order may be reinstated and the person again removed. This provision was found to be constitutional. *See Duran-Hernandez v. Ashcroft*, 348 F.3d 1158, 1162–63 (10th Cir. 2003); *but see Morales-Izquierdo v. Ashcroft*, 388 F.3d 1299 (9th Cir. 2004) (invalidating rein-statement procedure as ultra vires in conflict with the INA where order was entered by immi-gration official and not an immigration judge). There is no administrative review of reinstate-ment order. *Matter of G–N–C–*, 22 I&N Dec. 281 (BIA 1998).

[20] 8 USC §1231(a)(5), INA §241(a)(5); 8 CFR §1241.8(a). In addition, under 8 USC §1326(a), INA §276(a), a person may be subject to criminal prosecution for a subsequent attempt to return without having first received permission to do so by the government.

[21] *See* 8 USC §1101(a)(13)(C), INA §101(a)(13)(C). Cancellation of removal is discussed in this chapter, *infra.*

[22] *Rosenberg v. Fleuti*, 374 U.S. 449 (1963).

[23] *Id.* at 461.

[24] Fleuti was homosexual, which was a ground for inadmissibility but not deportability at that time; thus, based on the Court's ruling, he did not need to satisfy an inadmissibility ground *continued*

Whether one of the underlying principles of the *Fleuti* doctrine, that LPRs are entitled to greater protections upon their return to the United States, has survived IIRAIRA still may be in question.[25] While treating certain LPRs as persons seeking re-admission, courts also have acknowledged constitutional concerns, not normally recognized for other returning noncitizens.[26]

Parole

"Parole" is an important concept that allows the physical entry of a person into the United States without considering him or her to actually have been admitted to the country. Thus, parole is a "legal fiction." The use of parole also acts to preclude the person from asserting a legal right to admission even though he or she may be physically within the border of the United States. From its earliest usage in the 19th century, this device has been used as a convenient way to allow otherwise inadmissible persons to be free from detention while their formal admission was under consideration, or to permit them physically to gain admission.

Parole has been used over the years to deal with humanitarian situations, both on a large scale and in individual cases. Since the enactment of the Refugee Act of 1980,[27] the use of parole has been significantly curtailed. That is, one of the reasons for passage of the Refugee Act of 1980 was to regularize the admission process for refugees, which included using refugee visas instead of parole as the preferred way of dealing with a humanitarian crisis.

Pre-Hearing Detention

Beginning in 1988, Congress began to focus a great deal of attention on dealing with noncitizens in the United States who had been convicted of crimes. The Omnibus Anti-Drug Abuse Act of 1988 called for mandatory

---

that would have otherwise rendered him inadmissible.

[25] In *Matter of Collado-Muñoz*, 21 I&N Dec. 1061 (BIA 1997), the Board of Immigration Appeals (BIA) held that the *Fleuti* doctrine was no longer applicable. *See also Tineo v. Ashcroft*, 350 F.3d 382, 397 (3d Cir. 2003) (BIA's interpretation of 8 USC §1101(a)(13)(C), INA §101(a)(13)(C) was entitled to *Chevron* deference).

[26] In *Landon v. Plasencia*, 459 U.S. 21, 32 (1982), the Court, while allowing the application of inadmissibility provisions to a returning LPR, noted that "once an alien gains admission to our country and begins to develop the ties that go with permanent residence his constitutional status changes accordingly." *See also Ferraras v. Ashcroft*, 160 F. Supp. 2d 617, 627 (S.D. N.Y. 2001).

[27] Pub. L. No. 96-212, 94 Stat. 107.

detention of noncitizens, including LPRs, who had been convicted of aggravated felonies.[28] The law, which limited federal court review of mandatory detention, was successfully challenged in litigation following its passage.[29] Laws enacted in 1990 and 1991 restored the right to pre-hearing release under bond for permanent residents and persons lawfully admitted to the United States who were able to show that they were not likely to abscond.[30] In April 1996, however, Congress enacted the Antiterrorism and Effective Death Penalty Act of 1996 (AEDPA),[31] which barred all noncitizens with aggravated felonies or other criminal convictions from pre-hearing release. This resulted in court challenges that found many of the provisions unconstitutional.[32] Congressional bills passed one year later as part of IIRAIRA, however, reinforced the mandatory detention statute and eliminated the possible release of lawfully admitted noncitizens with aggravated felony convictions.[33]

In *Demore v. Kim*,[34] the Supreme Court heard a challenge to the mandatory detention statute by an LPR who had been in custody for six months without the benefit of a bond hearing. The Court held that Kim had not been deprived of his constitutional rights. It distinguished Kim's case from its decisions involving long-term detention of persons who already had their hearing and were awaiting removal (post-hearing detention). In contrast to those cases, Kim had not had his removal hearing and the Court held that the government had a legitimate interest in holding him during the pendency. While there was clear recognition by the Court that an LPR was entitled to constitutional protection, it held that the balance of interests weighed in favor of the government.[35]

---

[28] *See* Omnibus Anti-Drug Abuse Act of 1988, Pub. L. No. 100-690, sub. J, 102 Stat. 4181 (1988); 1988 *U.S. Code Cong. & Admin. News* 5937. Aggravated felonies—which are an immigration term of art—are discussed later in this chapter, at the section on criminal grounds; they are defined at 8 USC §1101(a)(43), INA §101(a)(43).

[29] *See, e.g., Kellman v. Dist. Dir.*, 750 F. Supp 625 (S.D. N.Y. 1990); *Agunobi v. Thornburgh*, 745 F. Supp. 533 (N.D. Ill. 1990); *Morrobel v. Thornburgh*, 744 F. Supp. 725 (E.D. Wa. 1990).

[30] *See* Immigration Act of 1990, Pub. L. No. 101-649, 104 Stat. 4978 (IMMACT90); Miscellaneous and Technical Immigration and Naturalization Amendments of 1991, Pub. L. No. 102-232, 105 Stat. 1733 (1991) (MTINA).

[31] Pub. L. No. 104-132, 110 Stat. 1214 (1996).

[32] *See Grodzki v. Reno*, 950 F. Supp. 339 (N.D. Ga. 1996); *Montero v. Cobb*, 937 F. Supp. 88 (D. Mass. 1996).

[33] *See* 8 USC §1226(c), INA §236(c). The pre-hearing mandatory detention statute was upheld as constitutional by the Supreme Court in *Demore v. Kim*, 538 U.S. 510, 529 (2003).

[34] 538 U.S. 510 (2003).

[35] *Id.* at 522–23. The claim in *Kim* was distinguishable from that made in *Zadvydas v. Davis*, 533 *continued*

Mandatory pre-hearing detention is required under the statute in cases involving persons who are removable on account of criminal activities (more discussion on criminal activity grounds, *infra*), *e.g.*, they are deportable for having committed two or more crimes involving moral turpitude, an aggravated felony, crimes involving drugs or firearms, or a miscellaneous crime under 8 USC §1227(a)(2)(D), INA §237(a)(2)(D). The only exceptions are for certain persons under the Witness Protection Program, or where the individual's release would protect other witnesses. The statute further requires that the Attorney General take into custody noncitizens released from parole, on supervised release, probation, or other custody after October 9, 1998.[36]

Similar detention provisions exist in the case of suspected terrorists. Under 8 USC §1226a, INA §236A, the Attorney General[37] is authorized to detain persons whom he has reasonable grounds to believe are persons described in 8 USC §§1182(a)(3)(A)(i), (A)(iii), or (B); INA §§212(a)(3)(A)(i), (A)(iii), or (B) (persons inadmissible for espionage or terrorism grounds). The Attorney General or the Deputy Attorney General may hold such persons for up to seven days before placing them in removal proceedings or charging them criminally. If a person is subsequently charged with immigration violations and the government wishes to hold the person, there must be periodic review of that person's detention at least every six months.[38] Thus, even if there is no reasonable likelihood of removal, the person may be held as long as he

---

U.S. 678 (2001), where the Court held that the removal statute did not contemplate detention beyond six months from the order of removal.

[36] *Matter of Adeniji*, 22 I&N Dec. 1102 (BIA 1999).

[37] While the Homeland Security Act of 2002, Pub. L. No. 107-296, 116 Stat. 2135, transferred functions of Immigration and Naturalization Service (INS) from the Department of Justice (DOJ) to the Department of Homeland Security (DHS), it did not change every authority-delegation reference in the INA and other laws. Instead, it included a savings provision (§1512(d) of the act) stating that statutory, regulatory, and other references relating to an agency that is transferred to DHS, or delegations of authority that precede such transfer shall be deemed to refer, as appropriate, to DHS (and its officers), or to its corresponding organizational units. Thus, for example, while INA §244 still states that the Attorney General has authority to designate Temporary Protected Status (TPS), that authority has in fact been transferred to the Secretary of Homeland Security, as evidenced by TPS regulations, which are issued by DHS (and not DOJ). *See, e.g.*, 70 Fed. Reg. 1450 (Jan. 7, 2005).

[38] *See Zadvydas*, 533 U.S. at 697 (citing 8 USC §1537(b)(2)(C), INA §507(b)(2)(C)). In *Zadvydas*, the Court stated "[w]e do have reason to believe, however, that Congress previously doubted the constitutionality of detention for more than six months." *Id.* at 701.

or she is determined every six months to pose a threat to the national security or the safety of the community or any person.

Detention of Persons in Removal Proceedings

Perhaps the most important thing for an individual facing detention is whether there is a possibility of release during removal proceedings.[39] Whether there is a reasonable possibility of freedom will depend on whether the noncitizen is seeking admission or has already been admitted. A person seeking admission does not have the right to be free on bond, and, under most circumstances, will face detention pending a determination of admissibility, while a person who already has been admitted must be considered for bond unless he or she meets the above criteria (criminal and terrorism grounds, etc.) for mandatory detention.[40] A final factor affecting whether a person will be detained is whether he or she is subject to proceedings under the 1996 amendments or under the law prior to 1996. A person released from criminal custody after October 8, 1998, is subject to mandatory detention.[41]

Post–Removal Order Detention

While pre-hearing detention has been allowed in many circumstances, post-hearing detention has been treated differently by the courts. In *Zadvydas v. Davis*,[42] a case involving a person previously admitted and ordered deported, the Supreme Court held that the removal statute does not authorize blanket detentions beyond six months. Following *Zadvydas*, the Court, in *Clark v. Martinez*,[43] held that the detention statute could not be interpreted differently in cases involving applicants for admission. In most cases, there is not a great deal of time that passes between an order of removal and the person's actual deportation. The question of post-hearing release only arises when the person is a sus-

---

[39] It is important to note that a removal proceeding can go on for a long period of time. It begins with the charging document called a Notice to Appear (NTA), and concludes only after a final order of removal has issued. A case that remains on appeal to the BIA does not have a "final order" of removal. *See* 8 CFR §1241.1.

[40] 8 USC §1226(a), INA §236(a).

[41] *See Adeniji*, 22 I&N Dec. 1102; *Matter of West*, 22 I&N Dec. 1405 (BIA 2000). For additional information regarding the policies on mandatory detention, see DHS Memorandum, HQDRO 50/10, "Follow Up Implementation of United States Supreme Court Decision in *DeMore v. Kim*" (May 15, 2003), *published on* AILA InfoNet at Doc. No. 03052340 (*posted* May 23, 2003).

[42] *Zadvydas*, 533 U.S. at 697.

[43] 543 U.S. 371 (2005).

pected terrorist or there is no reasonable possibility of deportation because no country will accept the person.

Where the person is suspected of having terrorist ties, the law authorizes post-hearing detention as long as the Attorney General (or his Deputy) certifies that the person poses a national security or safety threat.[44]

Alternatives to Detention

Persons who are subject to detention may be released on bond, under intensive supervision,[45] or if they are seeking admission, they may be paroled into the country.[46] Since persons in the posture of seeking admission have no constitutional rights, they are not constitutionally entitled to release on bond or parole. However, the statute confers authority on the Attorney General to exercise discretion and release persons on bond or parole.[47] At the same time that the statute confers authority, the regulations preclude IJs from hearing bond cases involving persons detained upon arrival.[48]

A bond is cash security posted to ensure that a person will appear at his or her proceedings or will not otherwise abscond. If the person absconds or fails to fulfill the requirement of the bond, termed a "breach of bond," the money is forfeited. The amount of a bond will depend on the underlying facts of a person's case, but, where required, the minimal amount of the bond is $1,500.[49] In the case where a person has been determined to be inadmissible and there are no prospects for removal, he or she may be paroled or detained for an indefinite period—or may move from parole to detention to parole periodically. Bond or parole may be revoked by the government, but the determina-

---

[44] *See* 8 USC §1226a(6) and (7); INA §§236A(a)(6) and (7).

[45] Under the Intensive Supervision Appearance and Electronic Monitoring Device Program (EMD), persons not subject to mandatory detention may be released with an electronic device attached to them, and their movements monitored—the person also is required to make periodic call-ins, and is subject to home visits. The program is operated on a pilot basis in several DHS districts. *See* "Overview of DHS Tethering Program," *published on* AILA InfoNet at Doc. No. 03111240 (*posted* Nov. 12, 2003).

[46] Persons seeking admission could include persons who entered the United States in violation of the immigration laws, since they have not yet been admitted to the country.

[47] *See* 8 USC §1226(a)(2), INA §236(a)(2).

[48] 8 CFR §§1003.19(h)(2)(i)(B) and 1236.1(c)(11).

[49] 8 USC §1126(a)(2), INA §236(a)(2).

tion must not be in violation of the agency's own regulations and is also subject to administrative review.

It was not until the 1980s that detention began to be used on a large scale. Between 1980 and the 1996 amendments, the standards for granting parole were for "emergent reasons" or reasons within the public interest; but parole also served as an alternative to detention as part of exclusion proceedings while an individual's admission request was considered.[50] The 1996 amendments changed the parole standard by requiring "urgent humanitarian reasons" or "significant public interest."[51] By limiting access to parole, the remaining alternative was detention—thus, greatly increasing its use. Moreover, the 1996 amendments further expanded the use of detention by making it mandatory for persons facing removal on grounds of criminal convictions.

Burdens of Proof

Regarding burdens of proof, the first concept to keep in mind is that the immigration laws are only applicable to persons who are not U.S. citizens, described as "aliens" under the INA. Those who are not citizens include LPRs, nonimmigrants, and undocumented persons. Included in the definition of U.S. citizen are all persons born in the United States and subject to U.S. jurisdiction, as well as naturalized citizens.[52] Therefore, in the case of a person present within the United States, the government bears the burden of establishing "alienage,"[53] a fact that may be established relatively easily upon a person's admission to an immigration officer that he or she was born outside of the United States. If the person admits to having been born abroad, the burden effectively shifts to the individual to show the time, place, and manner of legal entry.[54]

Where the person seeks admission, he or she has the burden of proof to show that he or she is either a citizen or not inadmissible under any

---

[50] This is so, even though the statute's language includes "the alien shall be detained for a proceeding under Section 240." *See* 8 USC §1225(b)(2)(A), INA §235(b)(2)(A).

[51] 8 USC §1182(d)(5)(A), INA §212(d)(5)(A).

[52] The phrase "subject to the jurisdiction" is meant to exclude persons born in the United States whose parents are assigned to the United States as diplomats; diplomats are not subject to the jurisdiction of the United States.

[53] *Murphy v. INS*, 54 F.3d 605, 608 (9th Cir. 1995).

[54] *See Manner of Benitez*, 19 I&N Dec. 173 (BIA 1984). Because alienage is jurisdictional, where the person is in the United States, the initial burden will be on the government. *Murphy*, 54 F.3d at 608.

provision of the INA.[55] If the individual presents evidence of citizenship such as a passport, the burden of proof shifts to the government to establish that the person had relinquished or lost his or her U.S. citizenship.

There is a question as to the precise burden of proof applicable in cases involving persons who are in the United States and subject to grounds of deportability. While the INA was amended in 1996 to provide that the government need only establish deportability by "clear and convincing" evidence, the Supreme Court previously held, in *Woodby v. INS*, that the standard must be by "clear, convincing and unequivocal evidence."[56] However, it is clear that the burden is on the government. At the same time, when the government has made out a prima facie case of deportability, the burden of going forward may, in some cases, shift to the person in proceedings to present rebuttal evidence.[57]

IIRAIRA changed the burden of proof for persons charged with not having been admitted or paroled into the United States. Before IIRAIRA, an alien's mere presence would have placed on the government the burden of establishing that the individual was deportable. Since IIRAIRA, once the government proves alienage, the burden is instead on the noncitizen to prove by clear and convincing evidence that he or she is in the United States pursuant to a lawful admission.[58] Failing this, the person must establish that he or she is "clearly and beyond a doubt entitled to be admitted," meaning that none of the grounds of inadmissibility is applicable or that he or she is otherwise entitled to some type of a waiver of the grounds of inadmissibility.[59]

Persons seeking admission must always show that they are clearly and beyond a doubt entitled to admission and are not inadmissible. A person in possession of a valid visa issued by a consular officer is prima facie eligible for admission. In cases where the person is a returning LPR, he or she will bear the burden of proving that he or she meets the definition, so that the person's return will not be treated as a new admission of a returning LPR pursuant to 8 USC §1101(a)(13); INA §101(a)(13).

---

[55] 8 USC §1361, INA §291 (including having the proper travel documents to show permission to be admitted).

[56] 385 U.S. 276, 286 (1966).

[57] *See Matter of Vivas*, 16 I&N Dec. 68 (BIA 1977).

[58] 8 USC §1229a(c)(2)(B), INA §240(c)(2)(B).

[59] 8 USC §1229a(c)(2)(A), INA §240(c)(2)(A).

Expedited Removal

Expedited removal is a special procedure established in 1996 that provides for the removal without a hearing for certain persons who are "arriving" in the United States and seeking admission who the inspecting officer determines to be inadmissible.[60] A person is considered to be "arriving" if he or she has not yet been admitted or paroled; when in transit through the United States; or when being brought to the United States after having been interdicted in international or U.S. waters.[61] Importantly, expedited removal is limited to arriving aliens who arrive without documents, or whose travel documents were obtained through possible fraud or willful misrepresentation. These individuals will be removed without a hearing;[62] furthermore, they are not entitled to release during the process. Expedited removal does not apply to persons who claim to be U.S. citizens or LPRs, or who have been granted refugee or asylum status or have a claim to it. A special clause in the law also exempts Cuban citizens who are seeking admission at an airport.[63]

Persons who fear persecution or torture must express that fear to an immigration inspector and then establish a "credible fear of persecution" to an asylum officer before they will be permitted to apply for asylum or torture relief. If the applicant is unable to make out a case to the officer, that person may request review by an IJ. "Credible fear" is different from "well-founded fear," which is the requirement for qualifying for asylum protection.[64] Credible fear is defined as "[a] significant possibility" that the person "could establish eligibility." Well-founded fear is the standard applied to asylum applicants—whether a reasonable person in the circumstances would have feared harm based on one of the five grounds provided for in the asylum statute.[65] A person who makes out a case for credible fear is placed in a regular removal hearing, and is per-

---

[60] The statute and regulations allow an inspecting officer at a port of entry to make the decision, which is reviewable only by the officer's supervisor. 8 CFR §1235.3(b)(7).

[61] 8 CFR §1.1(q).

[62] Inadmissibility based on 8 USC §§1182(a)(6)(C) and (7), INA §§212(a)(6)(C) and (7).

[63] 8 USC §1225(b)(1)(F), INA §235(b)(1)(F). Although the statute does not mention Cuba by name, it provides that the procedures are not applicable to a person who is a "native or citizen of a country in the Western Hemisphere with whose government the United States does not have full diplomatic relations."

[64] Well-founded fear is discussed in greater detail in Chapter 3.

[65] 8 USC §1101(a)(42)(A), INA §101(a)(42)(A).

mitted to apply for asylum, withholding of removal, and Convention Against Torture protection (each discussed in detail in Chapter 3).

When Congress established expedited removal, it also authorized the Attorney General (later the Secretary of DHS) to apply the procedure to persons who entered *illegally* and who had not been physically present in the United States for more than two years. For example, pursuant to the statute, the Attorney General, in 2002, issued a notice that all persons (except Cubans) found in the United States who had arrived by sea, unless they could prove that they had been in the United States for two or more years, would be treated as "arriving aliens" and, therefore, subject to expedited removal.[66] The 2002 regulation was further expanded by the DHS Secretary, in 2004, to include persons found within 100 miles of the border who could neither establish legal entry nor prove that they had been in the United States for at least two years.[67]

Whether a person will be subject to expedited removal may depend on the specific facts of the case. For example, one court has held that several persons who had been granted "advance parole"[68] into the United States and later found to have obtained their status by fraud, were improperly placed in expedited removal proceedings.[69] The district court reasoned that persons who had been granted advance parole were not "arriving aliens" as contemplated within the expedited removal statute, and that persons within the United States could not be deprived of their rights without some type of hearing.[70]

---

[66] 67 Fed. Reg. 68924 (2002).

[67] 69 Fed. Reg. 48877 (2004).

[68] Advance parole is a benefit that allows a person previously admitted to the United States to leave the country for a short period of time and return to continue processing whatever application that was pending at the time of his or her departure. *See* INS Operations Instruction 212.5(c); 8 CFR §212.5(f).

[69] *See American-Arab Anti-Discrimination Comm. v. Ashcroft*, 272 F. Supp. 2d 650, 669 (E.D. Mich. 2003) (citing *Rosales-Garcia v. Holland*, 322 F.3d 386, 409 (6th Cir. 2003)); *see also Matter of S–O–S*, 22 I&N Dec. 107 (BIA 1998) (for description of advance parole criteria in the Ninth Circuit).

[70] It should be noted further that this is the only case to hold expedited removal inapplicable.

Regular Removal Hearing[71]

The procedures to be followed in regular removal hearings are set forth in 8 USC §1229, INA §239. Jurisdiction with the immigration court is commenced by the government filing a Notice to Appear (NTA), or Form I-862, by personal service, by mail, or with a respondent's counsel.[72] If the person fails to appear, an *in absentia* hearing can take place, but only if there was personal service on the respondent or a responsible adult at his or her home.[73] The substance of the NTA provides notice to the person of his or her rights, the nature of the proceedings, and the allegations to which the person will have to respond. It sets forth the government's reasons for commencing the proceeding and states when and where the hearing will be (which must not be sooner than 10 days from the notice). The NTA also informs the respondent that he or she is required to immediately provide the government with an address and phone number, and that an *in absentia* order will be entered if he or she fails to appear.

The NTA is in English[74] and contains the following information:

- nature of proceedings;
- legal authority under which proceedings are conducted;
- acts alleged to be violations of law;
- section of INA allegedly violated;
- notice of right to representation (at no expense to the government);
- notice that the individual will be given a list of legal service organizations;
- notice of change of address requirement (failure to give correct address or change of address alleviates notice requirement);
- time and place of the hearing;
- consequences for failing to appear for hearing—removal *in absentia* under INA §240(b)(5) (note: an individual is ineligible for future forms of relief for a period of 10 years under INA

---

[71] For in-depth analysis of removal hearings, see J. Vail, *Essentials of Removal and Relief: Representing Individuals in Immigration Proceedings* (AILA 2006) (hereinafter Vail). Visit the AILA Publications website at *www.ailapubs.org* for more information or to see a table of contents.

[72] 8 CFR §1003.13.

[73] *In absentia* proceedings against minors are not proper. *See Matter of Gomez-Gomez*, 23 I&N Dec. 522 (BIA 2002). In cases of incompetents and minors under the age of 14, service is made upon the person with whom the incompetent or minor resides. 8 CFR §103.5a(c)(2)(ii).

[74] The NTA only need be issued in English.

§240(b)(7) if the individual was given oral notice of the time and place of the hearing and is ordered removable *in absentia*);

- name, alias, address, telephone number, and "A" number of individual.[75]

The hearing is conducted before an IJ—an employee of DOJ's Executive Office of Immigration Review (EOIR). The judge has the authority to administer oaths, receive evidence, interrogate, examine, and cross-examine witnesses.[76] The judge may issue subpoenas and has the power to sanction any action in contempt of his or her proper exercise of authority. While the respondent has the right to representation, the government will not provide counsel.[77] Strict rules of evidence are not followed in these hearings, and evidence will be admitted as long as it is probative and would not be fundamentally unfair to allow its admission.[78] A record of the proceedings is kept on tape, and if the respondent or witnesses are not English-speaking, a verbatim translation is made in order to ensure that there is a complete record in English of their testimony and statements.[79] At the conclusion of the hearing, it is common for the IJ to immediately decide the case and issue a decision. In more complicated cases, the judge will adjourn the proceedings and issue a written decision. An appeal of the decision must be made within 30 calendar days.[80]

---

[75] 8 USC §1229(a)(1), INA §239(a)(1).

[76] Hearings may be conducted telephonically by consent. 8 USC §1229a(b)(2), INA §240(b)(2). The statute also authorizes hearings to be held by video conference. 8 USC §1229a(b)(2)(A)(iii), INA §240(b)(2)(A)(iii). While hearings held telephonically or by video conference can raise serious questions about their fundamental fairness, no court since the passage of IIRAIRA has found them to be so flawed as to nullify a removal order. *See Beltran-Tirado v. INS*, 213 F.3d 1179, 1186 (9th Cir. 2000) (holding that telephonic testimony of out-of-state witness did not violate respondent's right to cross-examination); *Rusu v. INS*, 296 F.3d 316, 322–24 (4th Cir. 2002) (the court, while finding serious problems with video conference proceeding, found that the respondent was not prejudiced).

[77] 8 USC §1362, INA §292.

[78] *Exeagwuna v. Ashcroft*, 325 F.3d 396, 405 (3d Cir. 2003). *See also* 8 USC §1229a(c)(3)(A), INA §240(c)(3)(A).

[79] Translation also is important to make sure that the respondent understands the nature of the proceedings as well as questions posed to him or her by the judge.

[80] 8 CFR §1003.38(b). For more on appeals, see Chapter 6.

Summary Removal for Non–LPR Aggravated Felons

Under 8 USC §1228(b), INA §238(b), there is a summary procedure used to adjudicate cases involving persons who are not LPRs deportable for aggravated felonies. The proceedings are not presented to an IJ, but instead to a DHS officer.[81] The respondent is served with notice and has 10 days to respond, and must be afforded an opportunity to inspect the evidence and answer the charges. The regulations do not require that the proceedings be conducted in the respondent's language. Since an aggravated felon is barred from all forms of relief other than under the Convention Against Torture, the only questions are whether the underlying crime is an aggravated felony or if the person in proceedings is eligible for relief under the Convention Against Torture.[82]

While this summary removal procedure has been upheld as constitutional, there is some question whether in certain unique situations the aggravated felon might be able to qualify for some forms of *discretionary* relief.[83] For example, depending on when the person was convicted, the person might be able to avail him- or herself of cancellation of removal under the pre-1996 statute.[84] In addition, depending on a person's immigration status, and whether he or she was an applicant for admission, he or she might be eligible for a waiver. Federal habeas corpus review of summary removal determinations is available at the federal circuit courts.[85]

Terrorist Removal Hearing

Under AEDPA, Congress created a special procedure for the removal (after admission) of foreign terrorists, defined as persons who have engaged in, or are engaged, or after admission engage in a terrorist activity.[86] Removal is accomplished through the institution of proceedings in

---

[81] *See* 8 CFR §§238.1, 1238.1. The principal requirement under the regulation is that the deciding officer may not be the same one who issued the notice to appear. 8 CFR §§238.1(a), 1238.1(a).

[82] 8 CFR §§208.31, 1208.31.

[83] *U.S. v. Benitez-Villafuerte*, 186 F.3d 651 (5th Cir. 2002).

[84] *See INS v. St. Cyr*, 533 U.S. 289 (2001). *See* related discussion, *infra*.

[85] *Id. See also* discussion in Chapter 7 on the REAL ID Act of 2005, Emergency Supplemental Appropriations Act for Defense, the Global War on Terror, and Tsunami Relief, 2005, Division B, Pub. L. No. 109-13, 119 Stat. 231 (May 11, 2005) (REAL ID Act). While the REAL ID Act removes statutory and nonstatutory habeas claims, there is an argument that constitutional claims would not be precluded.

[86] *See* 8 USC §1227(a)(4)(B)(iii), INA §237(a)(4)(B)(iii). "Terrorist activity" is broadly defined at 8 USC §1182(a)(3)(B)(ii), INA §212(a)(3)(B)(ii), and can include the endorsement or encouragement of others to endorse terrorist activity, the solicitation of funds, or the provision of
continued

a special court composed of five federal district court judges appointed by the Chief Justice of the United States.[87] This court only hears terrorism cases. Proceedings are initiated by the government's filing of a petition, which states the facts and circumstances upon which the government relies to establish probable cause that the person is a terrorist physically present in the United States, and states the reasons that removal is necessary for purposes of national security.[88] The application is submitted *ex parte* and under seal to the special court.

A public hearing is conducted and the person charged is entitled to "reasonable notice" of the "nature" of the charges against him or her.[89] In the case of indigency, the person may have appointed counsel. In the case of LPRs, the rules provide for a panel of appointed counsel with security clearances.[90] Classified information may be used to support a deportation order, and the respondent is entitled to review an "unclassified summary" of the evidence prepared by the government.[91] However, the judge shall examine *ex parte* the classified information, and the Federal Rules of Evidence will not apply in the proceedings.[92]

The government must prove by a preponderance of the evidence that the accused is subject to removal because he or she is an alien terrorist.[93] Both the government and the accused may appeal the decision to the U.S. Court of Appeals for the D.C. Circuit by filing a notice of appeal within 20 days of the order of removal.[94] A decision on the appeal must be made by the appellate court within 60 days and is based on the record of the court below and the briefs submitted. Questions of law are reviewed *de novo*, and findings of facts may only be set aside if they are "clearly erroneous."[95] The respondent may not be deported pending his or her appeal to the D.C. Circuit. However, if the removal order is

---

support. The terrorism definition was expanded at Sec. 103 of the REAL ID Act of 2005, *supra* note 85. *See* USC §1182(a)(3)(B), INA §212(a)(3)(B).

[87] 8 USC §1533(a), INA §502(a).

[88] *See* 8 USC §§1532 and 1533; INA §§502 and 503.

[89] 8 USC §§1534(a)(2), and (b), INA §§504(a)(2) and (b).

[90] 8 USC §1534(e)(3)(F), INA §504(e)(3)(F).

[91] 8 USC §1534(e)(3)(A), INA §504(e)(3)(A).

[92] *Id.*; *see also* 8 USC §1534(h), INA §504(h).

[93] 8 USC §1534(g), INA §504(g).

[94] 8 USC §1535(c), INA §505(c).

[95] 8 USC §1535(a)(3), INA §505(a)(3).

affirmed, it may be enforced unless the individual is able to obtain a stay from either the D.C. Circuit or the U.S. Supreme Court.

As the preceding description demonstrates, the terrorist removal procedures include a number of elaborate measures to safeguard the rights of persons subject to grounds of removal relating to terrorism. Interestingly, there have not been any documented cases of the terrorist removal procedures being used.[96]

GROUNDS OF INADMISSIBILITY AND DEPORTABILITY AND WAIVERS[97]

While the inadmissibility and deportability grounds are presented in a list, it should be understood that when a person seeks admission, or the government attempts to make its case for deportability, there can be multiple bases for removal. Frequently, the Immigration and Customs Enforcement (ICE) attorney can allege numerous grounds of inadmissibility and/or deportability. In this chapter, the grounds are listed by category, with a discussion of each category's application to inadmissibility and deportability, followed by the relevant waiver, if any, for each ground.

With respect to waivers, some general points should be kept in mind. Waivers presented here relate to provisions in the statute itself that confer authority on the government to set aside or ignore a ground of inadmissibility or deportability. There are many forms of waivers that are available for immigrants; however, the broadest waivers—including the security grounds—are available for nonimmigrants (persons in the United States for short-term stays) seeking admission.[98] A waiver should be distinguished from relief from removal. Waivers may be sought when a ground of inadmissibility or deportability arises including while he or she is in removal proceedings.[99] However, relief from removal can only be sought from the IJ in a removal hearing, which allows the indi-

---

[96] See D. Steinbock, "Data Matching, Data Mining and Due Process," 40 Ga. L. Rev. 1, 73 n. 324 (2005).

[97] See Charts 1 and 2 in this chapter for grounds of inadmissibility and deportability, and waivers.

[98] See 8 USC §1182(d)(3)(B), INA §212(d)(3)(B). Under the REAL ID Act, the waiver for the terrorist grounds of inadmissibility is within the sole and unreviewable discretion of the Secretaries of State and Homeland Security. See REAL ID Act, supra note 85, §104.

[99] For example, an applicant who is seeking a visa overseas before a U.S. consul may seek a waiver of a relevant ground of inadmissibility. In addition, waivers often are sought in conjunction with other forms of immigration benefits, such as an immigrant or nonimmigrant visa or adjustment of status.

vidual facing removal to obtain or preserve permanent residency and thereby terminate the case against him or her. These forms of relief will be discussed in a separate section. Most waivers are discretionary, in the sense that while there are specific family relationships or other criteria that need to be established, the government is not required to grant the waiver in all cases.

The general criteria used in the exercise of discretion have been established by case law and require a balancing of positive and negative factors—*i.e.*, a balancing of equities. The positive factors include, but are not limited to: (1) the person's family ties in the United States; (2) how long the person has lived in the United States, especially if his or her residence began when the person was very young; (3) the evidence of hardship that the person and/or the person's family will experience as a result of the separation if removal occurs; (4) the person's employment, especially if it presents a stable history; (5) property or business ties in the United States; (6) value, service, and ties to the community; and (7) evidence of good moral character before, and especially following the disqualifying event.[100]

The negative factors include, but are not limited to: (1) the egregiousness of the underlying circumstances that rendered the person inadmissible or deportable; (2) the nature, seriousness, and recency of any criminal record; and (3) other evidence of bad moral character or undesirability for permanent residency.[101]

Health-Related Grounds

Inadmissibility. Persons who have a communicable disease of public health significance, who have not been immunized from certain diseases, who are HIV positive, or who have psychological problems that might render them dangerous to others or to themselves are inadmissible pursuant to the health-related grounds at 8 USC §1182(a)(1)(A), INA §212(a)(1)(A). In determining the application of the health-related grounds of inadmissibility, DHS relies on the determination of U.S. Public Health Service doctors (under the auspices of the Department of Health and Human Services (HHS)), whose certification is dispositive. An adverse determination, or Class "A" certification, may be re-

---

[100] *See Matter of Marin*, 16 I&N Dec. 578 (BIA 1978).
[101] *Matter of Tijam*, 22 I&N Dec. 408, 412 (BIA 1998).

viewed by a panel of physicians, and the applicant may bring his or her own medical expert to present information.[102] Also inadmissible on health-related grounds are drug abusers, defined as persons who engage in nonmedical use of a substance listed in §202 of the Controlled Substances Act[103] (not including single use or experimentation).[104]

Deportability Provisions. The immigration laws do not provide for the removal of a person for health-related reasons, but there is a deportability ground for an individual who—within five years of admission—becomes a public charge from causes that arose following their entry.[105]

Waivers. There is no waiver for an individual found to be inadmissible as a drug abuser. A person who is inadmissible because of a communicable disease may obtain a waiver if he or she is the spouse, parent, unmarried son or daughter, or the minor unmarried adopted child of a U.S. citizen or LPR, or person issued an immigrant visa.[106] The vaccination requirement may be waived according to regulations issued by the HHS Secretary where the vaccination would not be medically appropriate, or where it might be contrary to the person's religious beliefs or moral convictions.[107] Similarly, the mental or physical disorder clause may be waived at the discretion of DHS in consultation with the HHS Secretary, including the possible requirement of the posting of a bond.[108] Most persons who have family members in the United States who are LPRs or U.S. citizens, or who are accompanying a family member who is an admissible immigrant, may qualify for a waiver of these grounds of inadmissibility and deportability. The waiver is discretionary, so U.S. Citizenship and Immigration Services (USCIS) may require that the person also show that he or she has sufficient medical insurance to cover the cost of care should it become necessary. Refugees and asylees seek-

---

[102] Class "A" certifications are described at 42 CFR §34.2(d), and are medical determinations that the applicant has a communicable disease of public health significance or a physical or mental disorder or behavior that poses a threat to the property, safety, or welfare of the person or others as described in 8 USC §1182(a)(1)(A), INA §212(a)(1)(A). The review procedures are described at 42 CFR §34.8.

[103] Title II of the Comprehensive Drug Abuse Prevention and Control Act of 1970, Pub. L. No. 91-513, 84 Stat. 1255.

[104] A person investigated as a possible drug abuser will likely also be investigated as someone who may be inadmissible under the criminal grounds.

[105] 8 USC §1227(a)(5), INA §237(a)(5).

[106] 8 USC §1182(g), INA §212(g).

[107] 8 USC §1182(g)(2), INA §212(g)(2).

[108] 8 USC §1182(g)(1)(C), INA §212(g)(1)(C).

ing adjustment of status to permanent residency may obtain a waiver of the health-related grounds for humanitarian purposes, family unity, or when otherwise in the public interest.[109]

Criminal Grounds[110]

What Is a Conviction for Purposes of Inadmissibility and Deportability?

As a general matter, for the definition of conviction for immigration purposes to be met, there must be a final judgment of guilt.[111] A great deal of controversy has circulated around what constitutes a conviction under the INA as it relates to a variety of state deferred adjudication or ameliorative statutes. The 1996 amendments attempted to deal with deferred adjudications[112] entered on or after September 30, 1996. A person will be viewed as having been convicted if a judge or jury has found the person guilty, or if the person entered a guilty or *nolo contendere* plea and the judge has entered some form of punishment, penalty, or restraint on the person's liberty. Therefore, a state program in which the person admits to the factual predicates of a crime and is then granted probation, which after its successful completion results in the conviction being set aside would still amount to a conviction under the INA. A similar result occurs where the conviction is later vacated or expunged based on completion of a rehabilitation program.[113] However, where a conviction has

---

[109] 8 USC §1159(c), INA §209(c).

[110] For in-depth discussion on the criminal grounds of inadmissibility and deportability, see M. Kramer, *Immigration Consequences of Criminal Activity: A Guide to Representing Foreign-Born Defendants* Second ed. (AILA 2005) (hereinafter Kramer). See the AILA Publications website at *www.ailapubs.org* for more information and to see a table of contents.

[111] 8 USC §1101(a)(48), INA §101(a)(48); *Perez v. Elwood*, 294 F.3d 552, 561–62 (3d Cir. 2002). The formal judgment of guilt incorporates the definition found in the Federal Rules of Criminal Procedure R.32(d)(1), which provides that a judgment of conviction must set forth the plea, verdict or findings, the adjudication, and the sentence. If the defendant is found not guilty or for any other reason is entitled to be discharged, judgment must be entered accordingly. The judgment must be signed by the judge and entered by the clerk.

[112] Deferred adjudications commonly occur under state rehabilitation statutes where final sentencing is delayed for the completion by the defendant of certain requirements such as treatment or community service, at which time a final determination will be made. *See, e.g.,* Texas Code of Crim. Pro. art. 42.12, § 5.

[113] *See In re Marroquin-Garcia*, 23 I&N Dec. 705 (BIA 2005).

been vacated on the merits (for either substantive or procedural defects), it cannot be used for either inadmissibility or deportability grounds.[114]

The Board of Immigration Appeals (BIA), in *Matter of Roldan*,[115] took the position that a state rehabilitation of a person's conviction that did not result in vacating the decision on the merits or on a constitutional or statutory ground would be considered a conviction for purposes of meeting the INA definition, thus, making a person inadmissible or deportable. The Ninth Circuit, in *Lujan-Almendariz v. INS*,[116] held that a person whose offense qualified for treatment under the Federal First Offender Act,[117] but who was convicted and had his or her conviction expunged under state rehabilitative statutes, could not be removed based on those offenses. Following *Lujan-Almendariz*, the BIA, in *Matter of Salazar*,[118] refused to apply *Lujan* outside of the Ninth Circuit. However, if a person's conviction is vacated outside of a rehabilitative statute, it may still be sufficient and the conviction cannot be used to remove the person.

Juvenile adjudications do not constitute convictions triggering inadmissibility or deportability under the INA.[119] In essence, according to the BIA, juvenile delinquency proceedings are not criminal proceedings and acts of juvenile delinquency are not "crimes" within the meaning of the INA. A noncitizen's juvenile convictions will be evaluated under standards set by the Federal Juvenile Delinquency Act under 18 USC §5031–50. However, a juvenile tried as an adult will not be treated as a youthful offender and the conviction will trigger deportability or inadmissibility.[120]

Inadmissibility. These grounds of inadmissibility prohibit the admission of persons with certain criminal records. The INA prohibits the admission of persons who have committed or admit to the commission of acts (including attempts or conspiracy) that constitute the essential elements of a crime involving moral turpitude (CIMT) or a violation of (state, federal, or foreign) laws relating to a controlled substance.[121] Ex-

---

[114] *See Matter of Pickering*, 23 I&N Dec. 621 (BIA 2003).

[115] 22 I&N Dec. 512 (BIA 1999).

[116] 222 F.3d 728 (9th Cir. 2000).

[117] 18 USC §3607.

[118] 23 I&N Dec. 223 (BIA 2002). The BIA's position has been supported in other circuits. *See, e.g., Acosta v. Ashcroft*, 341 F.3d 218 (3d Cir. 2003); *Gill v. Ashcroft*, 335 F.3d 574 (7th Cir. 2003).

[119] *Matter of Devison-Charles*, 22 I&N Dec. 1362 (BIA 2001).

[120] *Vieira Garcia v. INS*, 239 F.3d 409 (1st Cir. 2001).

[121] 8 USC §1182(a)(2)(A)(i), INA §212(a)(2)(A)(i).

empted from this definition are "petty offense" exceptions—situations in which the person committed only one CIMT where: (1) the person was under the age of 18 when the crime was committed, and was released from confinement more than five years prior to the date of the application for admission; or (2) the maximum penalty for the crime did not exceed one year in prison and the person was not sentenced to a term of imprisonment of more than six months.[122] Any person convicted of more than one crime (even if the crime did not involve moral turpitude) where the aggregate sentence of confinement actually imposed was five years or more is inadmissible.[123]

In order for mere *admission* of certain acts to be sufficient to cause inadmissibility, the acts admitted to must constitute all of the essential elements of the crime. Furthermore, the applicant's admission to the crime must have been made voluntarily and knowingly; and the person must have been given a definition including the essential elements of the crime.[124]

Crimes Involving Moral Turpitude

A CIMT defies any absolute definition, but has been described as a crime that has a *mens rea* requirement and involves conduct that is inherently base or vile, and contrary to the accepted rules of morality—essentially a crime that is *per se* or intrinsically wrong.[125] While CIMTs often involve evil intent, a finding that the crime does not require evil intent does not render it outside the CIMT definition.[126] As one court has stated, "[a] crime involving the willful commission of a base or depraved act is a crime involving moral turpitude, whether or not the statute requires proof of evil intent."[127] In sum, the analysis requires a review of the criminal statute under which the person was convicted to determine if the acts evidenced an intrinsically bad act or something contrary to the existing moral standards.

---

[122] 8 USC §1182(a)(2)(A)(ii), INA §212(a)(2)(A)(ii). This is known as the "petty offense" exception.

[123] 8 USC §1182, INA §212(a)(2)(B).

[124] *See Matter of K*, 7 I&N Dec. 594 (1957); 9 FAM 40.21(a) N5.1.

[125] *Matter of L–V–C–*, 22 I&N Dec. 594 (BIA 1999); *Matter of Tran*, 21 I&N Dec. 291 (BIA 1996); *Matter of Danesh*, 19 I&N Dec. 669 (BIA 1988).

[126] *Matter of Torres-Varela*, 23 I&N Dec. 78, 83 (BIA 2001).

[127] *Gonzalez-Alvarado v. INS*, 39 F.3d 245, 246 (9th Cir. 1994).

Controlled Substances

Controlled substances offenses are defined in 21 USC §802 and include attempts as well as conspiracy to commit such offenses. The drugs are listed in §§802 and 812 of Title 21 and this ground includes other drugs designated by the Attorney General.[128]

The statute also allows a finding of inadmissibility where a consular or ICE officer has "reason to believe" that a person is a trafficker or knowing assister, abettor, conspirator, or colluder in trafficking in any controlled substance.[129] This does not require a conviction. Even the setting aside of a conviction might not preclude the government from denying the person's admission. In addition, the spouse or offspring of the offender could be found inadmissible if that person obtained financial or other benefits from the illegal activity within the previous five years and knew, or reasonably should have known that the benefit was from such activity.[130]

Other Criminal-Related Provisions

Similar provisions allow the government to prohibit the admission of persons whom it has reason to believe have engaged in, or are engaged in, or seek to engage in money laundering;[131] prostitution or commercialized vice;[132] who have asserted immunity from prosecution;[133] or are "significant traffickers" in persons.

Deportability Provisions. The grounds of deportability for criminal offenses at INA §237(a)(2)(C) cover more types of crimes than do the grounds of inadmissibility. Like inadmissibility grounds, the deportability provisions apply to individuals convicted of CIMTs, multiple criminal convictions, and controlled substance violations. Additionally, deportability grounds attach to crimes of domestic violence, firearms convictions, and, most importantly, aggravated felonies. Unlike the criminal grounds of inadmissibility, admission to crimes or acts that constitute the elements of a crime is not sufficient to meet the criminal grounds of deportability; a conviction of the underlying crime must be established.

---

[128] 21 CFR §1308.1, schedules I–V.
[129] 8 USC §1182(a)(2)(C)(i), INA §212(a)(2)(C)(i).
[130] 8 USC §1182(a)(2)(C)(ii), INA §212(a)(2)(C)(ii).
[131] 8 USC §1182(a)(2)(I), INA §212(a)(2)(I).
[132] 8 USC §1182(a)(2)(D), INA §212(a)(2)(D).
[133] 8 USC §1182(a)(2)(E), INA §212(a)(2)(E).

Aggravated Felony

Some of the more controversial provisions added to the immigration laws have been those dealing with aggravated felonies.[134] The aggravated felony provisions were first incorporated into the INA in 1990, and were further broadened in IIRAIRA. An LPR or any other noncitizen convicted of an aggravated felony is deportable, regardless of whether the person has left the United States since obtaining status. A person convicted of an aggravated felony will not be able to avail him- or herself of a waiver of deportability grounds or relief from removal. If the aggravated felon is deported after having been granted LPR status, he or she will not later be eligible for re-admission.[135] The definition of an aggravated felony is very broad and includes, but is not limited to crimes involving rape, sexual abuse, illicit trafficking in a controlled substance, money laundering, many firearm offenses, crimes of violence, theft offenses for which the term of imprisonment imposed is at least one year, and fraud or deceit crimes exceeding $10,000. Aggravated felonies are defined in the statute at 8 USC §1101(a)(43), INA §101(a)(43), and are incorporated into the deportability provisions at 8 USC §1227(a)(2)(A)(iii), INA §237(a)(2)(A)(iii). (A complete analysis of the aggravated felony provisions is beyond the scope of this discussion.)

To get a sense of the breadth of issues involved in interpreting whether a specific crime constitutes an aggravated felony, consider that a crime need not be a *felony* under state or federal law to be considered one for immigration purposes under 8 USC §1101(a)(43), INA §101(a)(43).[136]

Another area generating a great deal of controversy is the meaning of "crime of violence" in the context of determining whether a specific crime meets the aggravated felony definition. The BIA's standard for determining "crime of violence" looked at the generic nature of the offense as opposed to focusing on the intent and or recklessness element (if one ex-

---

[134] "Aggravated felony" is a term of art defined by INA §101(a)(43). What crimes constitute an aggravated felony is an area of law in flux. Several federal court and BIA precedent decisions have addressed the issue; most of these cases involve "crimes of violence" under INA §101(a)(43)(F) and "drug trafficking" crimes under INA §101(a)(43)(B). There are, however, more than 20 different types of aggravated felonies defined at INA §101(a)(43). To further complicate matters, an aggravated felony need not be "aggravated" and often is not a "felony."

[135] *See* 8 USC §1182(h), INA §212(h).

[136] *See, e.g., Matter of Small*, 23 I&N Dec. 448 (BIA 2002); *U.S. v. Marin-Navarette*, 244 F.3d 1284 (11th Cir. 2001). For a thorough analysis of the jurisdictional difficulties of labeling a crime as an aggravated felony, see Kramer, *supra* note 110, at 12–22.

isted) necessitated in the criminal statute.[137] In *Leocal v. Ashcroft*,[138] however, the Supreme Court construed the statute as requiring a review of the elements and nature of the offense of conviction rather than the facts of the crime.[139] In so doing, in this case, the Court held that a DUI conviction under a Florida statute that did not require any particular mental state with respect to the use of force against another person, was not a "crime of violence" within the meaning of 18 USC §16(b), and, thereby, not an aggravated felony under 8 USC §1101(a)(43)(F), INA §101(a)(43)(F).

Crimes Involving Moral Turpitude

A person may be deported for a CIMT if the crime was committed within five years of his or her admission—or 10 years if the person was granted permanent residence as the provider of essential information to law enforcement under 8 USC §1101(a)(15)(S), INA §101(a)(15)(S)[140]— and the crime could have carried a sentence of imprisonment of one year or more.[141] Under 8 USC §1227(a)(2)(A)(i)(I), INA §237(a)(2)(A)(i)(I), one looks to when the crime was committed, rather than to when the person was convicted—even though a conviction is necessary to trigger deportability. As for what constitutes the "admission" when there have been multiple admissions, the Ninth Circuit has held that the criminal act must have occurred within five years from the person's *last* admission in order for it to be applicable.[142]

A person also is deportable at any time after admission if he or she has been convicted of two or more CIMTs not arising out of a single scheme of criminal misconduct.[143] The burden is on the government to show that the two separate crimes were not part of the same criminal scheme. The BIA's position is that a "single scheme" means a lesser offense within the same crime; the Ninth and Third Circuits, however, focus on how the crimes were conceived and planned in order to deter-

---

[137] *See Matter of Palacios*, 22 I&N Dec. 434, 436 (BIA 1998); *Matter of Ramos*, 23 I&N Dec. 336 (BIA 2002); *U.S. v. Lucio-Lucio*, 347 F.3d 1202 (10th Cir. 2003) (Texas conviction was not an aggravated felony because it did not require intentional conduct).

[138] 543 U.S. 1 (2004).

[139] *Id.* at 7.

[140] *See* discussion of "S" visa at Chapter 4.

[141] 8 USC §1227(a)(2)(A)(i), INA §237(a)(2)(A)(i). This provision applies to persons whose proceedings commenced after April 24, 1996.

[142] *Shivaraman v. Ashcroft*, 360 F.3d 1142 (9th Cir. 2004). The alternative interpretation would allow counting from when the person became an LPR.

[143] 8 USC §1227(a)(2)(A)(ii), INA §237(a)(2)(A)(ii).

mine if they were part of a single scheme.[144] Under this provision, it does not matter what the sentence was for, or whether the second crime was a misdemeanor, so long as it involved moral turpitude. A conviction on foreign soil cannot provide the basis for deportability because the crime must have been committed *after* entry.

Firearms Offenses

A person is deportable if he or she is convicted of any law regarding the purchase, sale, offering for sale, exchange, use, owning, possessing, or carrying of any weapon, part, accessory of a weapon or destructive device as defined in 18 USC §921(a).[145] 8 USC §1227(a)(2)(C), INA §237(a)(2)(C) is broad and could include an offense that might not result in incarceration.[146] Where firearm possession was a separate element of an offense in furtherance of a crime, the deportability provision was triggered.[147]

Controlled Substances

Similar to the inadmissibility provisions regarding controlled substances, the penalties for the deportability grounds are severe. Unlike the inadmissibility provisions that do not require a conviction, a person must at least be convicted of a crime involving a controlled substance, even if the conviction was outside the United States.[148] The definition of controlled substance is the same as in the inadmissibility provisions, in that they are governed by Section 102 of the Controlled Substances Act. Exempted within the definition of controlled substance for deportability purposes is a single conviction for simple possession of 30 grams or less of marijuana.[149] Similar to the inadmissibility provisions, the deportability statute makes drug abusers and addicts subject to removal.[150]

---

[144] *See Gonzalez-Sandoval v. INS*, 910 F.2d 614 (9th Cir. 1990); *but see Matter of Adetiba*, 20 I&N Dec. 506 (BIA 1992).

[145] 8 USC §1227(a)(2)(C), INA §237(a)(2)(C).

[146] *Lemus-Rodriguez v. Ashcroft*, 350 F.3d 98 (7th Cir. 2003) (person convicted under Illinois law for reckless discharge of a firearm on New Year's Eve).

[147] *Matter of Lopez-Amaro*, 20 I&N Dec. 668 (BIA 1993), *aff'd*, 25 F.3d 986 (11th Cir. 1994).

[148] 8 USC §1227(a)(2)(B)(i), INA §237(a)(2)(B)(i).

[149] *Id.*

[150] 8 USC §1227(a)(2)(B)(ii), INA §237(a)(2)(B)(ii).

Other Deportable Offenses

A person also may be deportable if he or she is convicted: (1) under the Foreign Agents Registration Act;[151] (2) under the Trading with the Enemy Act;[152] (3) under the Selective Service laws; (4) under the Alien Registration Act;[153] (5) for a violation of the neutrality laws; (6) for submitting false information in registration; (7) for violating travel restrictions during war or national emergency; (8) for threats against the President, espionage, sabotage, or sedition; (9) for crimes involving domestic violence or stalking, or violation of a protective order (whether it was imposed by a civil or criminal court);[154] or (10) for high speed flight from an immigration checkpoint under 18 USC §758.

Waivers. The following grounds of deportability are not waivable: aggravated felonies or deportability for convictions under the Foreign Agents Registration Act;[155] the neutrality laws;[156] Trading with the Enemy Act;[157] the Selective Service laws;[158] the Alien Registration Act;[159] convictions for submitting false information during registration under the law and for violating travel restrictions during war;[160] threatening the President, espionage, sabotage, or sedition;[161] or crimes involving domestic violence or stalking or violation of a protective order.[162]

The broadest waiver of criminal grounds of inadmissibility is the §212(h) waiver.[163] Persons may obtain this waiver upon a showing of extreme hardship,[164] or if either 15 years have passed since the crime was committed or the crime was related to prostitution offenses that occurred within the 10 years prior to admission or application (if the pros-

---

[151] 22 USC §611.

[152] 8 USC §1227(a)(2)(D), INA §237(a)(2)(D).

[153] Pub. L. No. 76-670, 54 Stat. 670 (1940).

[154] 8 USC §1227(a)(2)(E), INA §237(a)(2)(E).

[155] 22 USC §611 *et seq.*

[156] 18 USC §960 (Neutrality Act).

[157] Trading with the Enemy Act of 1917, 50 USC App. 1 *et seq.*

[158] Selective Service Act, 50 USC App. 451 *et seq.*

[159] Alien Registration Act of 1940, Pub. L. No. 76-670, 54 Stat. 670 (codified as amended at scattered sections of 8 USC and 18 USC.

[160] 8 USC §1185, INA §215.

[161] 18 USC §871.

[162] 8 USC §1227(a)(2)(E), INA §237(a)(2)(E).

[163] 8 USC §1182(h), INA §212(h).

[164] 8 USC §1182(h)(1)(B), INA §212(h)(1)(B).

titution offense occurred more than 10 years before the application for visa, admission, or adjustment, it is not even a ground of inadmissibility).[165] A person who is a battered spouse or child eligible for self-petitioning also may be granted this waiver.[166] Where the waiver is sought based on the passage of 15 years, the person also must show that admission would not be contrary to the national welfare, safety, or security, and that he or she has been rehabilitated.[167] The extreme hardship basis for the waiver requires a showing that the person is the spouse, parent, son, or daughter of a U.S. citizen or LPR, and that the family member would suffer extreme hardship if the person was denied admission. Extreme hardship is defined narrowly.[168] Regulations that are based on the discretionary aspect of the waiver provide that in cases where the applicant committed violent or dangerous crimes, there must be a showing of "extraordinary circumstances" to overcome the presumption of denial.[169]

This waiver is not available for persons convicted of murder or criminal acts involving torture, or for crimes involving controlled substances—with the exception of a single conviction involving simple possession of marijuana of 30 grams or less.

In writing this statute, Congress has set up a scheme that allows non–LPRs seeking admission an opportunity to obtain a waiver of their crimes, even if they amount to aggravated felonies, while not allowing the same for LPRs.[170] Specifically, the final paragraph of 8 USC §1182(h), INA §212(h) states, "[n]o waiver shall be granted under this subsection in the case of an alien who has previously been admitted to the United States as an alien lawfully admitted for permanent residence." Whether this distinction amounts to a possible denial of equal protection as between LPRs and non–LPRs remains to be seen.[171] In any event,

---

[165] The statute provides a waiver if "the activities for which the alien is inadmissible occurred more than 15 years before the date of the alien's application for a visa, admission, or adjustment of status." *See* 8 USC §1182(h)(1)(A)(i), INA §212(h)(1)(A)(i).

[166] 8 USC §1182(h)(1)(C), INA §212(h)(1)(C).

[167] 8 USC §§1182(h)(1)(A)(ii) and (iii), INA §§212(h)(1)(A)(ii) and (iii).

[168] *Matter of Ngai*, 19 I&N Dec. 245 (1984) (requires showing of great and actual prospective injury).

[169] 8 CFR §212.7(d); *see also Matter of Jean*, 23 I&N Dec. 373, 383 (Att'y Gen. 2003).

[170] While non–LPRs are subject to inadmissibility for criminal convictions, there is no equivalent aggravated felony bar to admission as there is in the deportability provisions.

[171] Thus far, such challenges based on the 1996 amendments have not been successful. *See, e.g.,* continued

LPRs may take advantage of §212(h) through a form of relief from re-moval called re-adjustment of status, whereby they can request "admis-sion" (which will not invoke the aggravated felony definition) even if already an LPR if they leave the country and then arrive at a port of entry, request adjustment of status in conjunction with the §212(h) waiver (to waive the crime) and if granted, based on discretion, the dis-qualifying grounds are waived (this is risky, as it is based on discretion, but has been successful if the equities balance in favor of the respon-dent).[172]

Another waiver for criminal grounds exists for refugees and asylees seeking adjustment of status to permanent residency. They may obtain a waiver from most of the criminal grounds of inadmissibility for humani-tarian purposes, to ensure family unity, or when otherwise in the public interest.[173] The grounds excepted are those dealing with drug traffickers. Aggravated felons are ineligible for asylum.

Security and Foreign Policy Grounds

As noted earlier, the great majority of our modern immigration law traces its origin to 1952, a period in U.S. history when communism and similar political ideologies were viewed as the threats of the time. Today, we are living in a period in which the overwhelming fear is of terrorism coming from abroad and from within the United States. Many of the grounds of inadmissibility and deportability regarding security and for-eign policy reflect ideological fears of the past as well as the contempo-rary fears of terrorism.

Inadmissibility. The grounds for inadmissibility for security-related reasons pursuant to INA §212(a)(3) are quite expansive, and include general security grounds (espionage, sabotage, and illegal export of sensi-tive information, goods, and technology),[174] terrorism,[175] and Commu-nist membership or membership in a "totalitarian" political party.[176] The

---

Taniguchi v. Schultz, 303 F.3d 950 (9th Cir. 2002); *Moore v. Ashcroft,* 251 F.3d 919 (11th Cir. 2001); *Lara-Ruiz v. INS,* 241 F.3d 934, 947 (7th Cir. 2001); *but see Beharry v. Reno,* 183 F. Supp. 2d 584 (E.D. N.Y. 2002), *judgment rev'd on other grounds,* 329 F.3d 51 (2d Cir. 2003); *Francis v. INS,* 532 F.2d 268 (2d Cir. 1976).

[172] *See* Kramer, *supra* note 110, at 225. *See also* discussion in Chapter 5.

[173] 8 USC §1159(c), INA §209(c).

[174] 8 USC §1182(a)(3)(A)(i)(I), INA §212(a)(3)(A)(i)(I).

[175] 8 USC §1182(a)(3)(B), INA §212(a)(3)(B).

[176] 8 USC §1182(a)(3)(D), INA §212(a)(3)(D).

grounds also cover those whose admission is deemed to be contrary to the national interest vis-à-vis foreign policy interests.[177] Also inadmissible is a subcategory of persons who have caused harm to others, including Nazis or persons who have committed genocide,[178] violators of religious freedom,[179] Haitian nationals connected with human rights violations,[180] aiders and abettors of the Colombian insurgency,[181] and persons who have been involved in the establishment or enforcement of population control policies.[182]

As with drug traffickers and money launderers, the inadmissibility provisions regarding espionage and terrorism do not require more than that a government official "knows or has reasonable grounds to believe" that the person participated or will participate in the prohibited activity.[183]

In the case of terrorism, the broad bar encompasses membership in a terrorist organization, incitement of terrorism, the persuasion of others to support terrorism, endorsement of terrorism, the solicitation of funds, or the commission of acts that provide material support of a broad nature.[184] The provision also bars the spouse or child of a person found inadmissible if the activity occurred in the last five years, unless the spouse or child was not aware of or could not reasonably have been expected to know of the activity.[185]

Strict enforcement of the foreign policy grounds is often balanced against politics. For example, a person otherwise inadmissible for security reasons may be coming to the United States by invitation to address a domestic group sympathetic with his or her cause, or merely espouses controversial views that are at odds with those of the U.S. government.

---

[177] 8 USC §1182(a)(3)(C)(i), INA §212(a)(3)(C)(i).

[178] 8 USC §1182(a)(3)(E), INA §212(a)(3)(E).

[179] 8 USC §1182(a)(2)(G), INA §212(a)(2)(G).

[180] *See* Omnibus Consolidated and Emergency Supplemental Appropriations Act of 1999, Pub. L. No. 105-277, §616, 112 Stat. 2681 (1998) (prohibits the use of funds to issue visas to these persons).

[181] *See* Military Construction Appropriations Act, 2001, Pub. L. 106-246, §3205, 114 Stat. 511, 576 (2000) (prohibits the use of funds to issue visas to these persons).

[182] *See* Consolidated Appropriations Act, 2000, Pub. L. 106-113, §801(a), 113 Stat. 1501, 1501A-468 (1999) (prohibits the issuance of visas to these persons).

[183] 8 USC §§1182(a)(3)(A) and (B)(i)(II), INA §§212(a)(3)(A) and (B)(i)(II).

[184] 8 USC §1182(a)(3)(B)(i)(I)–(VIII), INA §212(a)(3)(B)(i)(I)–(VIII).

[185] 8 USC §§1182(a)(3)(B)(i)(IX) and 212(a)(3)(B)(ii), INA §§212(a)(3)(B)(i)(IX) and 212(a)(3)(B)(ii).

Restricting the admission of such a person implicates the free speech and associational interests of persons in the United States, thereby implicating the First Amendment.[186] The statute requires the Secretary of State, who makes the determination, to timely notify the chairs of the Senate and House Judiciary and Foreign Relations Committees of each case of inadmissibility for foreign policy reasons, and provide a basis for the determination.[187] The statute also exempts persons who are candidates for election from being excluded on the foreign policy basis during the period immediately preceding the election.[188] Thus, the foreign policy grounds are amenable to many exceptions.

Also prohibited under 8 USC §1182(a)(3)(D)(i), INA §212(a)(3)(D)(i) is the admission of immigrants who are or who have been members of the Communist or "any other totalitarian" party. A person is not inadmissible under this ground if his or her membership was involuntary, while under the age of 16, or necessary to secure employment or necessities.[189] If the membership preceded the application as an immigrant by two years (or five years, if the person was a member of a party that controlled the government), and the consular officer or Attorney General is satisfied that the individual is not a threat to the United States, then the person is not inadmissible.[190]

Persons who participated in the Nazi persecutions from March 23, 1933, to May 8, 1945, under the direction of or in association with the Nazi government of Germany (or any government in an occupied area) are inadmissible.[191] One court has held that the participation must not have been involuntary.[192] With respect to the commission of genocide, the United States, as a signatory to the International Convention on the Prevention and Punishment of Genocide, is prohibited from admitting persons who have engaged in acts committed with the intent to destroy, in whole or in part, a national, ethnic, racial, or religious group.[193] Per-

---

[186] See J. Scanlan, "Aliens in the Marketplace of Ideas: The Government, the Academy and the McCarran-Walter Act," 66 *Tex. L. Rev.* 1481 (1988).

[187] 8 USC §1182(a)(3)(C)(iv), INA §212(a)(3)(C)(iv).

[188] 8 USC §1182(a)(3)(C)(ii), INA §212(a)(3)(C)(ii).

[189] 8 USC §1182(a)(3)(D)(ii), INA §212(a)(3)(D)(ii).

[190] 8 USC §1182(a)(3)(D)(iii), INA §212(a)(3)(D)(iii).

[191] 8 USC §1182(a)(3)(E)(i), INA §212(a)(3)(E)(i).

[192] *Petkiewytsch v. INS*, 945 F.2d 871 (6th Cir. 1991); *but see Maikovskis v. INS*, 773 F.2d 435 (2d Cir. 1985).

[193] *See* Convention on the Prevention and Punishment of the Crime of Genocide, Dec. 9, *continued*

sons (and their immediate family) who, while serving as governmental officials, were responsible for—or carried out during the 24 months preceding their application for admission—acts that constitute particularly severe violations of religious freedom as defined in the International Religious Freedom Act of 1998 are inadmissible.[194] Severe violations include arbitrary prohibitions, restrictions, punishment, forced labor, and other acts because of a person's religious beliefs.

Deportability. The security and foreign policy grounds of deportability at 8 USC §1227(a)(4), INA §237(a)(4) are similar to the inadmissibility provisions. Like the inadmissibility provisions, a person may be deportable if he or she has engaged in any activity that violates laws relating to the export of goods, technology, or sensitive information—even if his or her acts do not amount to espionage.[195] A person also may be deportable for criminal activity that endangers the public safety and national security, or for activity that has as its purpose the overthrow of the U.S. government by force, violence, or other unlawful means.[196]

The terrorism provisions of the deportability statutes are wholly based on those of the inadmissibility statutes, making deportable anyone who meets 8 USC§§1182(a)(3)(B) or (F), INA §§212(a)(3)(B) or (F).[197] The foreign policy grounds for deportability are similar to the inadmissibility provisions. The deportability provisions regarding Nazis, or persons who have engaged in genocide, do not require that the person (Nazi) have misrepresented his or her past in securing admission.[198]

Waivers. There are broad waivers that may be granted at the sole discretion of the Secretaries of State and Homeland Security for the terrorism grounds of inadmissibility.[199] All grounds of inadmissibility with the exception of the provisions relating to the general security grounds of INA §212(a)(3)(A), but for violation of export rules, foreign policy, Nazis, and participants in genocide, may be waived for nonimmigrants by the Secretary of Homeland Security/Attorney General at the recom-

---

1948, 78 UNTS 277; 8 USC §1182(a)(3)(E)(ii), INA §212(a)(3)(E)(ii).

[194] Pub. L. No. 105-292, 112 Stat. 2787 (1998). This inadmissibility provision is found at 8 USC §1182(a)(2)(G), INA §212(a)(2)(G).

[195] *See Matter of Luis-Rodriguez,* 22 I&N Dec. 747 (BIA 1999).

[196] 8 USC §1227(a)(4)(A)(iii), INA §237(a)(4)(A)(iii).

[197] *Matter of Ruiz-Massieu,* 22 I&N Dec. 833 (BIA 1999).

[198] *Tittjung v. Reno,* 199 F.3d 393, 397 (7th Cir. 1999).

[199] 8 USC §1182(d)(3)(B), INA §212(d)(3)(B).

mendation of the Secretary of State.[200] No such waivers exist for the equivalent security-related grounds of deportability.

Economic Grounds

Inadmissibility. The major ground of inadmissibility within this category is for a person considered "likely to become a public charge."[201] The underlying purpose is to ensure that those being admitted will be able to support themselves while they are in the United States. To overcome this inadmissibility ground, the applicant is required to submit an affidavit of support from the family member sponsoring the person as a family-based immigrant.[202] The sponsor must show that he or she has an income 125 percent above the federal poverty line. A person may meet the income test by providing evidence of liquid assets, which when combined with other income, reaches the 125 percent figure.[203] If the sponsor is unable to establish sufficient income, he or she may satisfy the difference by showing other assets, such as real property or stock.[204]

Also inadmissible for economic grounds are immigrants who will be entering the labor market, unless the Secretary of the Department of Labor certifies that there are not enough qualified U.S. workers able, willing, and available to perform the work that will be performed by the immigrant, and that his or her employment will not have an adverse effect on the wages and working conditions of similarly employed U.S. workers.[205] The process, called a "labor certification," is headed by an employer-sponsor and must be satisfied to overcome this ground of inadmissibility.[206] The labor certification process is for immigrants entering the labor market and is inapplicable to persons who are immigrating based on a family relationship with a U.S. citizen or LPR, or to persons entering under the diversity visa program. It is also inapplicable to refugees and asylees.

---

[200] 8 USC §1182(d)(3)(A), INA §212(d)(3)(A).

[201] 8 USC §1182(a)(4), INA §212(a)(4).

[202] Family-based immigrants are discussed in greater detail at Chapter 5.

[203] In measuring whether assets meet the poverty income guidelines, the statute requires that the sponsor's assets be five times the amount needed by the beneficiary to meet the amount set by poverty income guidelines. 8 USC §1183a(f)(5), INA §213A(f)(5).

[204] 8 CFR §213a.1.

[205] *See* 8 USC §1182(a)(5)(A), INA §212(a)(5)(A). This provision is applicable to immigrant visa requests only.

[206] For more information on labor certification, see *The David Stanton Manual on Labor Certification* (AILA 2005), order at *www.ailapubs.org*.

Other workers are subject to additional requirements. For example, medical graduates of "nonapproved" foreign medical schools who have not passed the National Board of Medical Examiners (NBME) Parts I and II (or an equivalent examination) and who are not competent in oral and written English may not be admitted.[207] Similarly, persons seeking admission as health care workers must present proof of educational equivalency, must have passed a licensing or occupation examination recognized by a majority of the states, and must have a minimal level of proficiency in the English language.[208]

Deportability. The deportability provision equivalent to the public charge ground of inadmissibility is 8 USC §1227(a)(5), INA §237(a)(5). This provision makes deportable a person who within five years of admission has become a public charge (*i.e.*, receives specific public benefits) from causes not affirmatively shown to have arisen since entry.[209] The language of the statute attempts to shift the burden to the person to show "affirmatively" that the cause for becoming a public charge did not exist when the person was first admitted. In addition, the governmental entity that conferred the benefits must have made a demand for reimbursement, which the recipient has refused to repay.[210] However, not all benefits are prohibited, as the statute has been interpreted as only prohibiting what amounts to a cash payment. Whether a benefit is a cash payment is a complicated question, since many benefits are more akin to insurance than welfare.[211]

Waivers. The public charge bar to admission may be overcome by a waiver under 8 USC §1183, INA §213. This waiver allows a person who is believed likely to become a public charge to gain admission by posting a bond. However, by its terms, these bonds do not waive the affidavit of support requirement. The affidavit of support is not required of diversity immigrants, certain persons who are self-petitioning, special immigrants, asylees, refugees, persons who obtain permanent residency under the registry program, and employment-based immigrants.

---

[207] 8 USC §1182(a)(5)(B), INA §212(a)(5)(B).

[208] 8 USC §1182(a)(5)(C), INA §212(a)(5)(C); 8 CFR §§212.15, 1212.15.

[209] 8 USC §1227(a)(5), INA §237(a)(5). *See also* Field Guidance on Deportability and Inadmissibility on Public Charge Grounds, 64 Fed. Reg. 28689–93 (1999).

[210] 64 Fed. Reg. 28689, 28690 (1999).

[211] *Id.* at 28692–93.

The labor certification and foreign medical school graduate inadmissibility provisions, while not applicable to persons who meet the necessary criteria, may not otherwise be waived.

Immigration Law Violations

Inadmissibility. There are a broad range of immigration violations that can prevent a person from gaining future lawful admission; in other words, they constitute grounds of inadmissibility. Inadmissibility can attach due to violations at the time of entry (misrepresentation, smuggling, etc.); inadmissibility as a repercussion for prior removal; and violations occurring after proper entry that lead to unlawful status while within the United States.[212] Pursuant to INA §212(a)(6), inadmissibility attaches to persons in the United States who: (1) were not admitted or paroled; (2) failed to attend their removal hearing without reasonable cause; (3) committed fraud and misrepresentation; (4) are stowaways; (5) knowingly encourage, induce, assist, or aid another to enter the United States in violation of the law; (6) have been fined for making false documents or use someone else's lawfully issued documents; or (7) entered the United States to study at a private institution and improperly switched to a public institution in violation of the statute.[213]

Importantly, among the immigration violations that have the most serious consequences for inadmissibility are those having to do with fraud or willful misrepresentation.[214] The INA provides that where a person willfully misrepresents a material fact in obtaining or seeking to obtain a visa, documentation, or admission to the United States, he or she is thereafter inadmissible forever. Materiality is determined by whether the misrepresented fact closed off a line of inquiry or has a "natural tendency" to affect the decision that might have led to a denial of the visa or document.[215] The Ninth Circuit has held that the failure on the part of an applicant to disclose an arrest that resulted in a dismissal of charges was not

---

[212] 8 USC §1182(a)(6) (violations at entry) and (9) (later unlawful presence and inadmissibility as a result of prior removal), INA §§212(a)(6) (violations at entry) and (9) (later unlawful presence and inadmissibility as a result of prior removal).

[213] 8 USC §§1182(a)(6)(A)–(G), INA §§212(a)(6)(A)–(G). A person under INA §212(a)(6)(G) is inadmissible for five years (prohibition applies to attending public schools where the school has not been fully reimbursed for the cost of the educational program). *See* 8 USC §1184(m)(1)(B), INA §214(m)(1)(B).

[214] 8 USC §1182(a)(6)(C), INA §212(a)(6)(C).

[215] *U.S. v. Gaudin*, 515 U.S. 506, 521 (1995); *Kungys v. U.S.*, 485 U.S. 759 (1988).

material.[216] The fraud or misrepresentation must be willful and perpetrated on a U.S. government official. Furthermore, once a fraud or willful misrepresentation occurs, it cannot be cured unless there was a timely retraction.[217] For example, a person who entered into a fraudulent marriage and attempted to obtain immigration benefits, and later sought to annul the marriage, has still attempted to commit a fraud.[218]

A large number of persons are inadmissible for failure to have the proper admission documents, such as a valid passport, a valid immigrant or nonimmigrant visa, or other documentation necessary for entry. After 9/11, DHS instituted a program called National Security Entry-Exit Registration System (NSEERS).[219] In addition to requiring that males born in certain designated countries register with DHS for interviews, fingerprinting, and photographing, the regulation also required that the person register upon departure.[220] A person who has failed to register without good cause upon departure "shall be presumed to be inadmissible" as a person the Attorney General believes has engaged in unlawful activity under 8 USC §1182(a)(3)(A)(ii), INA §212(a)(3)(A)(ii).

As a result of a prior removal, inadmissibility can attach to someone who has been ordered removed in the past through summary (expedited) removal or regular removal proceedings initiated upon arrival and may not be readmitted for five years; where there has been a second removal, the period is extended to 20 years.[221] A person who fails to attend his or her removal hearing without "reasonable cause" and later seeks readmission is inadmissible for five years.[222] Someone who has been removed pursuant to a regular removal hearing that is not initiated upon arrival or who departed while an order of removal was outstanding may not return to the United States for 10 years (or 20 years in the case

---

[216] *Forbes v. INS*, 48 F.3d 439 (1995).

[217] At least this is the position taken by the Department of State. *See Foreign Affairs Manual*, 9 FAM 40.63 N.4.2.

[218] *See Garcia v. INS*, 31 F.3d 441 (7th Cir. 1994).

[219] While the NSEERS program was suspended in December 2003, persons who were subject to it must still notify DHS upon departure from the United States. *See* 68 Fed. Reg. 67577 (2003).

[220] Nationals from the following countries are subject to the NSEERS program: Afghanistan, Algeria, Bahrain, Bangladesh, Egypt, Eritrea, Indonesia, Iran, Iraq, Jordan, Kuwait, Lebanon, Libya, Morocco, North Korea, Oman, Pakistan, Qatar, Saudi Arabia, Somalia, The Sudan, Syria, Tunisia, United Arab Emirates, and Yemen.

[221] 8 USC §1182(a)(9)(A)(i), INA §212(a)(9)(A)(i).

[222] 8 USC §1182(a)(6)(B), INA §212(a)(6)(B).

of a second removal or for conviction of an aggravated felony) unless that person has first been granted permission by DHS.[223] According to INS, this section applies only if the person has departed the United States and is seeking re-admission.[224] Finally, a person who was previously removed as a result of an aggravated felony conviction is permanently inadmissible.[225]

Regarding inadmissibility for unlawful presence, persons who are unlawfully present in the United States for more than 180 consecutive days, but less than one year, and who voluntarily depart the United States before proceedings have commenced may not return for three years from their departure or removal; this provision does not apply if the person was granted voluntary departure by the IJ.[226] Persons who have been unlawfully present for one or more years are similarly prohibited from returning, but for 10 years.[227]

Deportability. There are several provisions that are unique to deportability and fall within the category of immigration violations. They are: (1) inadmissibility at time of entry;[228] (2) failure to maintain status;[229] and (3) failure to notify change of address, unless it was due to excusable neglect, or not willful.[230] A person who was inadmissible at the time of inspection but somehow managed to gain legal admission is nevertheless subject to removal as a deportable person. However, deportability is not presumed, and the burden rests on the government, as it does in other deportability cases.[231] Someone who is admitted to the United States and fails to follow the terms of his or her admission also is deportable. Terms of admission include departing by a specific date (or otherwise obtaining an extension of permission to remain), or fulfilling the specific

---

[223] 8 USC §1182(a)(9)(A)(ii)(II), INA §212(a)(9)(A)(ii)(II). The statute also imposes criminal penalties of up to two years' imprisonment for persons who return without permission. See 8 USC §1326, INA §276(a). This provision does not appear to apply to persons who departed following the commencement of removal proceedings but where an order of removal was not entered.

[224] INS Memorandum, "3/10 Year Bars and Section 245(i)" (May 1, 1997), *reprinted in* 74 *Interpreter Releases* 781, 791–94, *published on* AILA InfoNet at Doc. No. 97050191 (*posted* May 1, 1997).

[225] 8 USC §1182(a)(9)(A)(ii)(II), INA §212(a)(9)(A)(ii)(II). *See* Vail, *supra* note 71, at 44–45, 78.

[226] 8 USC §1182(a)(9)(B)(i)(I), INA §212(a)(9)(B)(i)(I).

[227] 8 USC §1182(a)(9)(B)(i)(II), INA §212(a)(9)(B)(i)(II).

[228] 8 USC §227(a)(1)(A), INA §237(a)(1)(A).

[229] 8 USC §1227(a)(1)(C), INA §237(a)(1)(C).

[230] 8 USC §1227(a)(3)(A), INA §237(a)(3)(A).

[231] 8 USC §1229a(c)(3), INA §240(c)(3).

requirements of the nonimmigrant visa under which the person has been admitted.[232] In addition, all noncitizens are required to notify DHS of a change of address within 10 days, and the failure to do so is a separate ground of deportability.[233]

A person may be deportable for "marriage fraud" if the person was admitted to the United States with an immigrant visa or documentation based on a marriage that was entered into less than two years prior to entry and terminated after entry, unless the person can establish that the marriage was not entered into to evade the immigration laws.[234] This statute was designed to shift the burden of proof in cases where a marriage was terminated within the period noted in the statute, and to facilitate the person's removal.

Waivers. The inadmissibility grounds for fraud or willful misrepresentation can be waived for the spouse, son, or daughter of a U.S. citizen or LPR upon a showing that the denial of the immigrant visa or permanent resident status would result in extreme hardship to the U.S. citizen or LPR spouse or parent.[235] An immigrant not in possession of a valid visa, passport, or admission document may obtain a waiver at the discretion of the government if the person either did not know or could not have reasonably known of the defect regarding the documentation.[236] There is no waiver for marriage fraud; the petitioning spouse and beneficiary bear the burden of showing that the marriage was *bona fide.*

The unlawful presence bars, with the exception of 8 USC §1182(a)(9)(C), INA §212(a)(9)(C) (relating to persons unlawfully in the United States for an aggregate period in excess of one year, or who have been ordered removed and return), may be waived for a person who is otherwise eligible for an immigrant visa and is the spouse, son, or daughter of a U.S. citizen or LPR and can show extreme hardship to the spouse or parent.[237] Section 1182(a)(9)(C) of 8 USC, INA §212(a)(9)(C) may be waived for a battered spouse or child who has been granted status as such, if he or she can establish a connection between the unlawful presence and

---

[232] The requirements for each nonimmigrant classification are discussed in Chapter 4.

[233] *See* 8 USC §§1305(a) and 1306, INA §§265(a) and 266.

[234] 8 USC §1227(a)(1)(G), INA §237(a)(1)(G).

[235] 8 USC §1182(i), INA §212(i).

[236] 8 USC §1182(k), INA §212(k).

[237] 8 USC §1182(d)(3)(A), INA §212(d)(3)(A) (denial of this waiver is not subject to review).

the extreme cruelty or battery to which he or she was subjected.[238] A person's failure to comply with the change of address requirements may be waived where it was reasonably excusable or not willful.[239]

The deportability grounds based on inadmissibility at the time of admission for a misrepresentation in procuring a visa or other documentation for entry may be waived for a person who is the spouse, parent, son, or daughter of a U.S. citizen or LPR. This waiver, like many others, is discretionary.[240] Refugees and asylees seeking adjustment of status to permanent residency or admission to the United States are not subject to the documentation grounds of inadmissibility and may seek a waiver for past immigration violations for humanitarian purposes—to ensure family unity or when otherwise in the public interest.[241]

Quasi-Criminal and Moral Grounds

Inadmissibility. Given both the wide latitude that courts have granted to Congress in exercising power over immigration and the historical roots of immigration exclusion provisions, it should not be surprising that many immigration restrictions are based on moral grounds. While the present statute, which was significantly amended in 1990, has fewer moral grounds of exclusion, it still retains those provisions that reflect contemporary values.[242] One provision that has been in the statute for a long time is the prohibition on the admission of polygamists.[243] While the present statute prohibits the admission of persons coming to practice polygamy, the earlier statute prohibited persons who had the status of a polygamist or who advocated polygamy. Also prohibited are persons who have engaged in, or seek to engage in prostitution, or who have sought to procure prostitutes within the last 10 years.[244] A person may be barred from admission even if he or she is moving to a part of

---

[238] 8 USC §1182(a)(9)(B)(iii), INA §212(a)(9)(B)(iii).

[239] 8 USC §1227(a)(3)(A), INA §237(a)(3)(A).

[240] *See* 8 USC §1227(a)(1)(H), INA §237(a)(1)(H). There is some question as to whether a person who entered into a fraudulent marriage is eligible for this waiver. *See Virk v. INS*, 295 F.3d 1055 (9th Cir. 2002); *but see Dallo v. INS*, 765 F.2d 581, 588 (6th Cir. 1985). The waiver is not available for persons who are Nazis. When considering the waiver, the nature of the fraud can be a factor in whether it should be granted.

[241] 8 USC §1159(c), INA §209(c).

[242] Earlier versions of the statute included inadmissibility grounds such as the prohibition on persons coming to perform immoral sex acts and the exclusion of homosexuals.

[243] 8 USC §1182(a)(10)(A), INA §212(a)(10)(A).

[244] 8 USC §§1182(a)(2)(D)(i) and (ii), INA §§212(a)(2)(D)(i) and (ii).

the United States where prostitution is legal (or if prostitution was legal in the person's own country).[245] A person who has been found to have committed document fraud for purposes of satisfying the verification requirements in seeking employment is inadmissible.[246]

Deportability. Earlier versions of the INA contained deportation provisions for persons engaged in prostitution or who were associated with a business of prostitution following their entry. Even though prostitution may not form the basis for establishing deportability, if the activity leads to other activity for which a person could be deported—such as criminal behavior or drug abuse—a person could face removal.[247]

A person who encourages, induces, or assists someone to enter, or try to enter the United States illegally at any time within five years of his or her entry is subject to removal.[248] Deportability provisions for document fraud mirror the inadmissibility provisions.[249]

Waivers. Inadmissibility for polygamy may not be waived. A person who assists or encourages someone to enter the country illegally and, as a result, becomes deportable, may seek a waiver for humanitarian purposes—if he or she is an LPR and the person assisted or encouraged to enter was the spouse, parent, son, or daughter.[250] Inadmissibility for prostitution may be waived pursuant to the waiver at 8 USC §1182(h)(1)(A), INA §212(h)(1)(A).

Inadmissibility for document fraud may be waived for humanitarian purposes for returning permanent residents and those seeking an immigrant visa or adjustment of status under the family preference or immediate relative category if (1) the person has not been previously fined and (2) the documents were obtained to support a spouse or child.[251] Deportability for document fraud may be waived for LPRs if the person has not had a previous civil monetary fine imposed and the offense was

---

[245] 22 CFR §40.24(c).

[246] 8 USC §1182(a)(6)(F), INA §212(a)(6)(F). Document fraud adjudications are conducted before an administrative law judge and have notice requirements. 8 USC §1324c(c)(2), INA §274C(c)(2).

[247] Generally, one's behavior will open a line of inquiry into other possible prohibited activities.

[248] 8 USC §1227(a)(1)(E), INA §237(a)(1)(E).

[249] 8 USC §1227(a)(3)(C), INA §237(a)(3)(C).

[250] The waiver is not available in the case of any other family member who might have been smuggled. *See* 8 USC §1227(a)(1)(E)(iii), INA §237(a)(1)(E)(iii).

[251] 8 USC §1182(d)(12), INA §212(d)(12).

to help the spouse or child obtain work.[252] Refugees and asylees seeking adjustment of status to permanent residency or admission to the United States may obtain a waiver of the quasi-criminal and moral grounds for humanitarian purposes.[253]

Miscellaneous Grounds

There are a number of inadmissibility and deportability provisions that defy categorization and can best be described as miscellaneous. Most of the grounds included in this category relate to classes of persons who captured the negative attention of a member of Congress. As a consequence, a special provision was inserted into the immigration laws, and, generally, the covered group does not include a large number of persons. These miscellaneous categories include: persons who are permanently ineligible for U.S. citizenship because they have made false claims to U.S. citizenship; persons who have unlawfully voted in violation of federal, state, or local law; those who have engaged in international child abduction; or persons who entered the United States as nonimmigrant exchange students subject to a two-year residency requirement in their home country.[254]

The false claim to U.S. citizenship and unlawful voting grounds of inadmissibility are not applicable to a person if his or her parents were or are U.S. citizens, the person permanently resided in the United States prior to reaching the age of 16, and the person believed at the time of voting or claiming citizenship that he or she was a U.S. citizen. The ground of inadmissibility for international child abduction applies in circumstances where a U.S. court has granted custody of a U.S. citizen child to a person and the child is kept outside the United States from the custodial parent in violation of the court order. The noncitizen who is responsible for the abduction is inadmissible until he or she complies with the custody order.[255] This ground does not apply where the child is in a country that has signed The Hague Convention on the Civil Aspects of International Child Abduction.[256]

---

[252] 8 USC §1227(a)(3)(C)(ii), INA §237(a)(3)(C)(ii).

[253] 8 USC §1159(c), INA §209(c).

[254] 8 USC §§1182(a)(6)(C)(ii), (a)(10)(C)–(D) and (e), 1227(a)(2)(D) and (a)(6), INA §212(a)(6)(C)(ii), (a)(10)(C)–(D) and 212(e), 237(a)(2)(D) and (a)(6).

[255] 8 USC §1182(a)(10)(C), INA §212(a)(10)(C).

[256] 8 USC §1182(a)(1)(C)(iii)(III), INA §212(a)(10)(C)(iii)(III).

The foreign exchange student residency requirement was designed to both promote U.S. foreign policy interests through educational programs and to aid developing nations by ensuring that persons who studied in the United States would use their education to support the development of their native countries, where either their skills were needed or their education was supported by the United States or their own government.[257] The inadmissibility is not an absolute provision since it is primarily designed to prevent the person from becoming an LPR until he or she has spent the requisite two years in the home country. The person may change nonimmigrant status to a limited group of visa categories.[258] Determining whether the residency requirement applies requires analyzing the individual case, but, generally, it will apply where the person was issued an exchange student, or "J" visa, and: (1) the person's education was financed in whole or in part, directly or indirectly by the government of the person's own country or an agency of the U.S. government; or (2) at the time of admission to the United States, the person was in a field of study that was on a Skills List kept by the Department of State (DOS); or (3) the person came to the United States or became a J student after January 10, 1977, in order to receive graduate medical education.[259]

Deportability. The provisions regarding false claims to U.S. citizenship and unlawful voting are the same as the inadmissibility provisions, except that the violation occurs after the person's admission.[260] These provisions are applicable after September 30, 1996. There is no comparable deportability provision for international child abductors or persons subject to the two-year foreign residency requirement. Presumably, a person who was in the United States in violation of the latter provision would be subject to removal just as someone who was inadmissible at entry would have their visa revoked and then be placed in removal proceedings.

Waivers. Refugees and asylees seeking adjustment of status to permanent residency or admission to the United States may obtain a waiver

---

[257] *See* C. Gordon, S. Mailman & S. Yale-Loehr, *Immigration Law and Procedure* §29.03 (2006); N. Schorr & S. Yale-Loehr, "The Odyssey of the J-2: Forty-Three Years of Trying not to Go Home Again," 18 *Geo. Imm. L.J.* 221, 224–28 (2004); C. Waller & L. Hoffman, "United States Immigration Law as a Foreign Policy Tool, The Beijing Crisis and the United States Response," 3 *Geo. Imm. L.J.* 313, 315 (1989).

[258] *See* discussion in Chapter 4.

[259] 8 USC §1182(e), INA §212(e).

[260] 8 USC §§1227(a)(3)(D) and (6), INA §237(a)(3)(D) and (6).

of these grounds of inadmissibility for humanitarian purposes.[261] Waiver of the two-year residency requirement for J visa holders is extremely difficult and requires a favorable recommendation from DOS and a showing that the denial of the waiver would cause exceptional hardship to the applicant's U.S. citizen (or LPR) spouse or child. The factors to be considered include, but are not limited to, economic, physical, emotional, employment, educational, and health consequences. An additional basis for obtaining the waiver is where a person's country has issued a "no objection waiver," or where the request comes from an interested U.S. federal or state agency.[262] DOS, however, must still issue a favorable recommendation.[263] Last, one can potentially obtain the waiver based on persecution for reasons of race, religion, or political opinion in the home country.[264]

ADDITIONAL RELIEF FROM REMOVAL

Earlier, this chapter discussed the grounds of removal, and how a person can have the grounds of inadmissibility and deportability waived. This section will discuss other remedies available for persons in removal proceedings. The remedies discussed here are forms of immigration relief or benefits that can be presented to an IJ or DHS to avoid removal.

These forms of relief can be placed into two broad categories: temporary and permanent. Some forms of relief lead to permanent residency, while others do not. Most of these forms of removal relief are discretionary—only a very few are mandatory. This section will explore these forms of relief in depth, in terms of their criteria and which governmental entity confers the benefit.[265]

---

[261] 8 USC §1159(c), INA §209(c).

[262] A "no objection waiver" refers to one of the conditions precedent to the waiver, which is that the person's government has "no objection" to the waiver being granted. *See* 8 USC §1182(e), INA §212(e).

[263] *Id.*

[264] *Id.*

[265] The REAL ID Act of 2005 includes language that attempts to further insulate IJ decisions on relief from removal claims from judicial review. It does this by making it more difficult for a court to overturn a decision based on credibility or lack of corroboration. *See* REAL ID Act, *supra* note 85, §101(d).

Temporary Relief

The principle characteristic of temporary removal relief is that it is of short duration or otherwise limited in some manner. Temporary forms of relief include (1) Temporary Protected Status; (2) withholding of removal; (3) stay of deportation; (4) voluntary departure; (5) Convention Against Torture relief; (6) deferred action; (7) deferred enforced departure; and (8) extended voluntary departure. All of these forms of relief—with the exception of the last three (deferred action, deferred enforced departure, and extended voluntary departure)—have a statutory basis.[266]

Stay of Removal. A stay of removal is a request to delay a removal order, and may be made to the ICE district director or to the IJ.[267] Congress's enactment of the REAL ID Act could foreclose judicial review for denials of stays of requests because the REAL ID Act attempts to remove habeas corpus relief in federal district court except for constitutional or detention claims; all other claims reviewing final orders of removal must be taken to the appropriate federal appeals court on a petition for review.[268] This stay of removal is a request for the exercise of a discretionary benefit in the form of temporary relief from removal.

Voluntary Departure. There are three different forms of voluntary departure depending on the stage of the proceeding when granted. Voluntary departure can be granted: (1) pre-removal hearing; (2) during the removal hearing; and (3) post-removal hearing. Pre- and post-hearing voluntary departure requests are determined by the local ICE district directors who may grant voluntary departure for a period not to exceed 120 days.[269] IJs make determinations on requests raised at the hearing and they may grant up to 120 days of voluntary departure.[270]

Persons who have been convicted of an aggravated felony or who are deportable as terrorists are ineligible for this form of relief.[271] A per-

---

[266] Temporary Protected Status, withholding of removal, Convention Against Torture relief, deferred enforced departure, and extended voluntary departure—all relief from harm—will be discussed in Chapter 3. It is Convention Against Torture relief that is mandatory should the applicant meet his or her burden of qualifying under the Convention.

[267] 8 USC §§1229a(b)(5)(C) and 1231(c)(2), INA §240(b)(5)(C) and 241(c)(2).

[268] REAL ID Act of 2005, *supra* note 85, §106(a).

[269] 8 CFR §1240.26.

[270] 8 CFR §1240.26(b)(1)(i)(A). Further extensions on voluntary departure usually are obtained from the ICE district director.

[271] 8 USC §1229c(a)(1), INA §240B(a)(1).

son who is applying for admission may request permission to withdraw an application in lieu of seeking voluntary departure.[272] Persons who have been granted pre-hearing voluntary departure, and fail to depart, will become ineligible for a range of immigration benefits, and also may expose themselves to civil penalties.[273]

Deferred Action. A decision to prosecute a case—that is, to initiate removal proceedings—is a wholly discretionary determination within the jurisdiction of the ICE district regional directors. Similarly, a decision not to execute a removal order is also within the power of the ICE district director. When such prosecution is indefinitely delayed, it is called "deferred action." This is not a benefit that can be granted by the IJ. Some of the factors ICE may consider in making such a decision are the likelihood of obtaining a removal order, the presence of sympathetic factors (especially if adverse publicity might cause difficulties for the agency), and whether the person is in a class of persons, such as aggravated felons, who are a high priority for removal.[274] While in earlier cases, courts expressed some willingness to review these determinations, the passage of IIRAIRA and a Supreme Court decision in 1999[275] presumably have closed the door on such review.

Permanent Relief

Permanent relief effectively terminates the removal proceedings and provides the person with a bar to removal that can later convert into permanent residency. This permanent relief is to be distinguished from waivers of grounds of inadmissibility and deportability, discussed earlier, which set aside a particular ground. A waiver merely provides a gateway to eventual status, but is not, in and of itself, a form of relief. The forms of relief discussed in this section grant the person either permanent residency or a means for obtaining it. They are: (1) cancellation of removal (formerly suspension of deportation) and (2) adjustment of status; asylum also enables permanent residency—it will be discussed in the next chapter. As will be explained in greater detail below, most forms of permanent relief have discretionary elements, meaning that those who meet

---

[272] This effectively achieves the same outcome, since voluntary departure avoids a removal order.
[273] 8 CFR §1240.26(a).

[274] These criteria were set forth in the Operation Instructions of the former INS; following its reorganization into DHS, the instructions have not been replaced. *See* OI 242.1(a)(22).

[275] *Reno v. American-Arab Anti-Discrimination Comm.*, 525 U.S. 471 (1999).

the eligibility requirements also must show that they merit a favorable exercise of discretion to receive the benefit.

Cancellation of Removal. Prior to the enactment of IIRAIRA in 1996, there were two major forms of relief that could be sought in proceedings before an IJ: "suspension of deportation" (based on continuous presence and family ties) and the "§212(c) waiver."[276] Both of these benefits continue to exist after the enactment of IIRAIRA, but they have been significantly modified. First, now that deportation and exclusion hearings have been merged into removal proceedings, suspension of deportation has been recharacterized as a cancellation of the proceedings— thus, "cancellation of removal." Second, the broad waiver of many grounds of inadmissibility and deportability that was §212(c) has been reformulated into another form of cancellation of removal proceedings. The main distinction between these two forms of cancellation is that one is a remedy for persons who have no permanent legal status, while the other is for persons who had permanent resident status and were at risk of losing it. The first grants the non–LPR beneficiary a termination of the proceedings and allows the person to become a permanent resident. The second terminates the proceedings and allows the person to retain permanent resident status.

Cancellation of removal for non–LPRs is available to persons who have resided continuously in the United States for at least 10 years, are of good moral character, and have not been convicted of any crimes described in the deportability and inadmissibility provisions.[277] They also must show that their removal would cause exceptional and extremely unusual hardship to their U.S. citizen or LPR child, spouse, or parent.[278] This form of cancellation is limited to 4,000 persons per year.

The cancellation of removal for permanent residents who risk losing status for actions that constitute grounds of deportability or inadmissibility is available to those who have been LPRs for a minimum of five

---

[276] Section "212(c)" relief referred to the former section of the INA in which the provision appeared. *See also* 8 USC §1182(c) (2001). The §212(c) relief was available to people facing grounds of inadmissibility and deportability. *See Francis v. INS*, 532 F.2d 268 (2d Cir. 1976); *Matter of Silva*, 16 I&N Dec. 26 (BIA 1976) (BIA applies the *Francis* decision nationwide).

[277] 8 USC §1229b(b)(1)(A)–(C), INA §240A(b)(1)(A)–(C). The 10-year time period is tolled by the service of the Notice to Appear. 8 USC §1229b(d)(1), INA §240A(d)(1).

[278] 8 USC §1229b(b)(1)(D), INA §240A(b)(1)(D).

years.[279] They must have resided in the United States in some status for at least seven continuous years, and have not been convicted of an aggravated felony.[280]

Following Congress' repeal of §212(c) relief, litigation arose over whether the provision was retroactive and, particularly, whether the repeal applied to persons who, at the time of their conviction, would have been eligible for the §212(c) waiver. The Supreme Court, in *INS v. St. Cyr*,[281] held that while Congress had the authority to enact a retroactive statute, it was not clear from AEDPA's and IIRAIRA's language that it actually precluded those who had been eligible to apply for §212(c) relief at the time of their guilty plea from doing so when placed in removal proceedings. Therefore, §212(c) relief is available for those who pleaded guilty prior to the statutory amendments. Those with aggravated felony convictions following the effective date of IIRAIRA are ineligible for §212(c) relief.

Adjustment of Status. Adjustment of status is a special benefit allowing a person to obtain permanent residency without having to travel abroad and be readmitted with an immigrant visa. A person may seek adjustment prior to the institution of removal proceedings or within the proceedings themselves. Therefore, this benefit may be sought before USCIS or an IJ. When the benefit is being sought in removal proceedings, it is a form of relief from removal. In addition to meeting the criteria for a favorable exercise of discretion, a person also must have been admitted or paroled, not be statutorily ineligible, and have an immigrant visa immediately available in order to qualify for adjustment.

---

[279] 8 USC §1229b(a)(1), INA §240A(a)(1).

[280] 8 USC §1229b(a)(2)–(3), INA §240A(a)(2)–(3). Also precluded are persons who have failed to register with USCIS authorities or have been convicted of visa or document fraud under 18 USC §1546. Criminal convictions may be waived where the person is a victim of domestic violence. 8 USC §1229b(b)(2), INA §240A(b)(2).

[281] *Supra* note 84.

Chart 1: Grounds of Inadmissibility and Deportability

Grounds	Inadmissibility	Deportability
General		
Application	Visa application, admission, adjustment of status, certain returns to the U.S. after permanent residency. Issues arise when seeking citizenship.	Following admission or entry, when seeking citizenship.
Unique Grounds	Admission of acts constituting a crime even without conviction, labor certification requirement, most health grounds, communists or totalitarian party, unqualified physicians or health care workers, persons asserting immunity from prosecution for "serious" crimes, polygamy, unlawful presence bars to returns, stowaways, student visa abusers, not in possession of proper documents, persons previously removed or unlawfully present, ineligible for citizenship, renunciation of citizenship to avoid taxation, accompanying certain inadmissible persons, international child abductors	Inadmissibility at entry, present in violation of law, violation of condition of entry, termination of conditional residence status, failure to register change of address, high-speed flight, selective service act crimes, violators of protection orders, domestic violence, stalking or child abuse or neglect crimes, false citizenship claim
Economic		
Public Charge	Likely to become public charge	Becomes a public charge within 5 years of admission
Political		
Foreign Policy	Secretary has reasonable ground to believe admission would have potentially serious adverse consequences	Same but person is in the U.S.
Health-Related		
Drug abuser	An abuser at the time seeking admission	At any time after admission
Criminal		
Crime Involving Moral Turpitude	A single crime involving moral turpitude except certain "petty offenses"	Convicted w/in 5 yrs of crime involving moral turpitude for which 1 year or more sentence could be imposed (10 years if admitted under "witness protection" visa)
Controlled Substance	Any such crime	Same, except simple possession of marijuana
Multiple Crimes Involving Moral Turpitude	2 or more offenses w/aggregate sentence imposed ≥ 5 yrs.	≥ 2 crimes involving moral turpitude
Petty Offense	Petty offense and juvenile exception to crimes	No equivalent
Aggravated Felonies	No similar provision	Conviction any time after admission (summary removal for non–LPRs)
Drug Traffickers	Where consular or DHS officer knows or has reason to believe is or has been trafficker in controlled substance or prior conviction for trafficking	Requires conviction for crime involving controlled substance
Prostitution and Commercialized Vice	Coming to engage in prostitution or has engaged in prostitution within 10 years prior to application for visa, admission, or adjustment	No basis
Firearms Offenses	No similar provision	Conviction any time after admission of purchasing, selling, offering, exchanging, using, owning, possessing, or carrying (or attempt or conspiracy) any weapon, part, or accessory

Chart 1: Grounds of Inadmissibility and Deportability, continued

Grounds	Inadmissibility	Deportability
Quasi-criminal		
Marriage Fraud	Permanently ineligible to receive family immigration visa	Marriage ends w/in 2 yrs unless *bona fides* established
Fraud or Misrepresentation	Seeks or has sought to procure visa, documentation, or admission into the U.S. Person admitted as nonimmigrant who obtains benefits for which ineligible through fraud or material misrepresentation is ineligible to return for 5 years	(See false documents below)
Smuggling	A person who at any time has engaged in "alien smuggling."	Smuggling within 5 years from "any entry"
Security		
Espionage	Government "knows or has reasonable ground to believe, seeks to enter to engage in"	Has or is engaged at any time after admission
Nazis	Participated in Nazi persecutions between 3/23/1933 – 5/8/1945	Same
Genocide	Engaged in genocide	Same
Terrorist	Has engaged in or consular officer or AG reasonably believes will or likely will engage in terrorist activities	Has engaged in, is or engages in terrorist activities
Miscellaneous		
Illegal Entrants	Exempts battered spouses or children	Persons illegally in U.S. subject to removal
Failure to Appear at Hearing	Inadmissible for 5 years	May be ordered removed *in absentia*
False Citizenship	False claim of U.S. citizenship for any purpose or benefit	Same
Document Fraud	Document fraud related to employer sanction compliance	Same

Chart 2: Factors and Grounds for Waivers

Factors	Grounds Waived
No Discretion	1. Prohibits the removal of a person where there is a "clear probability" that the persons life or freedom would be threatened on account of race, religion, nationality, membership in a particular social group, or political opinion
Discretion	
Pure discretion	1. Physical or mental disorder [8 USC §1182(a)(1)(A)(ii)]
	2. Previously removed persons under all forms of removal (expedited, arriving or after admission or self-removal) where the person seeks readmission within the applicable period [8 USC §1182(a)(9)(A)] [8 USC §1182(a)(6)(B)]
+ recommendation of consular officer	1. For nonimmigrants. Waives all grounds of inadmissibility except persons coming to engage in terrorism, persons whose admission would cause adverse foreign policy consequences. [8 USC §1182(d)(3)]
+ emergency or reciprocity, or person is in transit	1. Waives requirement of having a passport valid for 6 months or a valid nonimmigrant visa. [8 USC §1182(a)(7)(B)]
+ consideration of individuals' religious beliefs or moral convictions + bond or other assurances	1. Immigrants who fail to present proof of having received certain vaccinations for preventable diseases [8 USC §1182(a)(1)]
+ humanitarian purposes, family unity, or public interest	1. Waives inadmissibility for LPR who is returning (not under removal order) but subject to document fraud violation under §274C and is otherwise admissible. [8 USC §1182(d)(12)]
	2. Applicant for immigrant visa or adjustment who has had 1 document fraud violation under §274C where fraud was to support spouse or child (only). [8 USC §1182(d)(12)]
	3. Persons who have encouraged, induced, assisted, abetted, or aided an individual who at the time of such action was the alien's spouse, parent, son, or daughter (and no other individual) to enter the U.S. in violation of law. [8 USC §1182(d)(11)]
+ "no objection" waiver by diplomatic note from home country + favorable recommendation from Dept. of State	1. Waives the 2 yr. foreign residency requirement (no objection diplomatic note is not effective for J graduate medical trainees). [8 USC §1182(e)]
+ "would be subject to persecution" in home country	1. Waives the 2 yr. foreign residency requirement for persons who entered under a J (exchange visitor visa). [[8 USC §1182(e)]
+ well-founded fear of persecution	1. Waives all grounds except aggravated felons, persecutor of others, torturers. (Asylum)
Period of Time	
+15 years + rehabilitation and admission is not contrary to national welfare, safety, or security	1. For most crimes under 8 USC §1182(a)(2) including (A)(i)(I), (B), (D), and (E) of that subsection, including simple possession of 30g or less of marijuana but not including crimes involving murder or torture or for persons previously removed. Waiver is inapplicable to lawful permanent residents convicted of aggravated felonies or who have resided in the U.S. for less than 7 years immediately preceding the initiation of removal proceedings
+ lawful permanent resident for 5 years + resided continuously in the U.S. for 7 years	1. Waives all grounds of ineligibility and deportability except aggravated felony and terrorist provisions. Persons admitted as exchange or noncitizens obtaining graduate medical education or previously granted relief are ineligible. [8 USC §1229b(a)]
+ 10 years continuous physical presence + GMC + exceptional and extremely unusual hardship to the person's USC or LPR spouse, parent, or child	1. Waives all grounds except criminal and security grounds. [8 USC §1229b(b)]. Statute restricts benefits to only 4,000 people per year

Chart 2: Factors and Grounds for Waivers, continued

Factors	Grounds Waived
Relationship	
Spouse, minor unmarried child, or parent of U.S. citizen or LPR + discretion	1. Waives communicable disease of public health significance [8 USC §1182(a)(1)(A)(i)]—May require the posting of a bond. [8 U.S.C. § 1182(g)]
	2. Waives fraud or willful misrepresentation of material fact. [8 USC §1182(i)]
Spouse, parent, son or daughter of U.S. citizen or LPR, + discretion + not contrary to the national welfare, safety, or security + extreme hardship + rehabilitation	1. Waives crimes of moral turpitude [8 USC §1182(a)(2)(A)(i)(II)], 2 or more crimes irrespective of moral turpitude [8 USC §1182(a)(2)(B)], prostitution and commercialized vice [8 USC §1182(a)(2)(D)], persons having asserted immunity from prosecution (diplomats) [8 USC §1182(a)(2)(E)], controlled substance for simple possession of marijuana ≤ 30 g [8 USC §1182(a)(2)(A)(I)(II)]. *See* 8 USC §1182(h)]
	Unavailable to LPRs convicted of aggravated felony or hadn't lived in the U.S. for 7 years preceding the initiation of proceedings
Spouse, son or daughter of USC or LPR + extreme hardship to USC spouse or parent	Unlawful presence for more than 180 days (3 yr. bar) or greater than 1 year (10 yr. bar) [8 USC §1182(a)(9)(B).
Spouse or child if LPR or U.S. citizen + exceptional hardship + favorable recommendation from Dept. of State	1. Exchange visitor (J) program where subject to foreign residency requirement including persons coming to U.S. to obtain graduate medical training
	2. Inadmissible because of unlawful presence > 180 days but less than 1 yr

CHAPTER 3
Protection from Harm

Persecution for opinion is the master vice of society.
—Frances Wright

OVERVIEW

As described in the historical discussion in Chapter 1, protection under the immigration laws for those fleeing persecution did not fit under a neat statutory scheme. Historically, such persons were dealt with in emergency programs under the broad parole powers utilized by the Executive branch when those persons did not fit into a particular immigration category. Years after having granted parole in response to an emergent humanitarian crisis, Congress would grant a special adjustment of status to permanent residence for those who had been given the earlier special admission.

It was only in 1980 that Congress passed major legislation—the Refugee Act of 1980[1]—overhauling the way in which those fleeing persecution were to be protected. This statute created what was intended to be an orderly process for both the admission of refugees from overseas and the review of asylum applications by those who were either at the border or already in the United States. In keeping with other long-standing practices in U.S. immigration law, the refugees and asylees eventually would be eligible for permanent residency and, ultimately, for citizenship, if they qualified. Prior to the 1980 Refugee Act, only those persons from certain limited geographic areas or those fleeing from

---

[1] Pub. L. No. 96-212, 94 Stat. 102 (1980).

Communist-dominated countries could receive formal protection in what was called conditional entry status.[2]

The Refugee Act adopted the international definition of refugee, and removed the geographical and ideological restrictions that previously existed in the law. Contemporary immigration law now provides for five different avenues to, or forms of, relief. They include: refugee protection, asylum, withholding of removal, protection against torture (under the Convention Against Torture (CAT)),[3] and Temporary Protected Status (TPS). Refugee protection is available to designated persons *outside* the United States. Asylum and withholding of removal are available to certain persons who are either at a border or within the territory of the United States.[4] Protection against torture under the CAT is a broad prohibition preventing the expulsion or return of potential torture victims to any place where they may face torture; it is available to persons at the border or within the United States. TPS is available upon designation by the Department of Homeland Security (DHS), after consultation with other government agencies. TPS grants to its beneficiaries temporary protection from being removed to a specified country due to armed conflict, natural disaster, or conditions preventing a person's safe return.

THE STANDARDS OF THE REFUGEE DEFINITION AND BARS FROM MEETING IT

The sources of modern protections for refugees (and asylees) come from two major international instruments—the 1951 United Nations Convention Relating to the Status of Refugees (Convention)[5] and its 1967 Protocol,[6] and the CAT. The Convention and Protocol definition of refugee was incorporated into domestic law by the Refugee Act of 1980 (harmo-

---

[2] *See* Act of Oct. 3, 1965, Pub. L. No. 89-236, §20, 79 Stat. 912.

[3] *See* United Nations Convention Against Torture and Other Cruel, Inhuman or Degrading Treatment or Punishment, opened for signature Feb. 4, 1985, GA Res. 39/46 (Dec. 10, 1984), 39 U.N. GAOR Supp. No. 51 at 197, U.N. Doc A/Res/708 (1984), *reprinted in* 23 I.L.M. 1027 (1984), *modified in* 24 I.L.M. 535 (1985). The CAT was incorporated into U.S. law by the Fiscal Year 1999 Omnibus Consolidated and Emergency Supplemental Appropriations Act, Pub. L. No. 105-277, Div. G, Subdiv. B, Title XXI §2242 of the Foreign Affairs Reform and Restructuring Act of 1998, 112 Stat. 2681–822 (1998) (hereinafter FARRA).

[4] 8 USC §1158(a), INA §208(a).

[5] 19 U.S.T. 6577, 189 U.N.T.S. 137, 150, 152 (1951).

[6] 19 U.S.T. 6223, T.I.A.S. No. 6577, 606 U.N.T.S. 267 (1967). The United States is a party to the Protocol and not the Convention. However, the Protocol essentially adopts all of the Convention's definitions so that this distinction has little significance in terms of international obligations.

nizing U.S. law with its international treaty obligations).[7] The CAT was incorporated into domestic law through statutes enacted in 1998.[8]

The international definition of a "refugee," which the United States adopted, is a person outside of his or her country of nationality, who is unable or unwilling to return to his or her home country because of a "well-founded fear of persecution on account of race, religion, nationality, membership in a particular social group, or political opinion."[9] Under U.S. law, an "asylee" is a person who otherwise meets the refugee definition but who is either at the border or within the U.S. territory and who merits relief at the discretion of DHS or the Attorney General. The withholding of removal (or restriction on removal) form of relief also is premised on the five grounds of the refugee definition.[10]

While there have been efforts by Congress to restrict access to protections, asylum law has been the subject of much litigation and has been the one area within immigration law that has shown signs of possible positive development in the expansion of protections.[11]

In reviewing a particular set of facts to determine whether an individual meets the refugee definition, or in cases within the United States that would warrant a grant of asylum, it is helpful to go through an analysis of the elements of the statutory language. The statute provides for protection where the person

> is unable or unwilling to return to, and is unable or unwilling to avail himself or herself of the protection of,

---

[7] *See* 8 USC §1101(a)(42)(A), INA §101(a)(42)(A).

[8] *See supra,* note 3.

[9] 8 USC §1101(a)(42)(A), INA §101(a)(42)(A). U.S. law provides that the refugee definition includes persons who have suffered past persecution as well as a well-founded fear of future persecution and who are still within the country of persecution under special circumstances as the President may specify after consultation with Congress. 8 USC §1101(a)(42)(B), INA §101(a)(42)(B).

[10] 8 USC §1231(b)(3), INA §241(b)(3). For an in-depth discussion of asylum and refugee laws, see R. Germain, *Asylum Primer,* Fourth Ed. (AILA 2005), *www.ailapubs.org.*

[11] For example, while legislating expedited removal, Congress created exceptions to protect asylum-seekers. In 1998, Congress enacted the International Religious Freedom Act, Pub. L. No. 105-292, 112 Stat. 2787 (1998). The act required immigration judges and consular, refugee, and asylum officers to use the Department of State's Office of International Religious Freedom Annual Report as a resource when adjudicating cases. *Id.* at §601. More recently, the U.S. Commission on International Religious Freedom issued a report that was critical of the treatment of religious-based asylum applicants seeking admission to the United States. *See* U.S. Comm'n on Religious Freedom, *Study on Asylum Seekers In Expedited Removal* (Feb. 2005).

> that country because of persecution or a well-founded
> fear of persecution on account of race, religion, nation-
> ality, membership in a particular social group, or politi-
> cal opinion.[12]

First, the individual must be able to show a harm that rises to the level of persecution, which has been defined as the infliction of suffering or harm in a way regarded as offensive.[13] Courts have found a wide range of harms to be persecution—from physical harm to substantial economic deprivation.[14] The harm could have been inflicted in the past or be feared in the future. Furthermore, the harm need not be at the hands of the government, but can be by persons the government is unable or unwilling to control.[15] In order for a fear to be "well-founded," there needs to be a subjective as well as an objective element. The subjective element is the fact that the person has a fear, and the objective element is that the actual circumstances make the fear reasonable. Thus, a reasonable person in the circumstances of the applicant would fear persecution.[16]

In order to qualify for protection, the persecution must be "on account of" race, religion, nationality, membership in a particular social group, or political opinion.[17] The U.S. Supreme Court has ruled that "on account of" requires proof that the persecutor was motivated by one of the five grounds.[18] Courts still are providing additional guidance on the degree to which the applicant must establish the motivation or intent of the persecutor. Where there are mixed motives for the persecution, the BIA and federal courts have recognized that asylum still may be granted.[19] The REAL ID Act of 2005 specifically addresses mixed motive cases, and requires proof that one of the five grounds was or will be at least one *central reason* for the persecution.[20]

---

[12] 8 USC §1101(a)(42)(A), INA §101(a)(42)(A).

[13] *Matter of Acosta*, 19 I&N Dec. 21 (BIA 1985).

[14] *Kovac v. INS*, 407 F.2d 102, 106 (9th Cir. 1969).

[15] *McMullen v. INS*, 658 F.2d 1312, 1315 n. 2 (9th Cir. 1981).

[16] *INS v. Cardoza-Fonseca*, 480 U.S. 421 (1987); *see also Matter of Mogharrabi*, 19 I&N Dec. 439, 445 (BIA 1987).

[17] *INS v. Elias-Zacarias*, 502 U.S. 478 (1992).

[18] *Id.* at 482.

[19] *Matter of S–P–*, 21 I&N Dec. 486 (1996).

[20] *See* Emergency Supplemental Appropriations Act for Defense, the Global War on Terror, and Tsunami Relief, 2005, Division B, Pub. L. No. 109-13, §101(a), 119 Stat. 231 (May 11, *continued*

Whether persecution is on account of one of the five required grounds requires additional exploration of how these grounds are understood. One very helpful source of guidance is the *Handbook on Procedure and Criteria for Determining Refugee Status* published by the United Nations High Commission for Refugees (UNHCR).[21] The UNHCR provides guidance to countries that are parties to the Refugee Convention and Protocol as to how to interpret and apply the refugee definition.

According to the *Handbook*, race is meant to broadly include "all kinds of ethnic groups that are referred to as 'races' in common usage." Nationality is similar to race. There is some overlap between race and nationality, in that persecution also may be directed at a national minority or linguistic group. Examples of this would be Albanians in Yugoslavia and Kurds in Iraq, Iran, and Turkey. In other situations, there may be some overlap with political opinion grounds when political strife in a country is tied to a particular national origin identity. Persecution based on one's religion includes situations where someone is prohibited from religious practice, or where members of the religious group are subjected to harm and/or severe discrimination.

A "particular" social group includes persons of similar background, habits, or social status, and also may overlap with race, religion, etc. The social group category is one of the most potentially flexible of the five grounds. The BIA has defined social group-based persecution as "persecution that is directed toward an individual who is a member of a group of persons all of whom share a common, immutable characteristic."[22] It ruled that gender could be an element of a cognizable social group.[23] In

---

2005). The provision amended 8 USC §1158(b)(1), INA §208(b)(1).

[21] *See* Office of the United Nations High Commission for Refugees, *Handbook on Procedure and Criteria for Determining Refugee Status* (1979) (hereinafter *Handbook*). The *Handbook* has been cited as a resource in many cases. *See, e.g., INS v. Cardoza-Fonseca*, 480 U.S. 421, 439 n.22 (1987); *Perkovic v. INS*, 33 F.3d 615 (6th Cir. 1994); *Matter of Acosta*, 19 I&N Dec. 211 (BIA 1985).

[22] *Matter of Acosta*, 19 I&N Dec. at 233 ("the common characteristic that defines the group, must be one that the members of the group either cannot change, or should not be required to change."). This position has been accepted by the First, Third, Sixth, and Seventh Circuits. The Ninth Circuit has recognized a social group either by voluntary association or by immutable characteristics. *See Sanchez-Trujillo v. INS*, 801 F.2d 1571, 1576 (9th Cir. 1986) ("particular social group" implies a "voluntary associational relationship" among the purported members who are closely affiliated with each other); *Hernandez-Montiel v. INS*, 225 F.3d 1084, 1092 (9th Cir. 2000) ("particular social group" also may encompass an innate characteristic fundamental to a member's identity or consciousness that they cannot or should not be required to change).

[23] *Matter of Kasinga*, 21 I&N Dec. 357, 365–66 (BIA 1996). In *Matter of Kasinga*, the BIA held that "[y]oung women who are members of the Tchamba-Kunsuntu Tribe of northern Togo *continued*

December 2000, the Department of Justice (DOJ) issued proposed regulations that addressed social group, and that specifically recognized that a social group can be defined by gender.[24] The regulations originally proposed in 2000 have not yet become final and their promulgation has been further complicated by the concurrent jurisdiction over immigration matters between DOJ and DHS. Until these regulations are finalized, the role of gender in defining a particular social group is unclear but guided by *Kasinga* and its progeny.[25]

Political opinion encompasses a wide range of views held by a person. Guy Goodwin Gill, a scholar of international refugee law, has defined it as "any opinion on any matter in which the machinery of State, government, and policy may be engaged."[26] The statute specifically includes forcible abortion, forcible sterilization, and other forms of "coercive population control" as forms of political persecution.[27] Political opinion may be actual or imputed to an individual, and the opinion may be interpreted from actions as well as words. For example, a persecutor may interpret a person's affiliations as defiance of the state and, therefore, punish him or her even where the person did not intend to defy the government.

As noted earlier, under the INA's definition of refugee, eligibility for protection can be established by a showing of either past persecution or a well-founded fear of future harm. However, asylum *regulations* allow for a discretionary denial in cases involving past persecution when there has been a fundamental change of circumstances in the country such that

---

who have not been subjected to female genital mutilation, as practiced by that tribe, and who oppose the practice, are recognized as members of a 'particular social group.'" Thus, the feared persecution had a nexus to a social group that was partially defined by gender.

[24] "Asylum and Withholding Definitions," 65 Fed. Reg. 76588 (2000). The proposed regulations were issued following the BIA's denial in *Matter of R–A–* of an asylum claim from a woman who was fleeing domestic violence. *Matter of R–A–*, 22 I&N Dec. 907 (BIA 1999). Attorney General Janet Reno had vacated the BIA decision in *R–A–* in order to reassess gender-based persecution claims in light of her previously issued Gender Guidelines in 1995. *See* Memo, Phyllis Coven, Office of International Affairs (May 26, 1995), *reprinted* in 72 *Interpreter Releases* 781–90 (1995); *see also* 22 I&N Dec. at 906 (Attorney General order vacating decision (2001). As a result of that reassessment, the Attorney General promulgated the proposed regulations in December 2000, and later, in January 2001, remanded *R–A–* back to the BIA pending the promulgation of final regulations.

[25] *See, e.g., Niang v. Gonzales,* 422 F.3d 1187, 1198–200 (10th Cir. 2005); *Mohammed v. Gonzales,* 400 F.3d 785, 796–98 (9th Cir. 2005).

[26] G. Goodwin-Gill, *The Refugee in International Law* 49 (1996).

[27] 8 USC §1101(a)(42), INA §101(a)(42).

the person no longer has reason to fear,[28] or where the applicant could relocate to another part of the country to avoid persecution.[29] The relocation must be reasonable under all of the circumstances.[30] According to DHS's regulations, where there was past persecution or where the feared persecution is at the hands of the government, the burden shifts to DHS to show that the person can relocate.[31]

Even if an individual meets the requirement of showing a well-founded fear on account of one of the five grounds, he or she may be denied if he or she falls into special categories. The statute provides for mandatory denials of the asylum claim when (1) the applicant ordered, incited, assisted, or participated in the persecution of others;[32] (2) the applicant has been convicted of a particularly serious crime in the United States and constitutes a danger to the community (an aggravated felony is deemed to be such a crime);[33] (3) there are serious reasons to believe that the applicant has committed a serious, nonpolitical crime outside the United States;[34] (4) there are reasons to believe that the applicant constitutes a danger to the national security of the United States or is a suspected terrorist;[35] (5) the applicant has been firmly resettled in a third country;[36] (6) the applicant has previously applied for and been denied asylum in the United States or failed to file for asylum within one year

---

[28] 8 CFR §§208.13(b)(1)(i)(A), 1208.13(b)(1)(i)(A).

[29] 8 CFR §§208.13(b)(1)(i)(B), 1208.13(b)(1)(i)(B).

[30] *Id.*

[31] 8 CFR §§208.13(b)(1)(ii), 1208.13(b)(1)(ii). *See also Dandan v. Ashcroft*, 339 F.3d 567, 573 (7th Cir. 2003).

[32] 8 USC §1158(b)(2)(A)(i), INA §208(b)(2)(A)(i). When ineligibility is based on the person having participated in the persecution of others, such persecution must have been "on account of" race, religion, nationality, political opinion, or membership in a particular social group.

[33] 8 USC §§1158(b)(2)(A)(ii) and (b)(2)(B), INA §§208(b)(2)(A)(ii) and (b)(2)(B). The treatment of aggravated felonies as particularly serious crimes applies to removal proceedings commenced after April 1, 1997. The categorical application of the particularly serious crime provision only applies to conviction after October 1, 1990. *Kankamalage v. INS*, 335 F.3d 858, 864 (9th Cir. 2003).

[34] 8 USC §1158(b)(2)(A)(iii), INA §208(b)(2)(A)(iii).

[35] 8 USC §§1158(b)(2)(A)(iv) and (v), INA §§208(b)(2)(A)(iv) and (v).

[36] 8 USC §1158(b)(2)(A)(vi), INA §208(b)(2)(A)(vi). Firm resettlement amounts to an offer of some form of permanent status akin to permanent residency and does not include an offer of temporary protection or nonimmigrant status. *See Cheo v. INS*, 162 F.3d 1227 (9th Cir. 1998). 8 CFR §207.1(b). In cases where there are allegations of firm resettlement, the applicant should come forward with evidence that describes the lack of housing or other benefits in the country; limitations on his or her employment; and other restrictions such as on the ownership of property, travel, education, welfare, or citizenship. *See* 8 CFR §207.1(c).

after arriving in the United States;[37] or (7) the person may be removed under a bilateral or multilateral agreement to a safe third country where the person's life or freedom would not be threatened and where he or she would have access to a full and fair procedure for determining the asylum claim.[38]

In addition to mandatory denials, all asylum claims are subject to discretionary denials. Asylum is granted as a matter of discretion; even where a person can establish statutory eligibility, he or she must still convince the immigration judge (IJ) or asylum officer that discretion should be favorably exercised. There is little guidance on this issue; however, "the danger of persecution should outweigh all but the most egregious of adverse factors."[39] The test requires an evaluation of the totality of the circumstances, evaluating the possible persecution against the applicant's record, including but not limited to: (1) whether the applicant passed through and could have sought protection in a third country; (2) the length of time and the circumstances under which the applicant lived in a third country; (3) whether the applicant has personal ties or relatives legally in the United States; and (4) general humanitarian considerations, such as the applicant's age and health.[40] It is possible for an applicant who does not fall within the categories for mandatory denial to be denied in the exercise of discretion.

REFUGEE PROCEDURES

The 1980 Refugee Act created a procedure for persons outside the United States to be admitted as refugees. It permits the President to designate, under special circumstances, persons from specified geographical areas of the world to be admitted to the United States.[41] In order to be

---

[37] The one-year deadline may be waived for "changed circumstances" or "extraordinary circumstances" related to the failure to file within the one-year period. Changed circumstances include changes in the country conditions or in the applicable law or activities of the applicant that now place the person at risk. *Guan v. BIA*, 345 F.3d 47 (2d Cir. 2003). Extraordinary circumstances are factors or conditions that caused the applicant to miss the one-year deadline, such as post-traumatic stress or serious illness, disability, or ineffective assistance of counsel. 8 CFR §§208.4(a)(5), 1208.4(a)(5). *See also Matter of Y–C–*, 23 I&N Dec. 286 (BIA 2003).

[38] 8 USC §1158(a)(2)(A), INA §208(a)(2)(A). The United States entered into such an agreement with Canada on December 5, 2002, and the agreement became effective on December 29, 2004. *See* 69 Fed. Reg. 69480 (2004) (DHS regulations) and 69 Fed. Reg. 69490 (2004) (Executive Office for Immigration Review (EOIR) regulations).

[39] *See Matter of Pula*, 19 I&N Dec. 467 (BIA 1987).

[40] *Id.* at 473.

[41] In making the designation, the statute requires the President to consult with Congress. Addi-
continued

admitted, these persons still must meet, *as individuals*, the refugee definition discussed in the prior sections.

To receive protection, an individual may apply overseas before a
DHS officer who reviews the case and considers the categories of persons
designated by the President. For instance, for fiscal year 2004, the President designated that a maximum of 50,000 refugees could be admitted,
with the largest group from Africa (25,000) and the smallest group from
Near East/South Asia (2,000). An application is either submitted to a
DHS officer or at a U.S. consulate (which forwards the application to the
overseas DHS office).[42] In order to receive refugee status, the person
must have an individual or voluntary agency sponsor him or her and provide assurance that he or she will have a job and housing after arrival.[43]

As part of the determination of eligibility, a decision is made to determine if any grounds of inadmissibility are applicable and whether the
person has been firmly resettled. According to the statute, the public
charge, labor certification, and visa documentation requirements are inapplicable to refugees.[44] Other grounds of inadmissibility may be waived
for humanitarian reasons, to ensure family unity, or in the public interest, except for controlled substance traffickers, Nazis, and those inadmissible for security, foreign policy, or terrorism reasons.[45] Once the individual is issued a travel document, he or she has four months to come
to the United States to seek admission. Upon admission, the refugee receives work authorization, and after one year may apply for lawful permanent residency.

ASYLUM PROCEDURES

Asylum procedures are different from overseas refugee procedures as
the asylum claim is made by persons at or within the borders of the
United States. There are no limits on the numbers of persons who can
be granted asylum. A person seeking asylum at the border will be prescreened in the expedited removal process, described earlier. An asylum

---

tional refugees of "special humanitarian concern" may be admitted in response to an unforeseen emergency. *See* 8 USC §§1157(a) and (b), INA §§207(a) and (b).

[42] 8 CFR §§207.3(b), 1207.3(b).

[43] *See* J. Frederiksson, "Bridging the Gap Between Rights and Responsibilities: Policy Changes Affecting Refugees and Immigrants in the United States Since 1996," 14 *Geo. L.J.* 757, 768 (2000).

[44] 8 USC §1157(c)(3), INA §207(c)(3).

[45] *Id.*

officer will determine whether the person has a "credible fear" of persecution, and if so, the case will be set for hearing before an IJ. Credible fear is defined as "[a] significant possibility . . . that the alien could establish eligibility for asylum . . . ."[46] If the asylum officer does not believe that there is a "credible fear," the person may request review by an IJ on the question of credible fear. If it is determined that the person has a credible fear, the case will be set for a full hearing of the claim; if not, there is no further administrative review (nor is there judicial review from a denial).

A person who is already in the United States and not in removal proceedings may submit an "affirmative" application for asylum. A person submitting an application affirmatively will have the claim reviewed by an asylum officer and if the officer does not grant the claim, the case will be referred for the institution of removal proceedings. If a person already is in removal proceedings, he or she may submit a "defensive" claim for asylum and withholding of removal. A claim is termed "defensive" because it is a defense to the government's effort to remove them from the United States. As with persons in the overseas refugee process, one year after the person has been granted asylum, he or she may apply for adjustment of status to lawful permanent residency.[47]

Recent Enactments Affecting Asylum

In May 2005, Congress enacted the REAL ID Act of 2005, which includes several provisions that make it more difficult for asylum applicants to successfully present their claims.[48] Since the act is relatively recent, its impacts have not yet fully manifested. The law includes language that requires that the asylum applicant have as his or her "central reason" for persecution one of the five grounds.[49] The modification raises the burden of proof standard for "mixed motive" asylum claims, where one of the five grounds was not the only basis for the claim.[50] The

---

[46] 8 USC §1225(b)(1)(B)(v), INA §235(b)(1)(B)(v).

[47] In the original asylum statute, there was an annual quota of 10,000 asylees who could seek adjustment each year. The REAL ID Act of 2005, *supra* note 20, removed the asylum quota.

[48] *Id.*

[49] *Id.* at §101(a)(3). The actual language is that the burden of proof is on the applicant to establish that he or she is a refugee within the meaning of §101(a)(42)(A). To establish that the applicant is a refugee within the meaning of this section, he or she must establish that race, religion, nationality, membership in a particular social group, or political opinion was or will be a *central reason* for persecution.

[50] *See, e.g., Jahed v. INS*, 356 F.3d 991 (9th Cir. 2004); *Gafoor v. INS*, 231 F.3d 645, 50 (9th Cir. 2000).

REAL ID Act also allows the IJ greater independence in determining credibility and requiring corroborating evidence of the applicant.[51] Similarly, the credibility and corroboration language was designed to make it more difficult for federal courts to reverse IJ determinations.[52]

WITHHOLDING OF REMOVAL

The 1980 Refugee Act created a form of relief known as withholding of removal, which has its origins in the international law principle of *nonrefoulement*.[53] *Nonrefoulement* is the principle that a person may not be returned to a place where he or she faces persecution. It was incorporated into U.S. domestic law with the provision that the "Attorney General *may not remove* an alien to a country if the Attorney General determines that the alien's life or freedom would be threatened in such country because of the alien's race, religion, nationality, membership in a particular social group, or political opinion."[54]

Withholding is similar to asylum, in that it provides protection for persons fleeing persecution on account of one of the five grounds, but withholding, in fact, requires a higher standard of proof. Thus, in order to obtain mandatory withholding, which also is referred to as "restriction on removal," an individual must show by a "clear probability" that he or she faces the requisite harm of a "threat to life or freedom" in the proposed country of removal.[55] "Clear probability" means that it is "more likely than not" that the person would be subject to the harm.[56] The "clear probability" standard is a more difficult one to meet than the "well-founded fear" standard for asylum.

If a person is not able to qualify for asylum in the exercise of discretion or because of failure to meet the one-year deadline, he or she may be granted withholding if he or she can meet this higher standard. This relief only protects the person from being removed to the country where he or she faces harm, and it does not prevent the U.S. government from

---

[51] REAL ID Act, *supra* note 20, §101(a)(3).

[52] *See, e.g., Guo v. Ashcroft*, 361 F.3d 1194, 1200 (9th Cir. 2004); *Secaida-Rosales v. INS*, 331 F.3d 1245 (2d Cir. 2003).

[53] Refugee Convention, *supra* note 5, art. 33.

[54] 8 USC §1231(b)(3)(A), INA §241(b)(3)(A) (emphasis supplied). *See* note 37 in Chapter 2 concerning transfer of functions from Attorney General to Secretary of Homeland Security.

[55] *Janusiak v. INS*, 947 F.2d 46, 47 (3d Cir. 1991).

[56] *INS v. Stevic*, 467 U.S. 407, 429–30 (1987).

obtaining permission from a third country to accept the person (as long as the person faces no harm there and the third country will not remove the person to the country of nationality).[57] Restriction on removal does not qualify the person for permanent residency or allow the person to confer derivative status on his or her spouse or child, as is the case with asylum. Many of the statutory bars to asylum also apply to withholding of removal.[58]

CONVENTION AGAINST TORTURE

In 1994, Congress ratified the CAT, which among many other provisions, prohibits the removal of a person to a country where there are substantial grounds for believing that the individual would be in danger of torture or subject to inhuman or degrading treatment.[59] Subsequent to ratifying the CAT, the United States enacted legislation to implement it in U.S. law, and regulations were also promulgated.[60] Under the regulations, torture is defined as an

> act by which severe pain or suffering, whether physical or mental, is intentionally inflicted on a person for such purposes as obtaining from him or her or a third person information or a confession, punishing him or her for an act he or she or a third person has committed or is suspected of having committed, or intimidating or coercing him or her or a third person, or for any reason based on discrimination of any kind, when such pain or suffering is inflicted by or at the instigation of or with the consent or acquiescence of a public official or other person acting in an official capacity.[61]

An individual seeking CAT relief must establish that it is more likely than not that he or she will be tortured. Unlike the well-founded fear standard for asylum, CAT relief has no subjective component; it requires instead that the person establish, by objective evidence, that he or she is

---

[57] *Huang v. INS*, 436 F.3d 89, 95 (2d Cir. 2006) (citing *Cardoza-Fonseca v. INS*, 480 U.S. 428, 429 n.6 (1987)).

[58] 8 USC §1231(b)(3)(B), INA §241(b)(3)(B).

[59] CAT, *supra* note 3.

[60] FARRA, *supra* note 3.

[61] 8 CFR §§208.18(a)(1), 1208.18(a)(1). *See also Matter of J–E–*, 23 I&N Dec. 291, 297–99 (BIA 2002).

entitled to relief.[62] A person may be eligible for CAT relief even if he or she is barred from asylum, refugee status, or withholding of removal, as this statute is an absolute prohibition on the return of persons where they are likely to face torture. However, persons who are barred from relief because they have persecuted others or committed aggravated felonies, etc., may be held in detention. It is not clear whether someone who is ineligible for other relief and poses a danger to the community can be held in detention indefinitely.[63]

A person may apply for CAT relief in the removal process[64] whether he or she seeks admission or faces grounds of deportability. A person who is seeking CAT relief bears the burden of establishing "that it is more likely than not that he or she would be tortured if removed to the proposed country of removal."[65] A person may meet this objective evidence requirement with the person's own testimony, which, if credible, may be sufficient to sustain the burden of proof without corroboration. If a person meets this burden, he or she may not be removed to the country of feared torture, just as in withholding of removal.

TEMPORARY PROTECTED STATUS (TPS)

In the Immigration Act of 1990 (IMMACT90),[66] Congress established a provision for short-term protection known as Temporary Protected Status (TPS). The provision sets forth criteria for the extension of temporary protection to people from certain countries experiencing political or environmental upheaval.[67] For decades, during periods of civil strife, economic upheaval, or natural disaster, the Attorney General—in consultation with other agencies—exercised his or her discretion not to force nationals of countries experiencing these calamities to leave the United States. Individuals who were in the country illegally could present themselves and receive work authorization; those in proceedings had their cases put on hold; while those who already had orders of re-

---

[62] *Sevoian v. Ashcroft*, 290 F.3d 166, 175 (3d Cir. 2002).

[63] In *Zadvydas v. Davis*, 533 U.S. 678 (2001), the Supreme Court held that the immigration removal statute did not contemplate a post-removal order of indefinite detention. This case was extended to persons seeking admission in *Clark v. Martinez*, 543 U.S. 371 (2005).

[64] An applicant who submits the CAT request after the removal hearing must meet the requirements of a motion to reopen. *See* 8 CFR §1003.2(a).

[65] *Sevoian*, 290 F.3d at 174–75.

[66] Immigration Act of 1990, Pub. L. No. 101-649, 104 Stat. 4978.

[67] *See id.*, creating 8 USC §1254a, INA §244.

moval were not returned until the situation had stabilized. The relief was extra-statutory and was called "extended voluntary departure."[68] It was a pure form of prosecutorial discretion exercised on the part of the authorities.

In later years, the exercise of this prosecutorial discretion was given the designation of "deferred enforced departure."[69] TPS is the latest version of the statutory form of relief. Recent grants of TPS status have been to Liberians during specified periods of the civil war in that country; to nationals of El Salvador following a severe earthquake in 2001; and to nationals of Somalia as a result of its civil war.[70]

There are three bases for TPS under the statute: (1) existence of an ongoing armed conflict within a particular country that poses a threat to the personal safety of the general population;[71] (2) a flood, drought, epidemic, earthquake, or other natural disaster that causes a substantial temporary disruption in the living conditions in the country;[72] or (3) an extraordinary and temporary condition in a country that prevents its nationals from being able to return safely.[73] In order to qualify for TPS, a person must be physically present in the United States on the date of the designation and meet the requirements set forth in announcements issued by DHS.[74] The initial period for temporary status is from 6 to 18 months, and the decision whether to grant TPS is wholly discretionary and not subject to judicial review. Persons with a felony or two or more misdemeanor convictions are ineligible for TPS. In addition, those who are inadmissible for reasons of national security or terrorism also are in-

---

[68] *Hotel & Restaurant Employees Union, Local 25 v. Smith*, 846 F.2d 1499, 1510 (D.C. Cir. 1988) (*en banc*).

[69] For a listing of the many grants of extended voluntary departure dating back to 1960, see R. Boswell, *Immigration Law and Procedure: Cases and Materials* 558–59 (2d ed. 1992). Deferred enforced departure has been granted to nationals of certain countries such as Chinese students in the United States following the Tiananmen Square incident, during the Persian Gulf War, in 1991, for Persian Gulf evacuees, and, in 1997, for Haitians while Congress was considering legislation for their protection. *See* E.O. 12711, 55 Fed. Reg. 13897 (1990); "President Grants Relief for Persian Gulf Evacuees in U.S.," 68 *Interpreter Releases* 1649 (1991); "Clinton Orders Deferred Enforced Departure for Haitians," 75 *Interpreter Releases* 2 (1998).

[70] The official list of countries whose nationals may be eligible for TPS relief is posted on the DHS website at *http://uscis.gov/graphics/services/tps_inter.htm*.

[71] 8 USC §1254a(b)(1)(A), INA §244(b)(1)(A).

[72] 8 USC §1254a(b)(1)(B), INA §244(b)(1)(B).

[73] 8 USC §1254a(b)(1)(C), INA §244(b)(1)(C).

[74] Notice of grants and extension of TPS are made in the *Federal Register. See, e.g.,* "Extension of the Designation of Temporary Protected Status for Nicaragua," 71 Fed. Reg. 29166 (2006).

eligible.[75] Persons who qualify for relief may not be deported during the period of the grant, and are not precluded from applying for other immigration relief, such as asylum or cancellation of removal.[76]

---

[75] Most of the grounds of inadmissibility that cause the person to be ineligible may be waived for humanitarian reasons and family unity, or where it is otherwise in the public interest. *See* 8 USC §1254a(c)(2)(A), INA §244(c)(2)(A).

[76] The time that a person is in TPS does not cause a break in the period of continuous residency for purposes of cancellation relief; however, the only condition under which a person may use the period in which he or she was in TPS status to meet the minimal statutory requirement for relief is where the government determines that extreme hardship exists. 8 USC §1254a(e), INA §244(e).

CHAPTER 4
Nonimmigrant Visas: Temporary Admission to the United States

We become not a melting pot but a beautiful mosaic.
Different people, different beliefs, different yearnings,
different hopes, different dreams.
—Jimmy Carter

OVERVIEW

There are limited ways in which a person can gain admission to the United States. Individuals who come legally to the United States must have been prescreened by a consular officer and have obtained a travel permit or "visa" that gives them permission to seek admission at the border. The visa, however, does not provide a guarantee that the person will be admitted.

Broadly speaking, there are categories of visas for three types of entrants—refugees, immigrants, and nonimmigrants. Refugees and immigrants enter with the intention of remaining permanently in the United States. In contrast, most, if not all, nonimmigrants are coming for a temporary purpose. Due to the temporary nature of the visit, for most nonimmigrant visas, there are no numerical restrictions on the numbers of individuals who may be admitted.[1]

It is necessary to understand several important concepts before exploring each of the nonimmigrant visa categories. First, the immigration statute—the Immigration and Nationality Act (INA)[2]—operates under a

---

[1] The only nonimmigrant visas that have numerical restrictions are the H, Q-2, and S visas. (*See* discussion, *infra.*) There are, however, strict numerical limitations on immigrant visas.

[2] Immigration and Nationality Act of 1952 (INA), Pub. L. No. 82-414, 66 Stat. 163 (codified as *continued*

presumption that all persons coming to the United States—even on nonimmigrant visas—are intending immigrants and wish to remain permanently.[3] This presumption places a heavy burden on the applicant to convince the consular officer that he or she will depart the United States after completing his or her journey. Second, there are no catch-all nonimmigrant visas; each applicant must establish that he or she qualifies under one of the designated nonimmigrant categories. Third, each category of nonimmigrant visa may be obtained only by individuals who meet that category's specific criteria, and the individual receiving the visa must comply with all of its requirements for the entire time he or she is in the United States. A corollary is that regardless of the category of visa, the length of time a person may remain in the United States will be governed by the permission given when admitted by a Department of Homeland Security (DHS) official upon inspection at the port of entry.[4]

All of the nonimmigrant visas are listed and described at 8 USC §1101(a)(15), INA §101(a)(15).[5] The majority of visas allow the beneficiary to come to the United States with immediate family under the same visa.[6] However, most of the visa categories preclude the nonimmigrant or family member from working while in the United States. The statute further prescribes rules on the admission of nonimmigrants at 8 USC §1184, INA §214. An extensive set of federal regulations governs the issuance of nonimmigrant visas; the regulations set forth the requirements for qualification and maintenance of status, and provide the conditions under which a person may change from one nonimmigrant classification to another (a procedure called "change of status").[7]

---

amended at 8 USC §§1101 *et seq.*).

[3] 8 USC §1184(b), INA §214(b). There are ways, discussed *infra*, in which some nonimmigrants can avoid the consequences of this presumption.

[4] The inspection process is discussed in Chapter 2. The rules on the normal periods of time that a person may be allowed to remain under each visa category will be explored later in this chapter.

[5] There are currently 22 separate nonimmigrant visa categories at §§1101(a)(15)(A)–(V), INA §§101(a)(15)(A)–(V).

[6] However, the accompanying family member must not be inadmissible or must be able to qualify for a waiver. An accompanying family member enters on a "derivative" visa. For example, a person admitted as an F-1 student could bring family as F-2s—the derivative visa in this category.

[7] These regulations are contained in 8 CFR §214 (regulations governing DHS); 8 CFR §248 (regulations governing change of nonimmigrant classifications); 22 CFR §41 *et seq.* (regulations governing Department of State (DOS) issuance of nonimmigrant visas).

The nonimmigrant process can be difficult because the rules are not always clear, especially to the extent that the nonimmigrant has to navigate around the grounds of inadmissibility and deportability. Moreover, the individual often is attempting to maintain his or her nonimmigrant status with an eye toward extending his or her stay in the United States. These challenges have been heightened in the wake of the attacks of 9/11, for already-suspicious officials have become increasingly suspicious of noncitizens.[8]

DOCTRINE OF DUAL INTENT

In order to qualify for a nonimmigrant visa, a person must overcome the presumption of immigrant intent. The notion that an individual could simultaneously have the intent to remain in the United States temporarily and a future intent to be a lawful permanent resident (LPR) has been recognized, and is known as the "dual intent doctrine."[9] Just because the person has a desire to become an LPR in the future should not by itself disqualify the person from being admitted or cause a visa extension to be denied. This doctrine is recognized statutorily for H-1 (temporary workers), L (intracompany transferees), and V (family reunification) visa-holders.[10] While dual intent for E visa-holders does not specifically appear in the INA, it is recognized by DHS. This principle is not applied uniformly outside of these visa categories. Furthermore, evidence of an application for an immigrant visa can weigh against the applicant, justifying a conclusion that the person is not, in fact, a true nonimmigrant.[11] A further complicating factor is that decisions on nonimmigrant cases may be made by three different agencies.[12] Therefore, in many cases, any

---

[8] *See* M. Miyamoto, "The First Amendment After *Reno v. American-Arab Anti-discrimination Committee*: A Different Bill of Rights for Aliens?" 35 *Harv. C.R.-C.L. L. Rev.* 183, 209–11 (2000). Indeed, in both the World Trade Center bombing of 1993 and the attacks of September 11, 2001, the perpetrators were able to gain admission through the normal nonimmigrant visa issuing process. *See* F. Davies, "Fighting Terror: Many INS Failures Found on Suspects," *Boston Globe*, May 23, 2002, at A27.

[9] *Matter of Hosseinpour*, 15 I&N Dec. 191 (BIA 1975).

[10] *See* "INS Agrees to Dual Intent for E Visa Holders," 42 *Interpreter Releases* 1444 (1993).

[11] The statute presumes that all persons are immigrants unless the person can establish otherwise. 8 USC §1184(b), INA §214(b).

[12] DOS is responsible at the visa issuing point (consular posts and embassies); DHS at the port of entry and institution of charges for removal; and the Executive Office for Immigration Review (EOIR) (part of the Department of Justice (DOJ)) at the removal hearing and administrative review. Some employment-based visas involve decisions from the Department of Labor.

clear indication that the person desires or intends to remain permanently in the United States can cause problems in the person's ability to gain admission, obtain an extension, or change status unless he or she is in the statutorily recognized categories described above. Where recognized, dual intent will allow the beneficiary to pursue permanent residence in the United States at the same time that he or she is seeking a nonimmigrant visa, extension, or change of status.

VISA APPLICATION AND ADMISSION PROCEDURE

In the first step, the applicant presents him- or herself before a U.S. consul overseas, unless the individual is within a limited set of visa categories requiring that there be a petitioner in the United States. Depending on the nature of the visa, the "petitioner" is either someone who seeks the admission of the nonimmigrant (on behalf of the nonimmigrant), or the nonimmigrant him- or herself.[13] In these cases, the application is submitted in the place where the petitioner is located, and the approved petition is forwarded to the U.S. consul where the putative nonimmigrant lives, at which time he or she presents him- or herself before the consular officer. At the U.S. consular interview, the officer determines whether the person qualifies for the nonimmigrant visa; then, the officer ascertains whether any of the grounds of inadmissibility apply. If any are applicable, consideration is made as to the availability of waivers.[14]

Due to the events of 9/11, special permission is required for the person's admission if he or she is from a country designated as a state sponsor of terrorism;[15] even those not from designated countries can expect delays on account of the necessity of conducting security checks on individual applicants.[16] Visa denial rates and delays both have significantly risen since the 9/11 attacks.[17]

---

[13] Generally, where there is some type of employment relationship, there must be a U.S. petitioner. Otherwise, the nonimmigrant is the visa petitioner. A similar situation exists in cases involving persons seeking immigrant visas to come to the United States.

[14] All grounds of inadmissibility are waivable with the exception of those grounds that prohibit admission of persons engaged in espionage, sabotage, other unlawful activity regarding security grounds, overthrow of the government, Nazis, or individuals who have participated in torture. *See* 8 USC §1182(d)(3), INA §212(d)(3). As was noted earlier, the jurisdictional lines of authority in deciding questions involving many of the decisions under the INA are complicated. In an effort to resolve some of the potential jurisdictional conflicts, DOS and DHS have entered into a Memorandum of Understanding. *See* Chapter 1, note 6.

[15] Currently, the following are designated: Cuba, Iran, Libya, North Korea, Sudan, and Syria.

[16] Enhanced Border Security and Visa Entry Reform Act of 2002, Pub. L. No. 107-173, §306, *continued*

Once a person has been issued a visa, he or she may travel to the United States. However, all persons, including U.S. citizens, are subject to inspection at the border/port of entry. The inspection is to determine whether the person is an "alien" under the INA, whether he or she is "clearly and beyond a doubt" admissible, and whether the person is bringing in contraband or complying with customs and other regulations.[18] Only after the person has completed this process at the port of entry will he or she be admitted.

At the time of inspection, the individual is questioned regarding his or her intentions in coming to the United States. If the applicant has a valid nonimmigrant visa, the person will be questioned to determine whether he or she should be admitted under that visa and whether any of the grounds of inadmissibility are applicable. After making these determinations, the border inspector (an officer of U.S. Customs and Border Patrol (CBP)) decides how long the person will be allowed to remain in the United States. The length of time granted at border inspection should be distinguished from the validity period of the visa. The validity period on the visa document controls the period of time during which the person may make lawful attempts to seek admission, while the period of time that the person may actually remain in the United States is at the discretion of the CBP inspector. That period determines when the person must leave the United States, seek an extension or change of status, or seek an adjustment of status to lawful permanent residency.[19]

---

116 Stat. 543; 8 USC §1735(a). For an excellent explanation of the security procedures affecting nationals of up to 26 countries, see T. Loke Walsh & B. Wolfsdorf, "'Secure Borders, Open Doors': Consular Processing Issues in 2006," *The Visa Processing Guide and Consular Posts Handbook* 21 (AILA 2006–07 ed.). Visit *www.ailapubs.org* for more information or to order this or any other AILA publication.

[17] Consular officials who earlier could approve visa applications without a face-to-face interview were required to implement additional screening devices to review visa applicants. *See* L. Schwartz & M. Lazerow, "The Consul and Visas Condor: Closely Scrutinizing Visa Applicants," *Immigration Law Today* 24 (May/June 2003) (AILA). Additional background screening includes obtaining clearances from more government agencies than were used in the past—all of which results in longer adjudication times. *See* S. Macks, "Caught in the Middle: The Effect of Increased Visa Requirements on Non-Profit Performing Art Organizations," 15 *Seton Hall J. Sports & Ent. L.* 109, 123 (2005) (describing delays of up to eight months).

[18] 8 USC §1229a(c)(2)(A), INA §240(c)(2)(A).

[19] Changes of status and extensions of status are discussed in this chapter; "adjustment of status" is discussed further in Chapter 5.

ADVISORY OPINIONS

As part of the adjudication of an individual request for a nonimmigrant visa, a consular officer who denies an application is required to provide the person with a notice of the reasons for the denial.[20] The applicant may seek an internal review of the denial in the form of an advisory opinion from the Advisory Opinions Division (AOD) of the Visa Office of DOS,[21] but the case may only be reviewed on legal issues, not on factual findings or allegations. In the event that the *consular officer* requests an advisory opinion, the Visa Office will not issue a copy of the opinion to the applicant or his or her counsel since the AOD interprets 8 USC §1202(f), INA §222(f)—involving confidentiality of visa records—to govern advisory opinions. However, the Visa Office will send a letter to counsel or the applicant explaining the substance of the advisory opinion unless classified or sensitive information is involved.[22] As a matter of policy, advisory opinions are required where a consular official's denial is based on a finding that the person is inadmissible as a foreign government official who has engaged in a particularly serious violation of another person's religious freedom.[23]

In a strict sense, advisory opinions do not constitute administrative review, because the opinion rendered by the Visa Office is not binding on the consular officer. An advisory opinion is strongly persuasive, and, in most cases, will be followed by the consular officer. With the exception of the advisory opinion, there is no legal recourse for a person who has received a visa denial by a consular officer in a nonimmigrant case.[24]

---

[20] 8 USC §1182(b), INA §212(b). The officer should give the person a "timely" notice that states the reason for the denial with specific reference to the section of the INA under which he or she was found ineligible or inadmissible. The notice requirement may be waived by the Secretary of State; where the denial was on account of a criminal, security, or foreign policy grounds, notice is not required.

[21] *See Foreign Affairs Manual* (FAM) at 9 FAM 40.6 N.1; 22 CFR §41.121(d); 8 USC §1104(a)(1), INA §104(a)(1). *See* I. Kurzban, *Kurzban's Immigration Law Sourcebook*, Ch. 5, §II.B.1 (AILF 10th ed. 2006); L. Fuentes & E. Poh, "Advisory Opinions from the Visa Office," *The Visa Processing Guide and Consular Posts Handbook* 67 (AILA 2006–07 ed.).

[22] *Id.*

[23] 9 FAM 42.26 N.2.

[24] *See, e.g., Centeno v. Schultz*, 817 F.2d 1212 (5th Cir. 1987), *cert. denied*, 484 U.S. 1005 (1988). Some litigants have had success in cases involving visa revocations or the government's failure to adjudicate. *Wong v. Dep't of State*, 789 F.2d 1380 (9th Cir. 1986) (visa revocation); *Patel v. Reno*, 134 F.3d 929 (9th Cir. 1998). Administrative and judicial review are discussed in Chapter 6.

EXTENSION AND CHANGE OF STATUS

Extension and Reinstatement of Status

In order to avoid being placed in removal proceedings and found deportable, a person must maintain legal status at all times. One way of maintaining status is for the person to obtain an extension that effectively keeps the person in the same status. It is distinguishable from a change of status, which is a request to move from one nonimmigrant classification to another, or an "adjustment of status," which is a transition from nonimmigrant status to that of an LPR. (See Chapter 5 for discussion of adjustment of status.) A person must file his or her extension of status request in a timely manner; in other words, while he or she is still within the time period under his or her authorized stay.[25] A person may be eligible for extension of status even if he or she has fallen out of status through reinstatement of status. This is a discretionary determination by U.S. Citizenship and Immigration Services (USCIS) that the failure to maintain status was due to "extraordinary circumstances beyond [his or her] control"; moreover, there can be no other violations of status.[26] Alternatively, a reinstatement can occur where the violation was minor, excusable, and otherwise would result in extreme hardship.[27] A refusal to grant a reinstatement is a matter that is committed to agency discretion.[28] As a general rule, a person will not receive an extension of status if he or she has violated the terms of his or her status; an example of a common violation is unauthorized employment.[29] A person placed in removal proceedings will not be eligible for an extension of status; the immigration judge (IJ) does not have authority to grant these extensions. Each visa has its own rules and requirements; those specific requirements are discussed later in this chapter.

---

[25] There is an exception if the U.S. Citizenship and Immigration Services (USCIS) district director treats an untimely filing as excusable.

[26] 8 CFR §214.1(c)(4).

[27] *See, e.g.,* 8 CFR §§214.2(f)(16), 214.2(m)(10); 22 CFR §62.45. The regulations and INS Operations Instructions (OI) only provide for reinstatement of status in cases involving F-1, M, and exchange visa-holders.

[28] *See De Sousa v. Demore,* 169 F. Supp. 2d 1169, 1170–71 (N.D. Ca. 2001).

[29] 8 CFR §214.1(e).

Change of Status

The rules and regulations regarding change of status are at 8 USC §1258, INA §248; 8 CFR §248. The essential requirements are that the person be: (1) properly within status (not out of status) or be eligible for reinstatement of status; (2) within the classes of nonimmigrants that are not ineligible for change of status; (3) admissible to the United States;[30] and (4) considered as not having had the preconceived intent to seek the change of status before his or her original admission.[31] A person may be eligible for change of status even if he or she fell out of status, if the failure was due to "extraordinary circumstances beyond [his or her] control," and there are no other violations of status.[32]

Nonimmigrant visa categories that do not permit a change of status include: (1) persons who entered under the Visa Waiver Program (further discussion, *infra*); (2) C visas (transit); (3) D visas (crewman); (4) K visas (fiancé(e)s); (5) TWOVs (traveling without visa); and (6) S visas (informants). Other nonimmigrant visa categories carry their own special change of status restrictions; for instance, J (exchange visitor) visa-holders may be subject to a two-year foreign residency requirement and, if so subject, cannot change their nonimmigrant status except to an A visa (diplomatic); or G visa (international organization).[33] Persons admitted with an M visa (vocational students) may not change to an F visa (academic students) or to an H visa (temporary worker).

TRANSITION TO PERMANENT RESIDENCE: ADJUSTMENT OF STATUS

Certain persons who are in a lawful nonimmigrant status may transition to permanent residency. This process is called "adjustment of status," and is further described in Chapter 5. As with change of status, there are basic requirements in order to be eligible for this immigration benefit. In addition, some categories of nonimmigrants are ineligible for adjustment.

---

[30] Thus, they continue to be admissible.

[31] *Patel v. Minnix*, 663 F.2d 1042 (11th Cir. 1981). *See also* C. Gordon, S. Mailman & S. Yale-Loehr, *Immigration Law and Procedure* §12.09[4], n.17 and accompanying text (2006).

[32] 8 CFR §248.1(b)(1).

[33] 8 USC §1258(a)(3), INA §248(a)(3). Although the statute restricts the visa-holder's ability to change status, he or she may seek readmission under other nonimmigrant categories. *See* 8 USC §1182(e), INA §212(e). However, those previously admitted to obtain graduate medical training and who remain subject to the two-year residency requirement are ineligible for admission under the H or L visas. *Id.*

Maintaining status, properly changing status, and adjusting status pose special challenges to the immigration practitioner because of the expanding grounds of inadmissibility that have been enacted over the years.

VISA WAIVER PROGRAM

Beginning in 1986, Congress authorized nationals of specified countries to arrive in the United States under a blanket "Visa Waiver Pilot Program" without the necessity of first applying for a visa.[34] The program was made permanent in 2000.[35] Countries included in the Visa Waiver Program (VWP) are those with a low rate of visa denial, and have reciprocal arrangements with U.S. visitors. Although visas are unnecessary, the foreign nationals need passports, and there are additional requirements governing acceptable passports. For example, the issuing country must have a program to institute machine-readable passports with biometric identifiers (such as fingerprints, facial recognition, and iris scans).[36]

Persons from the visa waiver countries need not obtain visas when coming to the United States as tourists or visitors for business; when they arrive, they are inspected and at that time a decision is made as to whether they can be admitted. A person who arrives under the VWP must be able to overcome all of the grounds of inadmissibility, except for the visa requirement. If it appears that the person's request to be allowed into the United States will be denied, the person, like others arriving, may seek a withdrawal of his or her application in order to avoid future inadmissibility consequences.[37] If the person is allowed into the

---

[34] The Visa Waiver Program appears at 8 USC §1187, INA §217. Countries presently under the Visa Waiver Program are: Andorra, Australia, Austria, Belgium, Brunei, Denmark, Finland, France, Germany, Iceland, Ireland, Italy, Japan, Liechtenstein, Luxembourg, Monaco, New Zealand, the Netherlands, Norway, Portugal, San Marino, Singapore, Slovenia, Spain, Sweden, Switzerland, and the United Kingdom.

[35] Visa Waiver Permanent Program Act, Pub. L. No. 106-396, 114 Stat. 1637 (2000).

[36] As of June 26, 2005, all VWP travelers must possess machine-readable passports. Substantial fines will be imposed on carriers found to be in violation. DHS Press Release, *published on* AILA InfoNet at Doc. No. 05051269 (*posted* May 12, 2005). The original statute required that the biometric chips be in place by October 31, 2004. The biometric identifiers are set by standards established by the International Civil Organization and at present include iris scans, fingerprints, and facial images. "United States Visitor and Immigrant Status Indicator Technology Program," 69 Fed. Reg. 53318, 53327 (2004).

[37] Allowing a person to withdraw a request for admission is within the discretion of the CBP inspector.

United States, he or she is not entitled to a hearing if it is later determined that he or she should not have been allowed into the country.[38]

The VWP is convenient; however, persons admitted under the program may not remain for longer than 90 days and, depending on the decision of the inspector, an individual's permitted stay, in fact, may be for less time.[39] This period cannot be extended except for emergency reasons, and the person cannot change nonimmigrant status, or be allowed to adjust status to that of an LPR unless he or she is seeking permanent residency based on marriage to a U.S. citizen or as the child or parent of a citizen.[40]

CATEGORIES OF NONIMMIGRANT VISAS

In an effort to place the nonimmigrant visa categories into an easily understood conceptual framework, they have been organized below into six separate categories: (1) tourism; (2) educational; (3) special or family-related; (4) work or business; (5) governmental or quasi-governmental; and (6) miscellaneous.

Tourism

B-1. While this visa is for visitors, it is also for those with a business purpose and is described below under the work and business category.[41]

B-2. The largest of the nonimmigrant visa categories is this one, which is designed for the admission of tourists.[42] In any given year, the United States admits more than 13 million people as tourists. Tourists are defined in the statute as persons coming to the United States for "pleasure."[43] Over the years, the visa has expanded to include persons coming for health reasons, participating in amateur athletics, and accompanying U.S. Armed Forces personnel as dependents. The critical factor in qualifying for the visa is that the consular officer must be convinced that the person coming to the United States will not engage in work; is coming

---

[38] 8 CFR §217.4(b)(1).

[39] 22 CFR §41.2(l)(1).

[40] 8 USC §1255(c)(4), INA §245(c)(4). A U.S. citizen may petition for his or parent even if the parent entered under the visa waiver program if the U.S. citizen is over the age of 21.

[41] 8 USC §1101(a)(15)(B), INA §101(a)(15)(B).

[42] *See* DHS Report, "Temporary Admissions of Nonimmigrants to the United States" (May 2005), *published on* AILA InfoNet at Doc. No. 05051663 (*posted* May 5, 2005).

[43] 8 USC §1101(a)(15)(B), INA §101(a)(15)(B).

for a short period of time with a clear purpose; and unmistakably will depart at the end of the visit.[44] A person coming under this visa must have a definite plan for his or her trip and the ability to carry it out.[45]

Educational

Attracting foreign students has long been a part of U.S. foreign policy. The revenue that students bring provides benefits to the communities in which they reside, as well as to the institutions that receive their tuition dollars.[46] The categories described below share the characteristic of the visa recipient gaining academic, vocational, or other type of training.

F-1. This is the most common of the educational study visas and is designed for persons coming to engage in academic study in a full-time program at an approved institution.[47] The statute was amended in 1996, and prohibits persons seeking a student visa from studying at a public elementary, secondary, or adult education institution unless he or she will attend the school for less than 12 months and shows that he or she has paid the school district the full "unsubsidized per capita cost of the education[al program]."[48] The prospective student may attend education at any level, but will have to show that he or she has sufficient funds to pay for the education without having to work, and that he or she has sufficient preparation to complete the course of study. While students are allowed to work part-time under certain circumstances during their stay in the United States, it must not be seen as essential for their support, or as a way of paying for their educational program.[49]

---

[44] *See* 9 FAM 41.31 N.10–11.

[45] Where a visitor does not have sufficient funds to pay for the trip and little idea of where he or she is going, the application likely will be denied.

[46] *See* 8 USC §§1182(a)(6)(G) and 1184(m), INA §§212(a)(6)(G) and 214(m); *see also* A. Argetsinger, "Scramble to Protect Foreign Enrollment: Area Colleges Worry About Sept. 11 Fallout," *Washington Post*, Nov. 29, 2001, at B3 (estimates $11 billion in revenue to the U.S. economy and approximately 548,000 students); S. Dillon, "U.S. Slips in Attracting the World's Best Students," *N.Y. Times*, Dec. 21, 2004, at A1 (estimates revenue at $13 billion); A. Arroyo, "The USA PATRIOT Act and the Enhanced Border Security and Visa Entry Reform Act: Negatively Impacting Academic Institutions by Deterring Foreign Students from Studying in the United States," 16 *Transnat'l L.* 411, 429 (2003).

[47] 8 USC §1101(a)(15)(F), INA §101(a)(15)(F); 8 CFR §214.2(f).

[48] 8 USC §1184(m)(1), INA §214(m)(1). Failure to comply with this condition creates a separate ground for inadmissibility. *See* Chapter 2, "Miscellaneous Grounds."

[49] 22 CFR §41.61(b)(1)(ii); 9 FAM 41.61 N.7. There are circumstances under which a student who encounters an *unforeseen* change in circumstances *after being admitted* may be allowed to
continued

A person who wishes to study in the United States must be accepted by an approved institution that issues the prospective student a certificate document (SEVIS Form I-20).[50] The I-20 is then presented to the consular officer along with supporting information to establish that the person meets the F-1 requirements. The student is admitted for the duration of status according to the course of study indicated on the SEVIS I-20. After he or she has been admitted, the student is monitored by a "designated school official" (DSO) at the institution. The DSO is responsible for matters such as dealing with transfers between institutions, reduction of educational course load, and on-campus or off-campus employment. At the completion of the program, many students may be able to remain in the United States in order to obtain what is called "practical training" or postgraduate work related to their study.[51]

J-1. This is a broad visa category and it is for a person coming to the United States as a student, researcher, professor, nonacademic specialist, physician, international visitor, camp counselor, au pair, or summer student in a travel/work program. These programs are specifically approved by DOS under statutory authority granted to the agency in 1961.[52] A distinguishing feature of the J-1 visa is that some persons who are admitted under it are subject to a two-year foreign residency requirement before they may change to certain other nonimmigrant visa categories or before they may obtain permanent residency. The two-year foreign residency requirement is triggered where the person's program was financed in whole or part by the U.S. government, or by the government of the person's nationality or country of last residence; where the person was engaged in a field that was designated at the time of his or her entry as in short supply or needed in the person's home country; or where the person obtained medical training after January 10, 1977.[53]

---

work as a result. 8 CFR §214.2(f)(9)(ii)(C).

[50] The acronym "SEVIS" stands for the Student and Exchange Visitor Information System, which is an online system designed to keep track of foreign students in the United States. Each accredited educational institution that receives a foreign student is required to enter data relating to foreign students. Included in this reporting requirement is information relating to the students' maintenance of status and changes of address. *See* 70 Fed. Reg. 14477 (2005).

[51] OI 214.2(f)(10).

[52] *See* Mutual Educational and Cultural Exchange Act of 1961, Pub. L. No. 87-256, §109 (1961), *reprinted in* 1961 U.S. Code Cong. and Admin. News 2759, 2774–75.

[53] This ground of inadmissibility and its waiver are discussed in Chapter 2, "Miscellaneous Grounds." The two-year foreign residency requirement essentially means that one who falls within this requirement must reside and be physically present for a total of two years in either his or her country of nationality or country of legal permanent residence before being eligible *continued*

M-1. The M-1 visa is for vocational students—those who are coming to engage in a full-time program at a recognized nonacademic institution.[54] These students are not precluded from attending public institutions, and may attend a high school, community or junior college, or other post-secondary vocational or nonacademic program. Individuals who enter under this visa may not engage in any work until they have completed their studies. A full-time course load is considered to be 12 semester or quarter hours. The procedure for application, admission, and monitoring of the vocational student is similar to that of the F-1 student.[55]

Special and Family-Related Visas

The special and family-related visas are very different because they contemplate that the person will eventually become an LPR, and are based on a person's relationship with a U.S. citizen or LPR. Some of these visas were created due to the personal hardships caused as a result of the rigidity of the immigration laws, particularly the restrictions on a person who is seeking admission for a temporary period of time who does not have a fixed residence abroad due to his or her relationship with a U.S. citizen or LPR.[56]

K Visas. The K-1 visas are for fiancé(e)s of U.S. citizens who are entering for the sole purpose of getting married within 90 days of their admission.[57] Minor children of the K-1 visa-holder are eligible as derivatives for admission under the K-2 visa.[58] Individuals must establish that they have the legal capacity to marry, that they met the U.S. citizen within two years of filing the petition, and that they are otherwise admissible or eligible for a waiver.[59] The K-3 visa is a relatively new visa fashioned to get around the procedural difficulties of the immigrant visa process. It is designed for people already married to U.S. citizens, where the U.S. citi-

---

to change to certain other nonimmigrant visa categories or before obtaining permanent residency.

[54] 8 USC §1101(a)(15)(M), INA §101(a)(15)(M); 8 CFR §214.2(m).

[55] *See* 8 CFR §§214.2(f) and (m).

[56] S. Dizon, "The Child Status Protection Act: Does Immigration Math Solve the Family Unity Equation," 16 *Hastings Wom. L.J.* 117, 133 (2004); *see* Legal Immigration Family Equity Act (LIFE Act) Pub. L. No. 106-553, 114 Stat. 2762 (2000).

[57] 8 USC §1101(a)(15)(K)(i), INA §101(a)(15)(K)(i).

[58] 8 USC §1101(a)(15)(K)(iii), INA §101(a)(15)(K)(iii).

[59] 22 CFR §41.81(d).

zen spouse has filed an immediate relative immigrant petition, and the beneficiary seeks admission while awaiting its approval.[60] The children of a K-3 are issued K-4 visas;[61] K-3 and K-4 visa-holders are admitted for two years. A person who enters under a K visa is not eligible to change to another nonimmigrant status.

V Visas. The V visa is similar to the K-3 visa except that it is for someone who is married to an LPR, or who is the child of an LPR who filed a family petition on his or her behalf before December 21, 2000, and the petition has been pending for three or more years for any reason.[62] It also is for a person who has been waiting for three or more years for approval of a family-based immigrant petition due to the lack of availability of an immigrant visa because of quota restrictions.[63] The V visa applicant is not subject to the inadmissibility grounds due to unlawful presence or illegal admission to the United States, but must seek a waiver when he or she applies for adjustment of status. The V-2 visa is for the child of the V-1 visa-holder.[64]

Work or Business

These visas are characterized by the fact that they directly involve work or are of a "business" nature. But not all are considered to be work visas within the meaning of the INA.

B-1. A person on a B-1 visa is coming to engage in business other than "work."[65] The individual must have a foreign residency overseas that the person has no intention of abandoning. While a visit for pleasure is relatively easy to define,[66] the person coming to engage in business is frequently engaging in activity that is more akin to work, so the focus of this visa will often turn on the definition of "work." The distinction between business and work may be elusive. The following factors indicate

---

[60] 8 USC §1101(a)(15)(K)(ii), INA §101(a)(15)(K)(ii).

[61] The K-3 visa was created in 2000. *See* LIFE Act, *supra* note 56, and amendments, Pub. L. No. 106-554, 114 Stat. 2763.

[62] 8 USC §1101(a)(15)(V)(i), INA §101(a)(15)(V)(i).

[63] 8 USC §1101(a)(15)(V)(ii), INA §101(a)(15)(V)(ii).

[64] 8 USC §1101(a)(15)(V), INA §101(a)(15)(V).

[65] 8 USC §1101(a)(15)(B), INA §101(a)(15)(B). See INA §101(a)(15)(I) and *infra*, for information on I visas (visas for an alien who is a bona fide representative of foreign press, radio, film, or other foreign information media).

[66] See section on "Tourism," *supra*, for discussion of B-2 visas.

activities that constitute business, which is permitted under the B-1 (as opposed to work, which is not): (1) activities of a legitimate commercial or professional nature where the person is "not for hire;" (2) the accrual of profits is mostly overseas; (3) the activity furthers international commerce; or (4) the person is directed by a foreign employer, payment is abroad, and the services are not part of the U.S. labor market and not ones for which a U.S. worker would have to be hired.[67] Under these criteria, a person may be admitted as a B-1 visa-holder where he or she is coming to negotiate transactions or participate in a business conference; for example, missionaries may engage in their vocation but they may not sell items, solicit donations, or receive salary or remuneration.[68]

E Visas. These visas are for treaty traders (E-1) or treaty investors (E-2) and are in a special category to which some of the traditional nonimmigrant visa rules are inapplicable.[69] E visas allow the person to remain for an indefinite period of time under a reciprocal treaty of commerce and navigation between the United States and the country of nationality. The trader must be engaged in "substantial trade" between the United States and his or her home country. The treaty investor (E-2) must be developing or directing an enterprise in which he or she has invested a substantial amount of capital.

"Trade" is interpreted broadly and can include banking, tourism, transportation, consulting services, and insurance. "Substantial" is defined under the statute very vaguely, but has been interpreted for traders as constituting more than 50 percent of the activity, and, for investors, as an amount sufficient to establish a viable, and not a marginal, enterprise.[70] Treaty traders and investors are admitted for an initial period of

---

[67] 22 CFR §41.31(b); *Matter of Opferkuch*, 17 I&N Dec. 158 (BIA 1979); INS Memorandum, "Business Visitor Field Guidance," Johnny Williams, Reg. Dir., Western Reg., WRINS 70/20, *published on* AILA InfoNet at Doc. No. 03040190 (*posted* Apr. 1, 2003).

[68] *See* 9 FAM 41.31 N.9.1-3. There are some situations where persons enter as a B-1 even though they appear not to meet these criteria, such as domestic servants of U.S. citizens or of other nonimmigrants under a temporary assignment to the United States.

[69] 8 USC §1101(a)(15)(E), INA §101(a)(15)(E); 8 CFR §214.2(e). There is an E-3 visa category that is similar to the H-1B but solely for Australians and was created in May 2005. *See* 8 USC §1101(a)(15)(E)(iii), INA §101(a)(15)(E)(iii).

[70] 8 USC §1101(a)(45), INA §101(a)(45) provides that "substantial" is "such an amount of trade or capital as is established by the Secretary of State, after consultation with appropriate agencies of Government." *See also* 8 CFR §214.2(e)(14); 22 CFR §41.51(n).

two years and may receive extensions in two-year increments indefinitely as long as the business is maintained.

H Visas. H-1 and H-2 visas are for temporary workers, and the H-3 is for trainees. The H-1 visas are categorized below:[71]

H-1B. This classification allows persons who will engage in "specialty occupations," or are fashion models of distinguished merit and ability, or persons providing service related to the Department of Defense, to come to the United States to engage in work.[72] Even though temporariness is part of the description of this category, H-1Bs need not establish that they have a foreign residence.[73] Unlike most other visa-holders, H-1B nonimmigrants are not prejudiced if they are pursuing permanent residency under one of the immigrant visa categories. (*See* discussion on dual intent in this Chapter, *supra*.)

The definition of what is a "specialty occupation" is very expansive and is defined as a position that requires "the [t]heoretical and practical application of a body of highly specialized knowledge" and a bachelor's or higher degree (or its equivalent) for entry into the field.[74] In addition to the substantive criteria, the H-1B visa carries an annual quota of 65,000.[75] However, H-1Bs who are sponsored by educational institutions

---

[71] The H-1A visa no longer exists. The visa was to enable the admission of foreign nurses, but the program was discontinued. An H-1C category, discussed herein, exists for a limited number of nurses in very restricted circumstances. Otherwise, in order to gain temporary admission, nurses are required to fit under one of the other nonimmigrant categories or seek permanent residence through an immigrant work visa.

[72] 8 USC §1101(a)(15)(H)(i)(b), INA §101(a)(15)(H)(i)(b).

[73] *See* DOS Cable, 91 State 171115 (May 24, 1991), *reprinted in* 68 *Interpreter Releases* 681–84 (1991).

[74] 8 USC §1101(a)(15)(H)(i)(b), INA §101(a)(15)(H)(i)(b); *see also* 8 CFR §214.2(h)(4)(ii). *Cf.* M. Lawler, *Professionals: A Matter of Degree*, 4th Edition (AILA 2003), §11 fn. 6, and accompanying text for the history regarding the criteria for this visa.

[75] The statute places a quota of 65,000 per year, but the free trade visas for Chile and Singapore reduce the available visas by approximately 6,800 visas. However, unused Chile/Singapore free trade visas are added back into the quota at the beginning of the next fiscal year. Not subject to the quota are those who currently have H-1B status or have previously held the status and meet certain other criteria, employees of institutions of higher education or certain nonprofit organizations, and certain physicians. For fiscal years 2005 and 2006 only, visas awarded to those who have received a master's or more advanced degree from a U.S. institution of higher learning, up to a total of 20,000 per year, are not counted against the 65,000 quota. *See* L-1 Visa Reform Act of 2004, Pub. L. No. 108-447, 118 Stat. 2809.

are neither subject to the numerical cap, nor are required to pay the normal processing fee.[76]

In order to qualify for the H-1B, the U.S. employer must obtain a certification of a labor condition application (LCA) from the Department of Labor (DOL).[77] That application includes certain attestations,[78] a violation of which can result in fines, bars on sponsoring nonimmigrant or immigrant petitions, and other sanctions to the employer. The application requires the employer to state ("attest") that it will comply with the requirement that: (1) the employer will pay a wage that is no less than the wage paid to similarly qualified workers or, if greater, the prevailing wage for the position in the geographic area; (2) the employer will provide working conditions that will not adversely affect other similarly employed workers; (3) there is no strike or lockout at the place of business; and (4) notice of the DOL filing has been given to the bargaining representative or has been posted at the business.[79]

The H-1B nonimmigrant may be admitted for a period of up to three years and extensions generally cannot go beyond a total of six years except under certain circumstances. The H-1B employer must pay the reasonable cost of the employee's transportation abroad if the person is dismissed before the end of the period of admission.[80]

Some of the exceptions to the six-year limit are where the H-1B is the beneficiary of an immigrant labor certification application or employment-based immigrant petition that has been pending for more than 365 days prior to the end of the six years, or if he or she is the beneficiary of such a petition and is unable to obtain permanent residency due to quota restrictions.[81] The person is then eligible for extensions in one-year increments until the labor certification application or immigrant petition is decided, or a final decision is made on the individual's application for adjustment of status or an immigrant visa.

---

[76] 8 USC §1184(g)(5), INA §214(g)(5).

[77] 20 CFR §655.700(a)(3).

[78] 20 CFR §655.731(a)(1).

[79] 20 CFR §§655.705(c), 655.730(d).

[80] 8 CFR §214.2(h)(4)(iii).

[81] *See* American Competitiveness in the 21st Century Act, Pub. L. No. 106-313, §106, 114 Stat. 1251 (AC21).

H-1B nonimmigrants also may change employers upon the filing of a new application by the prospective employer as long as the H-1B was lawfully admitted into the United States and has not worked in the United States without authorization.[82] Similarly, an H-1B who has filed an application for permanent residency and whose application has been pending for 180 days may change jobs as long as the new job is is in the same or a similar occupational classification, which is known as "portability."[83]

H-1C. This visa is for professional nurses working in health care professional shortage areas; its availability will end in 2007.[84] It has been available to individuals coming to work temporarily as registered nurses who meet the requirements of 8 USC §1182(m)(1), INA §212(m)(1). A hospital is required to submit an attestation that the facility has taken significant steps to recruit and retain U.S. nurses. No more than 33 percent of the nurses at any given facility can be H-1C nurses. The H-1C category is limited to 500 visas per year and the recipient cannot have his or her status extended beyond three years. Given the constant shortage of available nurses in the health care profession, there have been renewed efforts to extend this visa or to allow its issuance under the H-1B category.[85]

H-2A and H-2B. Under the H-2A and H-2B programs, the person must be coming to the United States to perform service or labor of a temporary nature, and the employer must demonstrate that no U.S. workers capable of performing the work are available. Persons coming to perform agricultural labor or services must work in a job that is of a temporary or seasonal nature and are admitted as H-2A visa-holders; non–agricultural workers are admitted as H-2B visa-holders.[86] Agricultural employers can meet the certification requirements under the H-2A program if, by the half-way period in the season, they have been unable to find sufficient

---

[82] 8 USC §1184(n)(1), INA §214(n)(1). This provision became effective in October 17, 2000, and applies to all holders of H-1B status. *See* AC21, *supra* note 81.

[83] 8 USC §1184(j), INA §214(j).

[84] *See* The Nursing Relief for Disadvantaged Areas Act of 1999, Pub. L. No. 106-95, 113 Stat. 1312. The implementing legislation sunset the provision three years after the implementation of final regulations, which occurred in 2004.

[85] *See, e.g.,* Rural and Urban Health Care Act of 2005, (H.R. 248); "USCIS Instructs on Foreign Nurses: Outlines How to Qualify a Nurse as an H-1B," 81 *Interpreter Releases* 1742 (2005).

[86] *See* D. Lipinski, "The H-2s—A Class of Their Own," 2 *Immigration & Nationality Law Handbook* 84 (AILA 2001–02 ed.).

workers, thereby allowing them to fill the remaining positions with qualified foreign workers.[87]

The H-2B program is restricted to an annual quota of 66,000,[88] and is
for persons coming to perform non–agricultural work of a temporary or
seasonal nature (such as a unique construction job;[89] a trainer in stained
glass bending;[90] and summer camp or resort employees such as seasonal
cooks/chefs[91]) if U.S. workers cannot be found to take the position.
Regulations describe the positions as either satisfying a seasonal need,
peakload, or are for a one-time occurrence or an intermittent need.[92] A
position is considered temporary based on the nature of the employer's
need, not based on the nature of the duties.[93] The "temporary" certification, which is obtained from DOL, confirms that there are no U.S. workers available for the position, that the hiring of the foreign workers will
not adversely affect the wages and working conditions of similarly employed U.S. workers, and that there is no labor dispute in progress. The
application requires notice of the position for 60 to 120 days in the form
of advertising, consultation with labor unions where applicable, and
documentation to show that there has been an attempt to recruit U.S.
workers. The employer is required to pay the foreign worker for the cost
of his or her transportation home if the person is dismissed before the
end of the period for which the person was sought.[94]

H-3. The H-3 classification is for individuals who are receiving instruction or training in any field of endeavor, such as agriculture, commerce,
communications, finance, government, transportation, or the professions, as well as training in a purely industrial establishment, with the
exception of graduate medical training or education that falls within the
J visa (described above).[95] Often H-3 visa-holders are management
trainees from a large multinational company, medical externs,[96] and

---

[87] *See* 55 Fed. Reg. 29356 (1999).

[88] 8 USC §1184(g)(1)(B), INA §214(g)(1)(B).

[89] *Matter of General Dynamics*, 13 I&N Dec. 23 (Reg. Comm'r 1968).

[90] *Matter of Samarius Industries, Inc.*, 15 I&N Dec. 608 (Reg. Comm'r 1976).

[91] *In re Vito Volpe Landscaping*, 1991-INA-300 (Sept. 29, 1994) (*en banc*).

[92] 8 CFR §214.2(h)(6)(ii)(B).

[93] *See Matter of Artee*, 18 I&N Dec. 366 (Comm'r 1982).

[94] 8 CFR §214.2(h)(6)(vi)(E).

[95] 8 USC §1101(a)(15)(H)(iii), INA §101(a)(15)(H)(iii); 8 CFR §214.2(h)(7).

[96] 8 CFR §214.2(h)(7)(i)(A).

nurses who need a brief period of training that is unavailable in the native country.[97] The H-3 visa is only available where the equivalent training is not available in the home country, the foreign national will not be placed in a position where U.S. workers are regularly employed, and the training will help the foreign national pursue a career outside of the United States. Programs that are impermissible are those designed to recruit and train foreign nationals for staffing a U.S. operation, or programs in which the sponsor does not have the capacity or plan to provide the training. There is the potential overlap among H-3, B-1, and J-1 visas, and sometimes the person may more easily qualify for these other classifications (for example, in cases where he or she receives a salary from abroad and is receiving training). Persons admitted under this status may not remain for more than two years, and may not change or extend their stay, or be readmitted under an H or L visa until they have been outside of the United States for at least six months.[98]

I Visas. The I visa category is available to individuals who are representatives of foreign media.[99] The basis for this visa is a reciprocal arrangement between the United States and the applicant's home country allowing U.S. journalists to be admitted under similar conditions.[100] Individuals who are working for foreign press, radio, film, or other information media can enter under this category as long as they are employed with foreign media. In addition, those working in the information, documentary, or educational programming fields are eligible to enter under this visa category.[101]

I visa classification also may be granted to representatives from independent production companies who hold a credential issued by a professional journalism association.[102] However, those who are working in entertainment programming or commercial film may not enter in I status.[103]

L Visas. The L-1 visa for "intracompany transferees" has a long history under the INA. Like the H-1B, it is designed to facilitate the admission of

---

[97] 8 CFR §214.2(h)(7)(i)(B).

[98] 8 CFR §214.2(h)(13)(v).

[99] 8 USC §1101(a)(15)(I), INA §101(a)(15)(I).

[100] 22 CFR §41.52(a).

[101] 9 FAM 41.52 N.2.1.

[102] *See* OI 214.2(i).

[103] *Id.*

professionals into the United States. The visa specifically facilitates the
admission of multinational corporate executives and managers, or persons
with specialized knowledge.[104] The person must have been employed
abroad by the parent, branch, or subsidiary corporation of the company
continuously for one year out of the prior three years.[105] The benefit is
not limited to for-profit corporations or partnerships, so it may be sought
by a charitable, religious, or other nonprofit organization.[106]

Like the H-1B, the L-1 visa does not preclude the person from seeking lawful permanent residence while pursuing or being present in the
United States on an L-1 visa. The terms "managerial" and "executive
capacity" are defined in the statute and "specialized knowledge" is defined by the statute (the L-1 Visa Reform Act of 2004) and regulations.[107] The statute defines managers as persons who manage a function
or oversee a component of a company; establishes the goals and policies
of an organization or a major part or function of an organization; exer-
cises wide latitude of discretionary decision making; and receives only
general supervision or direction from higher level executives.[108] An employee with specialized knowledge is defined in the statute as a person
with "knowledge of the company product and its application in international markets or [with] . . . an advanced level of knowledge of processes
and procedures of the company."[109] The L-1 visa has no annual quota,
and the visa-holder may remain in the United States for a period of five

---

[104] 8 USC §1101(a)(15)(L), INA §101(a)(15)(L).

[105] Generally, the intracompany transferee must have been working for the company for one year
immediately preceding the filing of the application for admission. In some circumstances, employers request "blanket" permits, where they seek approval for a number of employees at the
same time, instead of filing separate petitions for individual employees. This generally is reserved
for larger corporations. See 8 USC §1184(c)(2)(A), INA §214(c)(2)(A). In applications filed before
June 6, 2005, where an employer was seeking a "blanket" permit, the employee need only have
worked overseas for the company for six months. The allowance for six months' previous employment was removed by the L-1 Visa Reform Act of 2004, supra note 75.

[106] See Matter of Church of Scientology Int'l, 19 I&N Dec. 593 (Comm'r. 1988); 9 FAM 41.54 N.7.3.

[107] 8 USC §§1101(a)(44)(A) and (B); INA §§101(a)(44)(A) and (B) (defining managerial and
executive capacities, respectively); 8 CFR §214.2(l)(1)(ii)(D). See also L-1 Visa Reform Act of
2004, supra note 75; 8 USC §1184(c)(2)(B), INA §214(c)(2)(B).

[108] See also 8 CFR §204.5(j)(2).

[109] 8 USC §1184(c)(2)(B), INA §214(c)(2)(B).

to seven years.[110] The spouse and children of the L-1 visa-holder are admitted as L-2s, and they are permitted to work.[111]

O Visas. The O-1 visa applies to two categories of persons. The O-1A visa is for people who, through sustained national or international acclaim, have demonstrated extraordinary abilities in the sciences, arts, education, business, or athletics.[112] The O-1B is for people in the motion picture or TV production business who have a record of extraordinary achievement.[113] The O-1 visa category has been interpreted to include a very broad range of fields. While there is no foreign residence requirement, the person must have an intent to remain temporarily. Extraordinary ability may be established either by a major international award or by at least three of the following criteria: (1) a national or international award; (2) membership in an organization in the field for which classification is sought requiring outstanding achievement; (3) published material about the person's work in professional or major trade publications; (4) having been called on to judge the work of others in the particular field; (5) original work of major significance in the field; (6) authorship and publication of scholarly work in the field; (7) evidence that the person has been in a critical or essential employment capacity with an organization of distinguished reputation; or (8) evidence that the person has or will command a high salary in the field.[114]

The O-2 is for persons who are accompanying and assisting the O-1 artist or athlete in the furtherance of his or her performance (the skills that are to be utilized in assisting must not be of a general nature).

The O-3 visa is for the spouse and children of the O-1/O-2 visa-holder.

P Visas. This visa is for athletes and entertainers.[115] The P-1A is for athletes who are themselves internationally recognized, or are part of a group that has achieved this recognition. The P-1B is for a person who performs with, or is an integral part of, an entertainment group that has been internationally recognized for a sustained period as being outstanding entertainers. The performer seeking admission in the category

---

[110] 8 USC §1184(c)(2)(D), INA §214(c)(2)(D).

[111] 8 USC §1184(c)(2)(E), INA §214(c)(2)(E).

[112] 8 USC §1101(a)(15)(O); INA §101(a)(15)(O); 8 CFR §214.2(o)(1).

[113] 8 CFR §214.2(o)(1)(ii)(A)(2).

[114] 8 CFR §214.2(o)(3)(iii).

[115] 8 USC §1101(a)(15)(P), INA §101(a)(15)(P).

must have had a substantial relation with the group for at least one year. A group of performers nationally recognized "for a sustained and substantial period" may obtain a waiver of the international recognition and one-year requirements under certain circumstances.[116] The waiver may be obtained for a quarter of the performers or entertainers in the group if they are replacing essential members of the group due to illness or other special circumstances.[117]

The P-2 visa is for a person performing as part of a group, or individually, or as an integral part of the performance, and is entering temporarily and solely to perform under a reciprocal exchange program.[118] The P-3 visa holder is entering as part of a "culturally unique program" (including coaching); the program may be commercial or noncommercial and need not be sponsored by an educational, cultural, or government agency.[119] The P-4 visa is for the spouse and children of other P nonimmigrants; they may not work.[120] Dual intent is permitted, but the P nonimmigrant must have an unabandoned foreign residence.

Q Visas. The Q visa is for persons participating in an international cultural exchange program approved for the purpose of providing employment, practical training, and the sharing of history, culture, and traditions of the entrant's country of nationality.[121] The program must take place in a school, museum, business, or other similar establishment.[122] The cultural component must be designed to exhibit or explain the attitude, customs, history, heritage, philosophy, or traditions of the person's country, and the program must be the vehicle to achieve the cultural objective. Q visas are limited to 15 months; the person must have a foreign residence and be employed under the same wages and conditions as U.S. workers.[123] Someone who already has been here for 15 months will not be readmitted until he or she has been physically outside the United States for at least one year.

---

[116] 8 USC §1184(c)(4)(B)(ii), INA §214(c)(4)(B)(ii).

[117] 8 USC §1184(c)(4)(B)(iii), INA §214(c)(4)(B)(iii).

[118] 8 USC §1101(a)(15)(P)(ii)(II), INA §101(a)(15)(P)(ii)(II).

[119] 8 USC §1101(a)(15)(P)(iii), INA §101(a)(15)(P)(iii).

[120] 8 USC §1101(a)(15)(P)(iv), INA §101(a)(15)(P)(iv).

[121] 8 USC §1101(a)(15)(Q), INA §101(a)(15)(Q).

[122] 8 CFR §214.2(q)(3)(iii)(A).

[123] 8 USC §1101(a)(15)(Q)(i), INA §101(a)(15)(Q)(i).

There is a special Q-2 program limited to 4,000 visas per year for persons 35 or younger from Northern Ireland and certain counties of Ireland.[124] The program is for culture and training, and provides practical training, employment, and experience, and conflict resolution; participants in the program may not stay in the United States for more than three years.[125]

R Visas. Ministers, persons working in a professional capacity for a religious organization, or others working for such an organization may enter as R-1 religious workers.[126] Religious occupations include activities that relate to religious functions. Examples of such occupations include liturgical workers, cantors, and religious broadcasters. Whether a position is religious relates to the religious function, *e.g.*, nun or monk. The spouse and children are allowed to enter under the R-2 visa.

In order to qualify, the person must be a member of a religious denomination (for a minimum of two years before the application filing) that has a bona fide nonprofit religious status in the United States.[127] In determining whether the organization qualifies as "religious," the consular officer will look to see whether there exists some type of ecclesiastical government, a creed and form of worship, a formal code of doctrine and principles, or religious services.[128] The initial period of admission is usually three years, and can be extended for an additional two years.[129]

TN Visas. The TN visa is for nationals of Canada or Mexico admitted under the North American Free Trade Agreement (NAFTA)[130] and who seek "temporary entry as a business person to engage in business activities at a professional level."[131] There is a list of professions for which persons may be admitted to the United States under this visa.[132] If the applicant is a professional, the visa is similar to the H-1B, but without a

---

[124] 8 USC §1101(a)(15)(Q)(ii), INA §101(a)(15)(Q)(ii).

[125] *Id.*

[126] 8 USC §1101(a)(15)(R), INA §101(a)(15)(R). *See Immigration Options for Religious Workers* (AILA 2005). Visit *www.ailapubs.org* for more information on AILA publications.

[127] 8 USC §1101(a)(15)(R)(i), INA §101(a)(15)(R)(i).

[128] 22 CFR §41.58(b).

[129] 8 USC §1101(a)(15)(R)(ii), INA §101(a)(15)(R)(ii).

[130] 8 USC §1184(e)(2), INA §214(e)(2). *See www.nafta-sec-alena.org* for text of NAFTA and other information relating to NAFTA.

[131] 8 CFR §214.6(a).

[132] 8 CFR §214.6(c), Appendix 1603.D.1 to Annex 1603 of NAFTA.

defined limit on the length of time that the person may remain in the United States. At the same time, the TN recipient will have to show that he or she will remain for a "temporary period," which is defined as a period with a "reasonable, finite end that does not equate to permanent residence.[133] "TN applicants must satisfy the inspecting immigration officer that the proposed stay is temporary. To establish the temporary nature of the employment, the TN applicant must demonstrate to the satisfaction of the inspecting immigration officer that the work or assignment in the United States will end at a specific time after which he or she will leave the United States."[134] A self-employed person may not be admitted as a TN.

Mexicans are treated differently from Canadians under this visa.[135] The Canadian need only show that he or she is a "professional" coming for work in his or her field based on a job offer, and may submit a request for admission at the border.[136] They must present proof of Canadian citizenship, description of the purpose for the entry, and evidence that they will be engaged in one of the occupations or professions listed in Schedule 1 of NAFTA or will perform appropriate B-1 activities. When traveling from Canada, entry may be made at CBP pre-flight inspection (PFI) at certain airports in Canada, including Toronto, Montreal, Vancouver, and Ottawa, or at a land border port of entry.[137]

The Mexican applicant, however, must present the application before a U.S. consul.[138] Business visitors who are citizens of Mexico must obtain a B-1/B-2 laser visa/border crossing card at a U.S. consulate abroad prior to entry to the United States.[139] To obtain a visa, the applicant must present a completed form DS-156, and if applicable, DS-157, the standard nonimmigrant visa application, evidence of Mexican citizenship and residence, passport or border-crossing card, and finger-

---

[133] 8 CFR §214.6(b).

[134] *See* J. Eiss & D. Rizzo, "Overview of the Temporary Entry Provisions in Chapter 16 of NAFTA," *Immigration Practice Under NAFTA and Other Free Trade Agreements*, Third Ed. 1, 10 (AILA 2006) (hereinafter Eiss & Rizzo). For more information on this or any AILA publication, visit *www.ailapubs.org*.

[135] 8 CFR §214.6(d).

[136] 8 CFR §214.6(d)(2).

[137] Eiss & Rizzo, *supra* note 134.

[138] 9 FAM 41.59 N.4; *see also* 8 CFR §214.6(d)(3).

[139] 8 CFR §214.2(b)(4). Eiss & Rizzo, *supra* note 134.

prints.[140] Only after a citizen of Mexico obtains a B-1/B-2 visa may he or she apply for admission at a U.S. port of entry.

However, the professional occupation range for Mexican TNs is the same as for Canadian applicants.[141]

Law Enforcement-Related Visas

In recent years, several new nonimmigrant visa categories were established to assist U.S. law enforcement. These visas provide temporary nonimmigrant status for the beneficiary and require the cooperation of law enforcement officials.

S Visas.[142] The S-5 and S-6 visas[143] are limited in number, and are for individuals who have important and reliable information concerning a criminal organization or enterprise. They must be willing to supply (or have supplied) information to state or federal law enforcement agents and their presence must be determined to be essential. (These are commonly referred to as "snitch" visas.) The S-5 visa is for people determined to be essential by the Attorney General and to have reliable and critical information about a criminal enterprise or organization.[144] The S-6 visa is for individuals determined jointly by the Secretary of State and Attorney General as having critical and reliable information concerning a terrorist organization where the person seeking the visa is, or will be, in danger if the visa is not granted.[145]

Two hundred visas are allocated to the S-5 category and 50 for the S-6 category.[146] These visas are limited to three years and may not be extended; however, the beneficiary may be granted permanent residency later as long as the information provided substantially contributes to the

---

[140] Eiss & Rizzo, *supra* note 134. *See also* 22 CFR §41.32(a)(2).

[141] 9 FAM 41.59, Exh. II; 8 CFR §214.6(c).

[142] The visa codes for this category are S-5 and S-6 because S-1 and S-2 were already in use when the legislation creating the visa was passed. *See* "Entry of Aliens Needed as Witnesses and Informants; Nonimmigrant S Classification," 60 Fed. Reg. 44260 (1995).

[143] 8 USC §1101(a)(15)(S), INA §101(a)(15)(S).

[144] 8 USC §1101(a)(15)(S)(i), INA §101(a)(15)(S)(i).

[145] 8 USC §1101(a)(15)(S)(ii), INA §101(a)(15)(S)(ii).

[146] 8 CFR §214(k)(1).

investigation's success.[147] These visas also are available to family members who are admitted as S-7s.[148]

T Visas. This visa was included in the implementing legislation to the UN Convention Against Torture.[149] The statute provides up to 5,000 visas for persons who have been the subjects of severe trafficking,[150] which is defined as "sex trafficking in which a commercial sex act is induced by force, fraud, or coercion, in which the person induced to perform such act has not attained 18 years of age" or "the recruitment, harboring, transportation, provision, or obtaining of a person for labor or services, through the use of force, fraud, or coercion for the purpose of subjection to involuntary servitude, peonage, debt bondage, or slavery."[151] The T visa is for victims who agree to assist in prosecutions or are under the age of 18 and would suffer "extreme hardship involving unusual and severe harm upon removal."[152] The T visa is for three years, and the individual may seek adjustment of status to that of an LPR if he or she has maintained status, been of good moral character, and complied with reasonable requests for assistance in prosecuting trafficking.[153]

U Visas. The U visa is for the individual who has been a victim of serious violent crimes (including domestic violence) as listed in the statute, and has suffered "substantial physical or mental abuse as a result."[154] In order to qualify for this visa, the victim must have been helpful, is being helpful, or likely will be helpful to a federal, state, or local law enforcement official.[155] The visa is limited to 10,000 issued per year,[156] and there

---

[147] 8 USC §1255(j), INA §245(j).

[148] 8 USC §1101(a)(15)(S), INA §101(a)(15)(S).

[149] Fiscal Year 1999 Omnibus Consolidated and Emergency Supplemental Appropriations Act, Pub. L. No. 105-277, Div. G, Subdiv. B, Title XXI §2242 of the Foreign Affairs Reform and Restructuring Act of 1998, 112 Stat. 2681–822 (1998).

[150] 8 USC §1184(o), INA §214(o).

[151] 22 USC §7102(8).

[152] 8 USC §1101(a)(15)(T), INA §101(a)(15)(T); 8 CFR §214.11(b).

[153] 8 USC §1255(l), INA §245(l).

[154] 8 USC §1101(a)(15)(U)(i)(I), INA §101(a)(15)(U)(i)(I). The visa also is available to the victim's minor unmarried children or, in the case of a minor, to his or her immediate family members. *See* 8 USC §1101(a)(15)(U)(ii), INA §101(a)(15)(U)(ii).

[155] 8 USC §1101(a)(15)(U)(i)(III), INA §101(a)(15)(U)(i)(III).

[156] 8 USC §1184(p)(2)(A), INA §214(p)(2)(A).

are provisions allowing the victim to adjust status to permanent residency after three years.[157]

Governmental or Quasi-Governmental

Just as U.S. government employees are able to travel overseas in their official capacity, so are foreign government officials and employees of international organizations. The United States is host to a number of international organizations, and thousands of their employees live in this country. The visas under this heading, for reasons of foreign policy, are partially under the jurisdiction of the Secretary of State.

A Visas. The A visa-holders enjoy diplomatic immunity and, under the Vienna Convention or a separate consular treaty with their country, they are not subject to the jurisdiction of the United States.[158] The A-1 visa is for heads of state, high military officials, certain officers assigned to diplomatic missions, and their immediate family. The A-2 visa is for other accredited officials of the foreign government and their immediate family. The A-3 visa is for attendants, servants, personal employees, and members of their immediate family.

G Visas. These visas are for officials, employees, and dependents of international organizations that are quasi-governmental.[159] Examples of such organizations are the United Nations (UN), the Organization of American States (OAS), the World Bank, and the International Monetary Fund (IMF). The G-1 visa is for the principal representative, family, and staff as long as they are assigned on a "resident basis."[160] The G-2 visa is for other (nonprincipal) representatives of a recognized government who are assigned to an international organization, and to members of their immediate family.[161] The G-3 visa is for officials of governments without *de jure* recognition by the United States, who are assigned to the international organization and members of their immediate family.[162] Persons included in this final category are nationals of nonrecognized

---

[157] 8 USC §1255(m), INA §245(m).

[158] *See* Vienna Convention on Diplomatic Relations, art. 33–36, Apr. 18, 1961, 23 U.S.T. 3227, 500 U.N.T.S. 95.

[159] 22 USC §288.

[160] 8 USC §1101(a)(15)(G)(i), INA §101(a)(15)(G)(i). Resident basis means that they are assigned to the organization's mission in the United States on a permanent basis.

[161] 8 USC §1101(a)(15)(G)(ii), INA §101(a)(15)(G)(ii).

[162] 8 USC §1101(a)(15)(G)(iii), INA §101(a)(15)(G)(iii).

countries or nationals of countries that are not members of the international organization.

Miscellaneous

There are additional visas that bear mention. The C visa is for persons traveling "in immediate and continuous transit" through the United States.[163] In order to be admitted, the person must have sufficient funds and permission to enter a third country.[164] The D visa is for persons working as crew members on airlines and shipping vessels.[165] Normally crewmembers are not allowed to remain for more than 29 days and may not be granted extensions or change of status.[166] NATO visas are for representatives of nations belonging to NATO, their staff, and immediate family.[167] The N visa is for parents of an undocumented person who is accorded special immigrant status.[168]

One additional category that is not really a visa is the transit without visa (TWOV) program, which began in 1952, and was temporarily suspended by DHS in August 2003.[169] The TWOV program previously allowed passengers arriving in the United States from a foreign country to transit through one or two U.S. airports en route to another foreign destination without a visa. DHS and DOS plan to reinstate the TWOV program as soon as additional security measures can be implemented to safeguard the program from misuse by terrorist organizations. The suspension of the TWOV designation did not affect the travel of persons from visa waiver countries, as they are not required to obtain visas if they are coming for a short stay.

---

[163] 8 USC §1101(a)(15)(C), INA §101(a)(15)(C).

[164] 22 CFR §41.71(a).

[165] 8 USC §1101(a)(15)(D), INA §101(a)(15)(D).

[166] 8 CFR §252.1(e).

[167] 22 CFR §41.25(a); *also see* 8 USC §§1101(a)(15)(G)(i), (iv), and (v), INA §§101(a)(15)(G)(i), (iv), and (v).

[168] 8 USC §1101(a)(15)(N), INA §101(a)(15)(N).

[169] 68 Fed. Reg. 46948 (2003). In September 2003, DHS began seeking comments; final regulations have not yet been issued.

CHAPTER 5
Immigrant Visas:
Lawful Permanent Residence

*Our attitude toward immigration reflects our faith in the American ideal.
We have always believed it possible for men and women who start at the
bottom to rise as far as their talent and energy allow. Neither race nor place
of birth should affect their chances.*
—*Robert Kennedy*

INTRODUCTION

Most countries provide noncitizens with a way of obtaining long-term residency, giving the person a right to remain and work. The United States has provided this form of benefit to noncitizens since the earliest days of the republic. The discussion in this section will deal with permanent residence: how it is obtained, and how it is preserved.

Lawful permanent residence is a status that a noncitizen may obtain in a number of ways:

- *Family-based immigrant visa.* Persons who have a familial relationship with a U.S. citizen or lawful permanent resident (LPR) may seek status through a petition filed by a family member or, under certain limited circumstances, through self-petitioning.[1]
- *Employment-based immigrant visa.* Foreign workers may obtain permanent residence if they are able to establish that they have unique skills, or are being offered a job in the United States

---

[1] 8 USC §1153(a), INA §203(a).

that will not displace a U.S. worker or have an adverse effect on the wages and working conditions of U.S. workers.[2]

- *Asylees and refugees.* Individuals admitted as refugees or granted asylum in the United States may be eligible to apply for LPR status within one year of admission (in the case of refugees) or of a favorable decision (in the case of asylees).[3]

- *Registry.* Persons who have been in the United States continuously for a set period of time and can show good moral character may obtain LPR status.[4]

- *Cancellation of removal.* Persons of "good moral character" who have been in the United States for 10 or more years and can show that their removal would result in exceptional and extremely unusual hardship to their spouse, parent, or child who is a U.S. citizen or LPR may become permanent residents.[5]

- *Diversity immigrant visas.* Winners of a visa lottery made available to citizens of a designated set of countries can become LPRs.[6]

- *Legalization and other special relief.* Specific categories of persons may obtain LPR status through special congressional enactments in the form of an amnesty or "legalization" for set groups of people.[7] Other individuals may obtain LPR status through private legislation.

In order to establish eligibility to apply for permanent residency, a person has to establish statutory eligibility as well as meet strict quota controls on the numbers of persons who may be granted the particular status in any given year.[8] In addition, the person must show that he or she is admissible or can qualify for a waiver of any applicable ground of inadmissibility. Whether and how a person may obtain LPR status will be determined by different procedures depending on an individual's immigration posture at the time that he or she is making the application and whether he or she is within or outside of the United States.

---

[2] 8 USC §1153(b), INA §203(b).

[3] 8 USC §§1159(a) and (b), INA §§209(a) and (b).

[4] 8 USC §1259, INA §249.

[5] 8 USC §1229b, INA §240A.

[6] 8 USC §1153(c), INA §203(c).

[7] An example is Congress's enactment of the Immigration Reform and Control Act of 1986, by which thousands of persons were granted amnesty and status in the United States. *See* Pub. L. No. 99-603, 100 Stat. 3359 (1986).

[8] *See, infra,* discussion on quotas in this Chapter.

A person who is an LPR may live and work in the United States and travel in and out of the country relatively easily. An LPR, by definition, is not a U.S. citizen, and, therefore, remains subject to all of the provisions of the INA. However, a person who has been admitted to LPR status for the statutorily prescribed period may be eligible to apply for U.S. citizenship.[9]

THE PETITION REQUIREMENT

In most cases, in order to obtain permanent residency through a family relationship or employment, there must be a petitioner (the person applying for LPR status is the "beneficiary"). Where status is being sought based on a familial relation, there must be a willing U.S. citizen or LPR who is seeking the admission of the applicant. Where there is an employment relationship, the U.S. employer is the petitioner. There are some limited exceptions to this petition requirement, including cases where the noncitizen has extraordinary employment qualifications; where the person has been the victim of extreme cruelty or battery by the family member who otherwise would be the petitioner; or, in some limited cases, where the petitioner has died.

The petition requirement can create harsh consequences where the petitioner no longer wishes, or is no longer able to seek the noncitizen's admission.[10] In situations where the petitioner has died, the statute provides that if the petitioner was a U.S. citizen and was married to the beneficiary for at least two years, the beneficiary may seek permanent residency within two years of the spouse's death.[11] Additionally, if the applicant has been a victim of extreme cruelty or battery at the hands of the U.S. citizen or LPR petitioner, he or she may be able to self-petition, and thus, not rely on the perpetrator.[12]

---

[9] Naturalization and citizenship are discussed in Chapter 7.

[10] As will be seen, the quota system has created long waiting periods. As a result, many changes can occur between the time the application is initially filed and when the beneficiary is admitted to legal status.

[11] 8 USC §§1151(b)(2)(A)(i), 1154(a)(1)(A)(ii); INA §§201(b)(2)(A)(i), 204(a)(1)(A)(ii).

[12] 8 USC §1154(a)(1)(A)(iii)–(iv), (a)(1)(B)(ii)–(iii), INA §§204(a)(1)(A)(iii)–(iv), (a)(1)(B)(ii)–(iii). There are additional self-petitioning situations set forth in other sections of the statute. *See, e.g.,* Pub. L. No. 108-136, §§1703(a) and (b), retroactively effective Sept. 11, 2001. For related provisions regarding posthumous benefits to surviving spouses, children, and parents of LPRs or victims of the 9/11 attacks, see Pub. L. No. 108-136, §§1703(c) and (d). *See also* Uniting and Strengthening America by Providing Appropriate Tools Required to Intercept and Obstruct Terrorism Act of 2001, Pub. L. No. 107-56, Title IV, Sub. C, §§421–428, 115 Stat. 272 (2001) (USA PATRIOT Act).

ROUTES TO PERMANENT RESIDENCY

The statute provides two main procedural routes to obtaining permanent resident status. The most common of these is the "immigrant visa" process, where the beneficiary seeking admission is outside of the United States. The other procedural route is where the person already is in the United States and attempts to have his or her status "adjusted" to that of an LPR without the necessity of first departing from the country.[13] This latter procedure is viewed as a special immigration benefit accorded only to a limited group of people.

Immigrant Visa Process

Under the immigrant visa process, an individual must first establish eligibility based on a family or employment relationship, or as a diversity immigrant, and then apply for a visa before a U.S. consul abroad. It is at the time of the consular interview that the grounds of inadmissibility and waivers are considered. Upon approval, the person may travel to the United States and be inspected to ensure compliance. Upon inspection and admission, the person is considered to be a permanent resident.[14]

Adjustment of Status

The "adjustment of status" route allows a person to obtain permanent residency without having to proceed overseas to apply for an immigrant visa. To qualify for adjustment, the applicant must have been inspected and admitted or "paroled," be in lawful status,[15] and not have worked illegally in the United States subsequent to January 1, 1977.[16] There also must be a visa number "immediately available" at the time of the application.[17] This requirement refers to the quota availability and preference category (discussed below) under which the person seeks permanent residency.

---

[13] 8 USC §1255, INA §245.

[14] Under some circumstances, such as where the visa is sought based on marriage to an LPR or U.S. citizen, the person may receive a two-year temporary or "conditional" status.

[15] The lawful status requirement does not apply to persons who are seeking adjustment as an immediate relative of a U.S. citizen (defined below), battered spouse or child, or in the case of certain special immigrants.

[16] The unauthorized employment bar is inapplicable to immediate relatives of U.S. citizens, asylees, or persons seeking permanent residency under the employment-based category who did not work without authorization for more than 180 days. 8 USC §§1255(c) and (k), INA §§245(c) and (k).

[17] *See* 8 USC §1255(a)(3), INA §245(a)(3).

The adjustment applicant must be able to overcome any and all grounds of inadmissibility. Even if a person meets these statutory eligibility requirements, his or her application still may be denied as a matter of discretion. The discretionary factors are family ties in the United States, hardship in traveling abroad, length of U.S. residence, previous immigration violations, and preconceived intent (which refers to the intent that a person may have had at the time of his or her last admission prior to pursuing adjustment of status). If a person is seeking adjustment based on an immediate relative petition, preconceived intent, standing alone, is not sufficient to deny the application.[18]

In 1994, Congress passed special adjustment of status provisions, commonly referred to as "§245(i)," based on INA §245(i),[19] which provided broad-based relief for persons who were otherwise ineligible for adjustment; thus, allowing them to become LPRs without having to go the route of the immigrant visa process abroad. In exchange for this benefit, they were required to pay a surcharge fee.[20] While the program ended in January 1998, those persons who had qualified under §245(i) as of that date were grandfathered in. On December 15, 2000, Congress extended the grandfathering date to April 30, 2001.[21] Thus, those individuals who were the named beneficiaries of either an application for labor certification (an additional requirement for employment-based immigration, discussed, *infra*) or an immigrant petition,[22] were eligible to adjust. Those who had a qualifying relationship or a job offer on that date, even if the petition was not approved until after that time, were grandfathered in under §245(i), so long as they did not depart the United States. While the existence of such a petition will not necessarily stop a removal proceeding, it will allow a person to file for adjustment if a visa number becomes available while in removal proceedings.

The current unavailability of adjustment of status under §245(i) presents more than just an inconvenience. Because many of those utilizing

---

[18] *See Matter of Cavazos*, 17 I&N Dec. 215 (BIA 1980).

[19] Department of Commerce, Justice, and State Appropriations Act, Pub. L. No. 103-317, Title V §506(b), 108 Stat. 1724 (1994); *see also* 8 USC §1255(i), INA §245(i).

[20] As originally enacted, §245(i) allowed most persons who had a basis for becoming LPRs, and who were otherwise admissible to become LPRs, to adjust upon payment of a fee of $1,000. This "grandfathering" provision also applied to children who "aged-out" (*i.e.*, turned 21) while the application was pending.

[21] Pub. L. No. 106-554, Title XV, 114 Stat. 2763 (2000).

[22] 8 CFR §1245.10(a)(2).

the former §245(i) entered the country without inspection, they accrued "unlawful presence" making them subject to the three- and ten-year bars against admissibility.[23] Thus, the need to go abroad to adjust necessarily means that they must travel to a port of entry and be readmitted—but, in fact, they generally will not be admitted because of the bars. In contrast, if they had been able to adjust, they would not have had to leave the country, and the three- and ten-year bars would not have been triggered.[24]

QUOTAS

Whether a person is able to become an LPR also will be controlled by whether he or she can satisfy the quota requirements. The statute exempts from the quota "immediate relatives" defined as the "children, spouses and parents" of a U.S. citizen; when a child petitions for his or her parent, he or she must be at least 21 years of age.[25] The quota for family immigrants is set at 480,000 less the number of immediate relative visas issued, with a minimum of 226,000 reserved for non–immediate relatives.[26]

The quota for employment-based immigrants is limited to 140,000 visas plus the unused numbers from the family preferences. Immigrant visas under the diversity lottery are set at 55,000. Other limits are country-based. No more than 7 percent of the total visas—or 25,600—can be used by nationals of any one country. In addition, no more than 2 percent—or 7,320—can be used by nationals from "dependent" areas (*i.e.*, colonies).[27]

FAMILY-BASED IMMIGRANTS

As noted above, the "immediate relative" category—spouses, parents, and children[28] of U.S. citizens—is not subject to numerical limitations. Other

---

[23] 8 USC §1182(a)(9)(B), INA §212(a)(9)(B).

[24] See discussion in Chapter 2 for more on inadmissibility.

[25] 8 USC §1151(b)(2)(A)(i), INA §201(b)(2)(A)(i).

[26] 8 USC 1151 §201(c)(1), INA §201(c)(1).

[27] For example, Guam and American Samoa are colonial territories of the United States. As prescribed in the INA, persons from colonial territories would be limited to 7,320 immigrant visas in any given year.

[28] A "child" is defined generally as an unmarried person under the age of 21. 8 USC §1101(b)(1), INA §101(b)(1). Under the statutory definition, a married person, or person over 21, would be a son or daughter rather than a child.

relationships, which are subject to a quota system, are divided into family-based "preferences." The family preferences include four categories:

- *First Preference*: unmarried sons and daughters of U.S. citizens;[29]
- *Second Preference*: spouses and children of LPRs (2A); and unmarried sons and daughters of LPRs (2B);[30]
- *Third Preference*: married sons and daughters of U.S. citizens;[31] and
- *Fourth Preference*: brothers and sisters of U.S. citizens.[32]

In all of the immigrant visa preference categories, only the primary beneficiary need establish the familial or employment relation; the person's spouse and minor children are eligible to immigrate under the same preference, but the total number of visas issued for that family count against the annual quota.

As noted above, the quota system precludes the issuance of visas to nationals of any one country in excess of 25,600. This means there must be a way of allocating the visas by nationality as well as by the order in which the applications are received. This allocation system uses the concept of a person's "priority date," which is described below.

The allocation of visas by nationality is called "foreign state chargeability."[33] Generally, a person's visa is charged to the country where he or she was born and not to the country of current nationality. Exceptions to this rule may be used to keep families together, especially where the use of an alternative method would ensure or quicken the person's admission. These exceptions include: (1) children, who may be charged to either of their parents' country of "chargeability," and spouses, who may be charged to the country of his or her accompanying spouse;[34] (2) persons who have lost their U.S. citizenship and are seeking to return are charged to the country of current citizenship; and (3) persons born in a place where neither parent is from may be charged to the country of either parent.[35]

In addition to the nationality allocation, the availability of visas under the quota system is determined by the person's "priority date." A

---

[29] 8 USC §1153(a)(1), INA §203(a)(1).

[30] 8 USC §§1153(a)(2)(A) and (B), INA §203(a)(2)(A) and (B).

[31] 8 USC §1153(a)(3), INA §203(a)(3).

[32] 8 USC §1153(a)(4), INA §203(a)(4).

[33] *See* 8 USC §1152(b), INA §203(b); 22 CFR §42.12.

[34] *See* 22 CFR §§42.12(c) and (d).

[35] *See* 22 CFR §42.12(e).

priority date is that date on which a person initially submitted documentation establishing eligibility for one of the preference categories under the immigrant visa scheme.[36] In the case of a family-based petition, the priority date would be the date on which the petitioner submitted the application showing that there existed a qualifying familial relationship with the beneficiary.[37]

While the establishment of a priority date may not be very complicated, the preservation and transfer of the priority date within preferences can amount to an arcane science. In an immigrant visa system where the visa applicants are fewer than the available quota, priority date rules are not critical. However, since the early 1980s, there have been far more visa applicants than the available quota allows, making a full understanding of priority dates important to the practitioner who must be very aware of how the dates impact the length of time it may take to immigrate.[38] An explanation of the use of the priority dates can be illustrated by the visa chart below, issued by the Department of State (DOS) for the month of June 2006. The visa charts are updated each month and can be found on DOS's website.[39]

	All Chargeability Areas Except Those Listed	China—mainland born	India	Mexico	Philippines
Family					
1st	22APR01	22APR01	22APR01	01JAN92	01SEP91
2A*	22APR01	22APR01	22APR01	22JAN99	22APR01
2B	01AUG96	01AUG96	01AUG96	22OCT91	08JUL96
3rd	01AUG98	01AUG98	01AUG98	01MAR93	01JUL88
4th	01MAR95	01MAR95	15AUG94	15AUG93	01NOV83

* [footnote omitted]

In the chart above, the furthest left hand column lists the particular preference categories; the remaining five columns list the geographical areas. The first column includes all areas except China, India, Mexico, and the Philippines, which have their own separate columns. The chart indi-

---

[36] An application must be properly filed with U.S. Citizenship and Immigration Services (USCIS) in order for a registration date to attach.

[37] 22 CFR §42.53(a); 9 FAM 42.53 N.1.

[38] H. Chang, "Migration as International Trade: The Economic Gains from the Liberalized Movement of Labor," 3 *UCLA J. Int'l L. & For. Aff.* 371, 406 (1998).

[39] DOS's Visa Bulletin website is *http://travel.state.gov/visa/frvi/bulletin/bulletin_1360.html.*

cates which registration or "priority dates" are currently being processed for immigrant visas as of the time that the chart was issued—the dates listed are the cut-off dates, and only dates *earlier* than those listed have numbers available. Accordingly, a person born in France with a priority date of April 21, 2001, as the unmarried son or daughter of a U.S. citizen (*i.e.*, first preference) should be able to apply for an immigrant visa. The April 21, 2001, date would be the date that the parent filed the necessary documentation on behalf of the son or daughter to establish parentage. The documentation might include a birth certificate indicating the child's name along with proof that the petitioner was a U.S. citizen. In contrast, a person born in the Philippines who is the unmarried son or daughter of a U.S. citizen who applied on September 1, 1991, still would not be able to apply for an immigrant visa because of the immigrant visa quota that only allows issuing immigrant visas to persons with priority dates earlier than the cut-off date listed in the chart.

One central theme in U.S. immigration law is that of family unification. The INA provides for the immigration of dependent family members who are either "accompanying" or "following to join" the primary immigrant under the same immigrant visa preference category and priority date.[40] A person is considered to be "accompanying" if he or she immigrates within six months of the primary beneficiary's immigration; otherwise, the individual is considered "following to join."[41]

In order for an individual to be able to immigrate as a "following to join" dependent under the same immigrant category and priority date as the primary beneficiary, he or she must either be the primary beneficiary's spouse or child as defined in the INA.[42] The following to join rules also allow dependent family members to charge the country quotas that would be most advantageous for assuring family unity.[43] For example, A, a native and citizen of France, immigrated to the United States in January 2000, as a married son of a U.S. citizen. If, when he came to the United States, he was unable to bring his spouse and child, the spouse and child could later immigrate as his dependents using the same visa preference and priority date that A used because they would be following to join.

---

[40] 8 USC §1153(d), INA §203(d).

[41] 22 CFR §40.1(a)(1).

[42] The person must meet the definition of spouse or child before the primary beneficiary is admitted to the United States with the immigrant visa. *See Matter of G*, 7 I&N Dec. 731 (BIA 1958).

[43] 8 USC §§1152(b)(1) and (2), INA §§202(b)(1) and (2).

Recognized Family Relationships

As is evident from the categories described above, not all family relationships are recognized for purposes of immigrating to the United States. A person could petition for his or her own parents or siblings, but a grandchild could not petition for a grandparent or a nephew for an aunt. The recognized family relationships for immigrating are determined by Congress pursuant to its plenary power.

For example, the immigration statute establishes a different set of requirements as between parents, such that a child can always immigrate through proof of relationship with his or her mother, but not necessarily from the father.[44] Immigration through the father could be precluded if the parents were not married and the child had not been legitimated or otherwise met the definition of child. In 1977, in *Fiallo v. Bell*,[45] the Supreme Court held this different treatment was constitutional even though it excluded the relationship between unwed fathers and "illegitimate" offspring as a basis for immigrating to the United States. More recently in *Miller v. Albright*,[46] and *Nguyen v. INS*,[47] the Supreme Court upheld such distinctions.

Spouse

Whether a spousal relationship exists for immigration purposes depends on a number of factors. First, the marriage must have been valid where it was celebrated. However, even marriages valid where celebrated may not be recognized for immigration purposes where such marriages are contrary to U.S. public policy, such as polygamous or incestuous marriages.[48] Moreover, if either of the parties to the marriage had been pre-

---

[44] *See, infra*, section on "child," for establishing proof of relationship to mother or father for immigration purposes.

[45] 430 U.S. 787 (1977).

[46] 523 U.S. 420 (1998).

[47] 533 U.S. 53 (2001).

[48] *Matter of H–*, 9 I&N Dec. 640 (BIA 1962). Whether an incestuous marriage is invalid for immigration purposes may depend on the state where the couple will reside, since these matters are normally the subject of state and not federal law. *See Matter of E–*, 4 I&N Dec. 239 (BIA 1951). Same sex marriages have not been recognized. *Adams v. Howerton*, 673 F.2d 1036 (9th Cir. 1982); Defense of Marriage Act, Pub. L. No. 104-199, 110 Stat. 2419 (1996). However, the BIA recently ruled that the Defense of Marriage Act does not preclude federal recognition of a state-recognized marriage between a postoperative transsexual and a person of the opposite sex, and accordingly approved an immediate-relative petition. *Matter of Lovo-Lara*, 23 I&N Dec. 746 (BIA 2005).

viously married, there must be a valid and final divorce before they can petition for immediate relative status.

Because of the premium placed on the marital relationship, and the fact that there is no quota on visas through marriages to U.S. citizens, there is a great deal of suspicion that individuals will enter into fraudulent or sham marriages to obtain LPR status. An attempt or conspiracy to enter into a sham marriage may be enough to trigger a statutory provision that precludes the granting of a preference petition where there has been a determination of fraud.[49] Whether a marriage is fraudulent will depend on genuine intent of the parties to be united in marriage.[50] In addition to the immigration consequences for a fraudulent marriage, there also are potential criminal penalties for visa fraud, false statements, and conspiracy.[51]

Persons who have not been married for at least two years at the time of applying for LPR status receive conditional resident status as opposed to permanent status. Within 90 days of the second anniversary of the grant of conditional residence, the couple must file a petition to remove the conditional status, and submit evidence that the marriage continues to be valid.[52] If the marriage has been terminated, the noncitizen may request a waiver if the marriage was entered into in good faith, and if he or she will experience extreme hardship if required to leave the United States.[53] Additionally, the applicant in a terminated marriage may request a waiver for removal of the conditional status if he or she is a victim of battery or extreme cruelty by the U.S. citizen or LPR spouse.[54]

If a marriage takes place while the beneficiary is in removal proceedings, the family petition may not be approved unless the parties are able to establish by clear and convincing evidence that the marriage

---

[49] 8 USC §1154(c), INA §204(c).

[50] *See Matter of McKee*, 17 I&N Dec. 332 (BIA 1980) (test is whether marriage was genuine, not whether the couple was living together at the time of the application); *Bark v. INS*, 511 F.2d 1200, 1202 (9th Cir. 1975).

[51] *See, e.g.*, 8 USC §1325(c), INA §275(c); 18 USC §§371, 1001, 1546. Conviction for marriage fraud can carry a sentence of up to five years' imprisonment and a fine of up to $250,000.

[52] 8 USC §§1186a(c) and (d)(2), INA §§216(c) and (d)(2). The failure to remove the condition within the 90-day period may be waived for good cause and extenuating circumstances. 8 USC §1186a(d)(2)(B), INA §216(d)(2)(B).

[53] 8 USC §§1186a(c)(4)(A) and (B), INA §§216(c)(4)(A) and (B).

[54] 8 USC §1186a(c)(4)(C), INA §216(c)(4)(C).

was entered into in good faith.[55] In other words, there is a presumption of fraud because of the timing of the marriage that the parties must overcome. The failure to establish the good faith basis to the marriage will result in the noncitizen's requirement to remain outside of the United States for two years[56] before he or she may return with an immigrant visa, at which time additional grounds of inadmissibility could be applicable, such as inadmissibility based on a prior removal order. Challenges based on constitutional grounds to these marriage fraud provisions have been unsuccessful.[57]

Child

A child is an unmarried individual under the age of 21, as described at 8 USC §1101(b)(1), INA §101(b)(1), and, according to the statute, includes a "legitimated" child, an adopted child, an orphan child, or a stepchild. A child is considered legitimated where the father marries the mother, or where a child born out of wedlock is placed legally in the same situation as a child born in wedlock[58]—according to the laws where legitimation takes place.[59] In order to be effective, the legitimation must occur before the child's 18th birthday, and the father must be the biological father.[60] There is no legitimation requirement for the mother.

An "adoption" is defined as a "[v]oluntary acceptance of a child of other parents to be the same as one's own child,"[61] and the adoption must become final before the child reaches age 16.[62] A law enacted in 2000 extended the age limit to 18, and provides that if a family adopts a child who is the natural sibling of another adopted child, and the adoption occurs at the same time or subsequent to the adoption of the first child, the second or subsequent child can still be considered a child if

---

[55] 8 USC §§1255(e)(2) and (3), and 1154(g). INA §§245(e)(2) and (3), and 204(g).

[56] 8 USC §1154(g), INA §204(g).

[57] *See, e.g., Azizi v. Thornburgh*, 908 F.2d 1130 (2d Cir. 1990); *Anetekai v. INS*, 876 F.2d 1218 (5th Cir. 1989).

[58] *See Matter of Cabrera*, 21 I&N Dec. 589 (BIA 1996).

[59] *Id.*; *Matter of Brennizon*, 19 I&N Dec. 40 (BIA 1984).

[60] 8 USC §1101(b)(1)(C), INA §101(b)(1)(C); *Matter of Cabrera*, 21 I&N Dec. at 591. By definition, legitimation is the process through which the father acknowledges paternity and confers rights and incurs responsibility vis-à-vis the child and placing the child in the same position as a child born in wedlock.

[61] *Matter of Chan*, 14 I&N Dec. 127 (BIA 1972).

[62] 8 USC §1101(b)(1)(E)(i), INA §101(b)(1)(E)(i).

under the age of 18.[63] As in other situations, the law of the place of adoption will be controlling, such that a customary adoption may be sufficient if it is equivalent to a full and complete adoption according to the laws of the place where it occurs. The biological parents may not receive any benefits under the immigration laws where there has been an adoption under 8 USC §1101(b)(1)(E), INA §101(b)(1)(E).[64]

Special provisions have been created in the statute allowing orphan children to be adopted abroad, and allow the entry of a child that a U.S. citizen will adopt after admission.[65] The biological parents must have died or abandoned the child; or if there is one parent, that parent must be unable to care for the child and irrevocably release the child (via writing) for adoption.[66] An orphan child adopted abroad before being issued an immigrant visa is eligible for immediate citizenship.[67]

A stepchild relationship takes place regardless of whether the parent petitioning is the biological parent, as long as the parents marry before the child's 18th birthday.[68] A stepparent relationship can continue even after the parents divorce, as long as the relationship continues; this will also apply to step-sibling relationships.[69]

Parent

A parental relation is established through one of the different methods described above in relation to the discussion of the definition of a "child."[70] The child may only petition for a parent when he or she reaches the age of 21—in other words when the child becomes a son or daughter as defined pursuant the statute.[71] If the son or daughter is a U.S. citizen, he or she can petition for the parent as an immediate relative.[72] The only

---

[63] *See* Amendment to Definition of Adopted Child, Pub. L. No. 106-139, 113 Stat. 1696 (1999). *See also* 8 USC §1101(b)(1)(E)(ii), INA §101(b)(1)(E)(ii).

[64] 8 USC §1101(b)(1)(E)(i), INA §101(b)(1)(E)(i).

[65] 8 USC §1101(b)(1)(F), INA §101(b)(1)(F); *Matter of Greenwood*, 18 I&N Dec. 417 (BIA 1983).

[66] 8 USC §1101(b)(1)(F), INA §101(b)(1)(F).

[67] *See* Child Citizenship Act of 2000, Pub. L. No. 106-395, §101, 114 Stat. 1631.

[68] 8 USC §1101(b)(1)(A), INA §101(b)(1)(A). *See also Palmer v. Reddy*, 622 F.2d 463 (9th Cir. 1980); *Matter of McMillan*, 17 I&N Dec. 605 (BIA 1981); *Matter of Awwal*, 19 I&N Dec. 617 (BIA 1988).

[69] *Matter of Mowrer*, 17 I&N Dec. 613 (BIA 1981); *Matter of Mourillon*, 18 I&N Dec. 122 (BIA 1981).

[70] 8 USC §1101(b)(2), INA §101(b)(2).

[71] 8 USC §1151(b)(2)(A)(i), INA §201(b)(2)(A)(i).

[72] 8 USC §1151(b)(2)(A)(i), INA §201(b)(2)(A)(i). A petitioning son or daughter must be a U.S. citizen in order to accord immigration benefits on his or her parents.

overarching requirement is that the parental relationship have been established in accordance with the statute.

Sibling

In order for a person to qualify as a brother or sister of a U.S. citizen for purposes of the fourth family preference, the person—at some point in time—must have been the "child" (as defined at 8 USC §§1101(b)(1) and (2), INA §§101(b)(1) and (2)) of a common parent.[73] The burden of proof will be on the petitioner to establish the legal relationship by a preponderance of the evidence.[74] Regardless of the biological relationship, an adoption severs the relationship with the natural family members if the adoption was sufficient to meet the requirements of 8 USC §1101(b)(1)(E).[75]

Preservation of Benefits for Children of Immigrants

In 2002, Congress passed the Child Status Protection Act (CSPA).[76] The CSPA is designed to ameliorate problems that result when the dependent children "age-out,"[77] marry, or otherwise become ineligible for derivative beneficiary status while a visa petition is pending.[78] Often, between the time that a visa petition was filed and when the parent was eligible for the visa, the child may have reached the age of 21, and, therefore, was no longer eligible for derivative status.

The CSPA preserves the ability of a child derivative beneficiary to the extent that his or her "aging-out" was due to backlogs in adjudication of visa petitions. Under the CSPA, a calculation is done by subtracting the amount of time that it took DHS to adjudicate the petition from the child's age at the time that visa numbers became available. If that number is less than 21 years, the person may proceed as if he or she still were a "child" under the INA.[79] The CSPA, however, is not retroactive

---

[73] *Matter of Heung*, 15 I&N Dec. 145 (BIA 1974). The same applies for other preferences requiring that a person establish that he or she is the son or daughter of a U.S. citizen or LPR, or where the child—upon reaching the age of 21—is petitioning for a parent as an immediate relative. *See Matter of Coker*, 14 I&N Dec. 521 (BIA 1974).

[74] *Matter of Bueno-Almonte*, 21 I&N Dec. (BIA 1997).

[75] *See Young v. Reno*, 114 F.3d 879 (9th Cir. 1997).

[76] Pub. L. No. 107-208, 116 Stat. 927 (2002).

[77] An individual ceases to be a "child" when he or she reaches the age of 21; hence, "aging out."

[78] For most derivative beneficiaries, their ability to immigrate is dependent on their age (under 21) or their marital status (single).

[79] H. Gordon & T. Niedzwiecki, "CSPA: Leaving No Child Behind," 1 *Immigration & Nationality Law Handbook* 289, 291 (2003–04 ed.).

and is implemented prospectively from August 6, 2002. Furthermore, it does not apply to V or K visas, nor does it allow for visa backlogs due to the oversubscribed immigration quotas that exist in many of the family-based preference categories.

EMPLOYMENT-BASED IMMIGRANTS

As with the family-based immigrant selection system, the employment-based category is organized into preferences. The current system was established by IMMACT90,[80] and was an adaptation of the previous two preferences that existed for most of the 20th Century. The total number of employment-based visas allowed each year is 140,000.[81] In a case involving an employment-based preference, the priority date would be the date on which the application for labor certification (discussed, *infra*) was submitted, or, if a certification was not required, the date on which the preference petition was submitted.

Employment Preferences

First Preference (EB-1). Approximately 28.6 percent of the total employment-based visas are allocated for the first preference.[82] This category does not require that the beneficiary obtain a certification from the Secretary of the Department of Labor (DOL) that the work in which he or she will engage will not displace U.S. workers—*i.e.*, a labor certification.

The first subcategory within this preference (a/k/a EB-11, EB-1-1, or EB-1-A) is for persons of extraordinary ability in the sciences, arts, education, business, or athletics; the extraordinary ability is to be demonstrated by sustained national or international acclaim and by extensive documentation.[83] Such persons are not required to have a prospective employer,[84] but they must be entering to continue to work in their chosen field, and they must "substantially benefit prospectively the U.S."[85]

Evidence of an individual's sustained national or international acclaim may include one-time achievement of a major international award,

---

[80] Immigration Act of 1990, Pub. L. No. 101-649, 104 Stat. 4978.

[81] 8 USC §1151(d)(1)(A), INA §201(d)(1)(A).

[82] 8 USC §1153(b)(1)(A), INA §203(b)(1)(A).

[83] 8 USC §1153(b)(1)(A)(i), INA §203(b)(1)(A)(i).

[84] 8 CFR §204.5(h)(5).

[85] *Id.*; *see also* 8 USC §§1153(b)(1)(A)(ii) and (iii), INA §§203(b)(1)(A)(ii) and (iii).

or, alternatively, three of the following (although not dispositive): (1) lesser national or internationally recognized prizes or awards; (2) membership in an association that requires outstanding achievement in the field for which the classification is sought; (3) published material about the person or his or her work in professional or trade journals; (4) participation in judging the work of others in the field; (5) evidence of original scientific, scholastic, artistic, athletic, or business-related significant contributions; (6) authorship of scholarly articles; (7) artistic exhibitions; (8) performance in a leading or critical role for a distinguished organization; (9) high salary or remuneration in relation to others in the field; and (10) commercial success in the performing arts.[86]

Another subcategory within the first preference is that of outstanding professors and researchers with a minimum of three years' experience in teaching or research who are recognized internationally in an academic discipline (a/k/a EB-12, EB-1-2, EB-1-B).[87] These individuals must be coming for a tenure or tenure-track position, or for a comparable position at a university, institute, or with a private employer to conduct research.[88] While no labor certification is required, there must be an offer of ongoing employment from the sponsoring employer.[89]

The final subcategory for the first preference is that for multinational executives or managers who have been employed abroad in that capacity for one year in the last three years prior to entry with the firm, corporation or legal entity, affiliate, or subsidiary (a/k/a EB-13, EB-1-3, EB-1-C).[90] As with the other two EB-1 subcategories, no labor certification is required; however, the prospective employer must submit a statement that the beneficiary will perform as an executive or manager.[91]

Second Preference (EB-2). The employment-based second preference is for members of the professions holding advanced degrees, or for persons with exceptional ability in the arts, sciences, or business who will substantially benefit the national economy or culture who are "sought by an employer in the United States."[92] The visa allocation is 28.6 percent

---

[86] 8 CFR §204.5(h)(3).

[87] 8 USC §§1153(b)(1)(B)(i) and (ii), INA §§203(b)(1)(B)(i) and (ii).

[88] 8 USC §1153(b)(1)(B)(iii), INA §203(b)(1)(B)(iii).

[89] 8 CFR §204.5(i)(3)(iii).

[90] 8 USC §1153(b)(1)(C), INA §203(b)(1)(C).

[91] 8 CFR §204.5(j)(5).

[92] 8 USC §1153(b)(2)(A), INA §203(b)(2)(A). *See also* 8 CFR §204.5(k)(1).

of the total, and applicants may obtain a "national interest" waiver of the labor certification requirement that otherwise is required for the EB-2 category.[93]

"Exceptional ability" is defined as an expertise beyond that which is normally found in the profession.[94] Proving "exceptional ability" can be accomplished by demonstrating three of the following: (1) an official academic record showing a degree, diploma, certificate, or similar award from a college, university, school, or other institution of learning relating to the area of exceptional ability; (2) at least 10 years of full-time experience in the occupation, documented by letters from current or past employers; (3) a license to practice the profession or certification for the particular profession or occupation; (4) evidence that the person has commanded a salary or other remuneration for services demonstrating exceptional ability; (5) membership in professional associations (there is no requirement that the professional associations require outstanding achievement for admission); or (6) recognition for achievements and significant contributions to the industry or field by peers, governmental entities, or professional or business organizations.[95] An advanced degree could include a bachelor's degree plus five years of progressive work experience in their field.[96]

Third Preference (EB-3). Approximately 28.6 percent of the visas allocated for this employment-based category are for skilled workers, professionals, and "other workers"—all of which require approved labor certifications.[97] An EB-2 applicant also may apply under the EB-3 preference (this is an option during a retrogression in a particular EB-2 category and geographic quota). "Skilled workers" are persons whose position requires a minimum of two years' training or work experience.[98] "Professionals" are positions requiring a baccalaureate degree or university equivalent.[99] The "other workers" subcategory is for persons in positions that require

---

[93] 8 USC §§1153(b)(2)(A) and (B), INA §§203(b)(2)(A) and (B). The "national interest waiver" may be obtained when the Attorney General "deems it to be in the national interest" to waive the requirement that the individual be "sought by an employer in the United States."

[94] 8 CFR §204.5(k)(2).

[95] 8 CFR §204.5(k)(3)(ii).

[96] 8 CFR §204.5(k)(3)(i).

[97] 8 USC §1153(b)(3), INA §203(b)(3). There is no national interest waiver to the certification requirement available in this category.

[98] 8 USC §1153(b)(3)(A)(i), INA §203(b)(3)(A)(i).

[99] 8 USC §1153(b)(3)(A)(ii), INA §203(b)(3)(A)(ii).

less than two years' training to engage in the work; it is limited to 10,000 visas.[100] This preference category is complicated by the fact that the labor certification process has been plagued by extensive delays and the "other worker" subcategory often has been backlogged.[101] For example, as of June 1, 2006, numbers in this subcategory were unavailable.[102]

Fourth Preference (EB-4). This preference is for "special immigrant" visas; the statute includes many enumerated special immigrants, of which only the major ones are mentioned here.[103] About 7.1 percent of the total numbers of immigrant visas are allocated to these special immigrants. The categories include certain religious workers, Panama Canal Treaty employees, Amerasian children, certain employees of U.S. foreign service posts abroad, certain retired employees of international organizations admitted to the United States under the G-4 nonimmigrant visa, and dependents of juvenile courts.[104]

Fifth Preference (EB-5). This preference is for employment-creation (a/k/a investor) visas. It provides conditional residency for those who after November 29, 1990, invest $1 million in a new commercial enterprise that employs at least 10 full-time U.S. workers.[105] Conditional residency means that the beneficiary receives temporary residency for a two-year period, at which time an application is made to remove the condition and grant permanent residence.[106] Within 90 days of the anniversary of the grant of conditional resident status, the person may request that

---

[100] 8 USC §§1153(b)(3)(A)(iii) and (b)(3)(B), INA §§203(b)(3)(A)(iii) and (b)(3)(B).

[101] *See* A. Paparelli and G. Pigeaud, "Read My Lips: No New National Interest Waivers," *11th Annual California Conference Handbook* 1 (AILA 1998). This is further exacerbated by Congress's willingness to charge visa numbers from immigrant relief programs, such as NACARA to this category. The NACARA program reduced the "other worker" category by 5,000 visas. See discussion under Special Relief Programs Granting Permanent Residency in this chapter.

[102] *See* DOS's Visa Bulletin, at *http://travel.state.gov/visa/frvi/bulletin/bulletin_2924.html*. Unavailability means that no visas irrespective of the priority date will be issued under that particular category. Visa numbers can become unavailable for a number of reasons such as the period during the allocation (fiscal) year, and may be a temporary situation. Similarly, there can be forward or backward movement of visa numbers from one month to the next according to the bulletin.

[103] 8 USC §§1153(b)(4) and 1101(a)(27), INA §§203(b)(4) and 101(a)(27).

[104] *See* 8 USC §1101(a)(27), INA §101(a)(27). The terms "certain employees" at foreign service posts abroad and "certain retired employees" of international organizations is used because the statute has very specific requirements and does not cover all employees for special immigrant status. *See* 8 USC §§1101(a)(27)(D) and (I)(iii), INA §§101(a)(27)(D) and (I)(iii).

[105] 8 USC §1153(b)(5)(A), INA §203(b)(5)(A).

[106] 8 CFR §§216.6, 1216.6.

the condition be removed, and the individual will be an LPR. In order to receive permanent residence, the applicant must have "substantially met the capital investment requirement."[107]

The visa allocation for this category is 7.1 percent of the total number of employment-based visas set aside annually, of which 3,000 are reserved for "targeted employment areas."[108] A lesser investment of $500,000 may qualify the investor if the investment is in one of the targeted employment areas that includes rural areas with populations of less than 20,000, or locations that have experienced unemployment at 150 percent of the national average.[109] The investment must be personally connected to the person seeking the status and may be made from jointly held accounts with a spouse.[110]

Under the Departments of Commerce, Justice, and State, the Judiciary, and Related Agencies Appropriations Act of 1993,[111] a pilot investor program was established that relaxes the standards for the investor.[112] The pilot program permits investments through "regional centers" with a relaxed job-creation requirement. The regional centers apply to USCIS demonstrating how the program will promote economic growth.[113] Upon approval, a foreign investor's investment in one of these centers may qualify him or her for the immigrant visa.[114] This program has since been extended to 2008 and is limited to 3,000 visas annually.[115]

Below is the June 2006 visa bulletin issued for the employment-based preferences, which shows whether there is a wait for the various visas. The "U" designation signifies that visas are unavailable, and the "C" designation signifies that visa issuance is current at the time of the issuance of the bulletin.

---

[107] 8 CFR §§216.6(a)(4)(iii), 1216.6(a)(4)(iii); *Matter of Izummi*, 22 I&N Dec. 169 (Assoc. Comm'r. 1998).

[108] 8 USC §§1153(b)(5)(A) and (B), INA §§203(b)(5)(A) and (B). Targeted employment areas are geographic or political subdivisions designated by a state government as areas of high unemployment. *See* 8 CFR §204.6(i).

[109] *Id.*

[110] 8 CFR §204.6(g)(1). *See also Matter of Ho*, 22 I&N Dec. 206 (Assoc. Comm'r. 1998).

[111] Pub. L. No. 102-395, §610, 106 Stat. 1828.

[112] 8 CFR §204.6(m).

[113] 8 CFR §§204.6(m)(3) and (4).

[114] 8 CFR §204.6(m)(7).

[115] *See* Pub. L. No. 108-156, 117 Stat. 1944 (2003).

Employment-Based	All Charge-ability Areas Except Those Listed	China-mainland born	India	Mexico	Philippines
1st	C	01JUL05	01JAN06	C	C
2nd	C	01JUL04	01JAN03	C	C
3rd	01JUL01	01JUL01	08APR01	22APR01	01JUL01
Other workers	U	U	U	U	U
4th	C	C	C	C	C
Certain Religious Workers	C	C	C	C	C
5th	C	C	C	C	C
Targeted Employment Areas/Regional Centers	C	C	C	C	C

The "other worker" category is unavailable for all countries and the third employment-based preference is only available for persons from all countries with priority dates before April 8, 2001. The categories without waitlists are the fourth, fifth, relgious workers and targeted employment visas.[116]

Labor Certification Procedures

Some of the preference categories require a labor certification, whereby a U.S. employer who is "sponsoring" an immigrant is required to obtain verification from the Secretary of DOL that there are insufficient available, qualified, and willing U.S. workers to fill the position, and that the employment will not have an adverse effect on the wages and working conditions of similarly situated U.S. workers. The requirement of this certification has long been a part of immigration law; it can be found at 8 USC §1182(a)(5)(A), INA §212(a)(5)(A), which establishes that persons seeking admission as employment-based immigrants must obtain a certification to gain admission. Effectively, the certification process is one where the employer, through a recruitment effort, "tests" the market to establish that the person for whom a certification is sought meets the above statutory standard. In December 2004, DOL issued final regulations that established a new labor certification procedure, termed "Pro-

---

[116] Since visas are issued depending on an applicant's priority date and visa category under which he or she is proceeding, the priority date of visa applicants that are being processed in any given month could move backward or forward.

gram Electronic Review Management" (PERM).[117] PERM took effect on March 28, 2005, with the intent to facilitate faster determinations. For cases submitted before March 28, 2005, a petitioner would use the pre-PERM labor certification process ("traditional labor certification).[118] Applicants who had pending labor certifications were given the option to re-file under the PERM procedures.[119]

While it remains to be seen whether PERM's objective of expediency is accomplished, PERM was intended to streamline the labor certification process that had been broadly criticized as being inefficient and time-consuming for employers and the state agencies involved. More measures designed to protect U.S. workers also were established under PERM. For instance, if there was a layoff within six months prior to the filing of the application for labor certification, the employer must attest to and document notification and consideration of U.S. workers who were laid off and who worked in the same occupation or a related occupation to the one for which certification is being sought.[120] A U.S. worker who does not meet all of the requirements of the job cannot be rejected (and, thus, a certification cannot be issued), if that U.S. worker could receive job training or if he or she is able to perform the job duties in a normally acceptable manner given his or her background.[121]

The employer is required, through an individual job offer, to test the labor market by engaging in a variety of recruitment efforts. For example, for a professional position, the employer must post a notice of the job opportunity in-house,[122] place a 30-day job order with the state workforce agency (SWA),[123] post notice with any/all in-house media typically used by the employer in filling job openings,[124] run an advertisement in two

---

[117] See 69 Fed. Reg. 77326–421 (2004) codified at 20 CFR Parts 655 and 656. For the proposed regulations, see 67 Fed. Reg. 30466, 30468–69 (2002).

[118] For more information on PERM and labor certification, see *The David Stanton Manual on Labor Certification*, 3rd Ed. (AILA 2005). Visit the AILA Publications website at *www.ailapubs.org*.

[119] 20 CFR §656.17(d). Re-filing under PERM requires that the employer withdraw the previously filed labor certification request; the new application must be filed within 210 days of the withdrawal. 20 CFR §656.17(d)(2).

[120] 20 CFR §656.17(k).

[121] 20 CFR §656.17(g)(2).

[122] 20 CFR §656.10(d)(1)(ii).

[123] 20 CFR §656.17(e)(1)(i)(A). The role of the SWA has been reduced to determining the prevailing wage and receiving the job order. See 69 Fed. Reg. 77330.

[124] 20 CFR §656.10(d)(1)(ii).

Sunday editions of a newspaper of general circulation,[125] and select and fulfill three additional forms of recruitment from a list of 10 possibilities.[126] The advertised position must include the job location, the employer's name, a job description of the position that is specific enough to apprise U.S. workers of the position, and direct applicants to report to, or send résumés to the employer;[127] there is no requirement that the salary be mentioned in the advertisement. The salary for the labor certification must be higher than the prevailing wage as determined by the SWA.[128]

The PERM regulations allow for electronic filing (although the application may be submitted by mail). Supporting documentation is not submitted with the application; rather, the employer retains the documentation in the event of an audit. If, as a result of the recruitment efforts, the employer is unable to locate a U.S. worker who is able, willing, qualified, and available to fill the position, the DOL certifying officer may issue the labor certification. DOL estimates that an application not selected for audit will be approved within 45–60 days.[129] In cases selected for audit, the employer will be required to submit supporting documentation establishing compliance with each of the requirements of the labor certification, including additional "reasonable" requirements imposed by the DOL certifying officer.[130] The burden will be on the employer seeking certification to show why the U.S. workers who responded to the recruitment efforts were not suitable for the position.[131] A denial may be appealed to the Board of Alien Labor Certification Appeals (BALCA).[132]

The labor certification is not an authorization of any kind (*i.e.*, work authorization), and only serves the limited purpose of establishing that there are insufficient available, qualified, and willing U.S. workers to fill the position and that the noncitizen's employment will not have an adverse effect on the wages and working conditions of similarly situated

---

[125] 20 CFR §656.17(e)(1)(i)(B).

[126] 20 CFR §§656.17(e)(1)(ii)(A)–(J).

[127] 20 CFR §656.17(f).

[128] 20 CFR §656.10(c)(1). *See also* 20 CFR §§656.40–41. The salary for traditional labor certification cases must be within 5 percent of the prevailing wage as determined by the SWA.

[129] 69 Fed. Reg. at 77328 (2004).

[130] 20 CFR §656.20.

[131] 20 CFR §§656.21(d)–(f).

[132] 20 CFR §656.26.

U.S. workers.[133] The certification, once issued, is valid indefinitely as long as the job remains available.[134]

There is a large backlog of 350,000 traditional labor certification applications that still are awaiting adjudication, some dating back to April 2001. To address this backlog, DOL has established two Backlog Elimination Centers (BEC); these centers are tasked with reviewing each application, sending out a "45-day letter" asking for confirmation that the employer wishes to continue with the processing of the application, and ultimately adjudicating the application.[135] The goal of the BECs is to have all pending cases adjudicated by approximately March 2007.

The labor certification process may be shortened or avoided altogether by qualifying the position as a "Schedule A" position or a position designated for "special handling," or by obtaining a national interest waiver.

The Secretary of DOL has issued a blanket determination that certain occupations do not have an adverse effect on the wages and working conditions of U.S. workers, and that workers generally are unavailable for these positions; these are known as Schedule A positions.[136] Schedule A Group I includes physical therapists and nurses.[137] In order to use Schedule A for a nurse or a physical therapist, an employer need only show that the applicant meets the criteria of the position including licensure or certification.[138] Schedule A Group II includes persons of exceptional ability in the sciences or arts; the PERM regulations have now added performing artists to Schedule A Group II.[139]

Special handling procedures have been developed for cases involving certain college and university teachers.[140] A college or university

---

[133] *Matter of Raol*, 16 I&N Dec. 466 (BIA 1978).

[134] 20 CFR §656.30.

[135] "ETA Issues Third Round of PERM FAQs; Backlog Processing FAQs," 82 *Interpreter Releases* 817, 818 (2005).

[136] 20 CFR §656.15. Schedule A refers to the section of the Code of Federal Regulations describing these precertified occupations, 20 CFR §656.5.

[137] 20 CFR §656.5.

[138] 20 CFR §§656.15(c)(1) and (2). For physical therapists, qualification to sit for a state's written licensing exam is sufficient. For nurses, either a certificate from the Commission on Graduates of Foreign Nursing Schools (CGFNS), a full and unrestricted license to practice nursing in the state of intended employment, or having passed the National Council Licensure Examination for Registered Nurses (NCLEX-RN) is needed. *Id.*

[139] 20 CFR §656.5.

[140] 20 CFR §656.18.

wishing to sponsor a foreign worker must show that it recruited the person under its normal nationally competitive process, including national advertising.[141] The request must be submitted within 18 months of the selection.[142]

In order to obtain a national interest waiver (*i.e.*, a request that the job offer and labor certification requirements be waived), it must be shown that the person for whom the waiver will be sought is employed in an area of "substantial intrinsic merit," that he or she would benefit the United States to a "substantially greater degree" than a U.S. worker, and that the benefit to the United States outweighs the interest inherent in the labor certification process.[143]

DIVERSITY IMMIGRANTS

In an effort to allow the immigration of persons from regions and states that traditionally have had a lower admission of immigrants, Congress established the "diversity immigrant" category.[144] The diversity program allows for 55,000 annual admissions,[145] giving a preference to persons from countries or regions that have not had a large number of persons immigrating to the United States in a five-year period. The process begins with an individual's submission of an application for the diversity "lottery"; then, if the person is successful, he or she is considered for ranking.[146] Applicants are given priority depending on the number they are assigned in the lottery process. To qualify, an applicant must have at least the equivalent of a high school education, or at least two years' work experience within the five years prior to applying in a field requiring at least two years of training or experience.[147] Persons who are admitted under this program may bring his or her spouse and minor children.[148] The diversity visa category does not use the system of priority dates.

---

[141] 20 CFR §656.18(b).

[142] 20 CFR §656.18(c).

[143] 8 USC §1153(b)(2)(B)(i), INA §203(b)(2)(B)(i). *Matter of New York State Department of Transportation*, 22 I&N Dec. 215 (Assoc. Comm'r 1998). This area of the law is not settled.

[144] *See generally* 8 USC §1153(c), INA §203(c).

[145] 8 USC §1151(e), INA §201(e).

[146] Applications are submitted online and are selected on a random basis. 22 CFR §§42.33(b) and (e). *See also* 8 USC §1153(c)(1), INA §203(c)(1).

[147] 22 CFR §42.33(a); 8 USC §1153(c)(2), INA §203(c)(2).

[148] 8 USC §1153(d), INA §203(d).

SPECIAL RELIEF PROGRAMS GRANTING PERMANENT RESIDENCY

From time to time, Congress has established special provisions for the adjustment of status to permanent residency for targeted groups of people. Since 1997, a number of these programs have been enacted, including the Nicaraguan Adjustment and Central American Relief Act (NACARA),[149] the Haitian Refugee Immigration Fairness Act of 1998 (HRIFA),[150] the Vietnam, Cambodia and Laos Adjustment Act,[151] and several provisions of the USA PATRIOT Act that apply to the spouses and children of persons killed in the 9/11 attacks.[152]

NACARA established special adjustment of status to permanent residency for Nicaraguans and Cubans who were in the United States between December 1, 1995, and April 1, 2000. It waived many of the grounds of inadmissibility, even allowing the benefit for persons ordered removed or who failed to depart. HRIFA was enacted in response to the failure to provide equal treatment for Haitians who had come to the United States under similar circumstances as Nicaraguans and Cubans. It allowed those who had filed for asylum or who were paroled into the United States before December 31, 1995, to become LPRs through adjustment of status if they could show that they had a credible fear of persecution. Similar laws were enacted for Vietnamese, Cambodian, and Laotians who were paroled into the United States before October 1, 1997.[153] These laws are consistent with the tradition of allowing people from certain countries who were paroled into the United States in refugee crisis situations to become LPRs.

There also are specific sections of the USA PATRIOT Act that provide for the adjustment of status for nonimmigrants injured in the 9/11 attacks, or who were otherwise prevented from completing the process under the diversity immigrant lottery. The USA PATRIOT Act also provided for adjustment of status for the spouses and children of U.S. citizens and LPRs who were killed in the 9/11 attacks.[154]

---

[149] Pub. L. No. 105-100, 111 Stat. 2160, 2193 (1997).

[150] Pub. L. No. 105-277, 112 Stat. 2681 (1998).

[151] Pub. L. No. 106-378, 114 Stat. 1442 (2001).

[152] Uniting and Strengthening America by Providing Appropriate Tools Required to Intercept and Obstruct Terrorism Act of 2001, Pub. L. No. 107-56, §§1421–28, 115 Stat. 272 (2001).

[153] This program was limited to 5,000.

[154] Implementing regulations can be found at 8 CFR §1245.15.

VISA PROCESSING PROCEDURES

Immigrant visa processing refers to the process through which a person receives his or her permanent residency by obtaining a visa issued by a U.S. consul overseas, and then proceeds to the United States for admission, at which time the person is inspected and admitted as an LPR.[155] This is contrasted with adjustment of status, where a person is able to remain in the United States for all of the processing and has his or her status "adjusted" to that of an LPR.

Immigrant Visa Processing. All processing begins with a family- or employment-based preference petition filed with USCIS. For employment-based categories requiring a labor certification, the certification must be obtained from DOL. Where the position is eligible for a blanket waiver, the documents establishing qualification for Schedule A are filed with USCIS along with the preference petition. In the case of diversity immigrants, the initial application is the filing for the diversity lottery with DOS.[156]

After the preference petition is approved, the remainder of the process is completed with the U.S. consul in the person's country of nationality or of last permanent residence. The consul waits for a visa number to become available according to the visa priority date chart.[157] The applicant is then interviewed for eligibility based on the underlying qualifications for the preference and the inadmissibility grounds. If the visa is denied, there is no formal appeal, other than obtaining an advisory opinion from the DOS Visa Office.[158]

Adjustment of Status. An applicant for adjustment of status must be in the United States, as this is a benefit that can only be applied for within the United States. A person with a pending application may leave the United States temporarily under "advance parole," which allows him or her to re-enter the country to continue the application.[159] The adjust-

---

[155] For detailed information on visa processing at U.S. consulates, see *The Visa Processing Guide and Consular Posts Handbook* on the AILA Publications website at *www.ailapubs.org.*

[156] *See* DOS website at *http://travel.state.gov/visa/immigrants/types/types_1318. html.*

[157] *See* DOS Visa Bulletin at *http://travel.state.gov/visa/frvi/bulletin/bulletin_1360.html.*

[158] *See generally* discussion on review of consular decisions in Chapter 6; 22 CFR §42.81(d). *See also* L. Fuentes and E. Poh, "Advisory Opinions from the Visa Office," *The Visa Processing Guide and Consular Posts Handbook* 67 (AILA 2006–07).

[159] Advance parole is described in more detail in Chapter 2.

ment application can be submitted only if there are immigrant visa numbers available according to the visa priority charts. The procedure for adjustment of status is similar to the process for the immigrant visa, although permanent residency is pursued with USCIS through an adjustment application, or before an immigration judge in removal proceedings, rather than before a U.S. consul abroad. In adjudicating the adjustment application, USCIS or the judge will determine if any inadmissibility grounds are applicable, and, if so, whether waivers are available. In the event that an application is denied by USCIS, it may be renewed before the immigration judge at the removal hearing. If it is denied by the immigration judge, it may be appealed to the Board of Immigration Appeals (BIA).[160]

REVOCATION OF PETITIONS

A preference petition is deemed to be revoked automatically where (1) the petitioner withdraws the application;[161] (2) the petitioner dies;[162] (3) the business ceases to exist (employment-based); (4) the beneficiary marries, where the preference was based on being single;[163] or (5) divorce, where the preference is based on marriage (except in cases of battered spouses or children).[164] USCIS also has the authority to revoke its approval with notice for "good and sufficient cause."[165] The burden in revocation is on the petitioner since the applicant must show eligibility for the immigration benefit.[166]

LOSS OF PERMANENT RESIDENCY

There are three ways that a person can lose permanent residency: (1) rescission of adjustment; (2) removal; and (3) abandonment of status. Rescission of adjustment is a special procedure applicable only to persons who obtained their lawful permanent residence through adjustment of status. Rescission can be sought by the government within five years of the adjustment of status if the person was not eligible for the status at

---

[160] 8 CFR §1003.1(b)(3).

[161] 8 CFR §§205.1(a)(3)(i)(A), 1205.1(a)(3)(i)(A).

[162] 8 CFR §§205.1(a)(3)(i)(C), 1205.1(a)(3)(i)(C).

[163] 8 CFR §§205.1(a)(3)(i)(G) and (H), 1205.1(a)(3)(i)(G) and (H).

[164] 8 CFR §§205.1(a)(3)(i)(D), 1205.1(a)(3)(i)(D).

[165] 8 USC §1155, INA §205.

[166] *Matter of Estime*, 19 I&N Dec. 450 (BIA 1987).

the time it was obtained.[167] The rescission also will apply to all persons who received derivative status based on the primary grant of permanent residence.[168] The burden is on the government to establish ineligibility based on clear, convincing, and unequivocal evidence pertaining to the original adjustment.[169] The process begins when the USCIS district director sends notice of intent to rescind. The person has 30 days to respond, and the case will be set for a hearing before an immigration judge.[170] Adverse decisions can be appealed to the BIA.[171]

Permanent residency also can be lost in removal proceedings where the government alleges deportability or inadmissibility.[172] Proceedings can be brought against persons granted adjustment or admitted to the United States with an immigrant visa. These proceedings can be brought at any time, so long as the person has not become naturalized.

An LPR can seek readmission or travel in and out of the United States indefinitely as long as he or she is returning to an unrelinquished lawful permanent residence. Under USCIS regulations, a permanent resident card (Green Card) may not be used as an entry document after absences of greater than one year.[173] However, case law indicates that abandonment is more a question of intent, and a person may be treated as having abandoned status with absences of less than one year, or may be found to have retained permanent residence even if the absence exceeded one year.[174] Whether there has been abandonment will turn on whether the trip overseas was temporary, which can be shown by the actual facts, the purpose, and the dates of the trip abroad.[175] Examples of temporary trips would include trips for the purpose of taking care of a sick relative, attending a funeral, temporary employment abroad, or visiting with family

---

[167] 8 USC §1256(a); INA §246(a).

[168] *In Re M–S–*, 22 I&N Dec. 349, 353 n. 4 (BIA 1998); *Matter of Valiyee*, 14 I&N Dec. 710 (BIA 1974).

[169] *Yaldo v. INS*, 424 F.2d 501 (6th Cir. 1970).

[170] A failure to respond results in rescission without a hearing. 8 CFR §1264.

[171] 8 CFR §§1003.1(b)(8) and 1246.7

[172] See 8 USC §1101(a)(13), INA §101(a)(13), for a definition of admission and when a permanent resident may be prevented from readmission. The grounds of deportability include inadmissibility at entry. 8 USC §1227, INA §237.

[173] 8 CFR §211.1(a)(2).

[174] *See, e.g., Khodagholian v. Ashcroft*, 335 F.3d 1003 (9th Cir. 2003); *Moin v. Ashcroft*, 335 F.3d 415 (5th Cir. 2003); *Matter of Guiot*, 14 I&N Dec. 393 (1973).

[175] *Chavez-Ramirez v. INS*, 792 F.2d 932 (9th Cir. 1986); *Matter of Huang*, 19 I&N Dec. 749 (BIA 1988).

for a holiday. The burden of proof is on the government to prove abandonment by clear, convincing, and unequivocal evidence.[176] In any event, lawful permanent residence is not lost until there has been a final administrative order of removal, unless the status was taken away by rescission.[177]

---

[176] *Singh v. Reno*, 113 F.3d 1512 (9th Cir. 1997).
[177] 8 CFR §§1.1(p), 1001.1(p).

CHAPTER 6
Administrative and Judicial Review

Judges must beware of hard constructions and strained inferences,
for there is no worse torture than that of laws.
—Francis Bacon

INTRODUCTION

This chapter will provide a synopsis of administrative and judicial review over immigration-related decisions. At the outset, it is helpful to understand that the rules relating to both administrative and judicial review have undergone a long, evolutionary process.

The control of immigration falls under a variety of federal agencies that themselves have been subject to reorganization. The most substantial organizational revision in recent history was the abolition of the Immigration and Naturalization Service (INS), and the creation of the Department of Homeland Security (DHS) and its components: U.S. Customs and Border Protection (CBP), U.S. Immigration and Customs Enforcement (ICE), and U.S. Citizenship and Immigration Services (USCIS).

Historically, immigration decisions were made deep within the government bureaucracy and were rarely the subject of much scrutiny.[1] Furthermore, until very recently, the immigration enforcement and adjudicatory arms were within the same agency (discussed, *infra*), which, arguably, raised potential conflicts between their missions. Thus, the jurisdictional boundaries within and between agencies are confusing and not always easily distinguished.

---

[1] For more background on this subject, see P. Schuck, "The Transformation of Immigration Law," *Colum. L. Rev.* 1 (1984).

Because much of federal court review is controlled by the principle that courts may only review matters where the applicant has either exhausted available administrative remedies or where it would be futile to do so, it is necessary to first understand the scope of administrative review. Rules regarding the available administrative review are the creation of agency promulgations that do not necessarily fall within a cohesive regulatory scheme. Thus, an overview of the multiple government agencies involved in immigration cases is warranted.

ADMINISTRATIVE REVIEW

There are five federal agencies involved in decision-making on immigration-related issues: the Departments of Homeland Security (DHS), Justice (DOJ), State (DOS), Labor (DOL), and Health and Human Services (HHS). Prior to the government reorganization creating DHS, adjudication, enforcement, and service functions were all within DOJ. Because only the enforcement (ICE and CBP) and service functions (USCIS) were moved to DHS, the hearing functions carried out by immigration judges (IJ) and the Board of Immigration Appeals (BIA) remain within DOJ's Executive Office for Immigration Review (EOIR).

The reorganization that occurred through the creation of DHS, aside from creating ICE, CBP, and USCIS, also impacted the jurisdiction of the other federal agencies involved in immigration law matters—DOS, DOL, and HHS. Most of the immigration-related functions of DOS are divided among its consular officers, the Bureau of Consular Affairs, and the Passport Office. At DOL, the implementation of the labor certification authority is within its Employment Training Administration (ETA), and its Board of Alien Labor Certification Appeals (BALCA). The immigration functions at HHS are carried out by physicians in its Public Health Service who determine matters relating to the health grounds of inadmissibility.

The most straightforward approach to understanding complicated jurisdictional issues is to focus on the decision-making sequence—that is, who makes the initial decision, and then what body or bodies may review that determination (if it is reviewable). If judicial review is even permissible, it will be review of the final administrative decision by the federal court that has jurisdiction.

Most applications/petitions for immigration benefits submitted to DHS for review may be appealed to the Administrative Appeals Office (AAO).[2] The majority of matters heard by IJs—removal cases and defensive benefit applications—are reviewed by the BIA.[3] Other decisions, such as passport applications, are reviewed by the DOS Board of Appellate Review, which is part of the Office of the Legal Advisor. BALCA reviews labor certification matters. Applications that are made to consular officers are not reviewable. Following is a list of common applications with descriptions of the administrative body having appellate jurisdiction:

Admissions Process. A person who is seeking admission to the United States at a port of entry (or in limited circumstances within the United States or at sea) and who is believed to be inadmissible for false statements or for lack of proper documents is subject to expedited removal;[4] the decision regarding expedited removal is made by a DHS officer. This decision may not be reviewed by an IJ unless the person expresses a fear of persecution, or makes a claim to U.S. citizenship or lawful permanent resident (LPR) status.[5] A person seeking admission who is not subject to expedited removal, but who is placed in regular removal hearings will have his or her case determined by an IJ and may seek review by the BIA.[6]

Asylum. A person not in removal proceedings who is seeking asylum may apply "affirmatively" before DHS. Affirmative asylum applications are submitted to an asylum officer.[7] If asylum is not granted, a denial of asylum does not issue, but instead the asylum office decision is characterized as a "referral" to an IJ.[8] By way of that referral, the person is placed in removal proceedings, and may pursue his or her asylum application as a "defense" to removal. This defensive application technically is not an appeal of the asylum office's decision, although it allows the person the opportunity to raise his or her claim again. A denial of the asylum application by the IJ may be appealed to the BIA.[9] A defensive

---

[2] With the creation of DHS, Title 8 of CFR was amended and the jurisdictions are no longer listed. *See* 8 CFR §§103.1 and 1103.3(a)(ii) (nonexistent section of Title 8 and a reference to it).

[3] 8 CFR §§1003.1(b)(1)–(3).

[4] 8 USC §§1225(b)(1)(A)(i), 1182(a)(6)(C), (a)(7), INA §§235(b)(1)(A)(i), 212(a)(6)(C), (a)(7).

[5] 8 USC §1225(b)(1)(C), INA §235(b)(1)(C).

[6] 8 USC §1229a, INA §240; *see also* 8 CFR §1003.1(b).

[7] 8 USC §1158, INA §208; 8 CFR §§208.4(b), 1208.4(b).

[8] 8 CFR §§208.14(c), 1208.14(c).

[9] 8 CFR §1003.1(b)(9).

asylum claim that is submitted at a removal hearing as a form of relief from removal is heard first by an IJ, and may be appealed to the BIA.[10]

Not all persons who arrive in the United States are permitted to affirmatively apply for asylum. If a person is subject to expedited removal at a port of entry, he or she must (1) express his or her fear of persecution to a DHS officer upon arriving; and (2) establish a "credible fear" of persecution in an interview with an asylum officer in order to be allowed to seek asylum.[11] An asylum officer's denial of the credible fear claim may be reviewed by an IJ.[12] If such persons establish a credible fear, they will be able to seek asylum in removal proceedings before an IJ.[13] If asylum is denied by the IJ at the removal hearing, that decision may be appealed to the BIA.[14]

Claims to U.S. Citizenship. When the DOS Bureau of Consular Affairs issues a certificate of loss of nationality, or when there is a decision to deny or revoke a passport, such decision can be reviewed before DOS's Board of Appellate Review.[15] A certificate of loss of nationality can be issued when the government believes that the person has committed an act of expatriation.[16] Few acts will result in the loss of U.S. citizenship, as citizenship can be relinquished only through a knowing and voluntary renunciation.[17] A decision in favor of the person claiming U.S. citizenship may not be further challenged; however, an adverse decision against the individual may be reviewed in federal court.[18] A person seeking admission to the United States at a port of entry who claims U.S. citizenship will have his or her claim heard initially by an IJ and then reviewed by the BIA.[19]

---

[10] *Id.*

[11] 8 USC §1225(b)(1)(B), INA §235(b)(1)(B). *See also* 8 CFR §208.30.

[12] 8 USC §1225(b)(1)(B)(iii)(III), INA §235(b)(1)(B)(iii)(III). 8 CFR §§208.30(g), 1208.30(g).

[13] 8 USC §1225(b)(1)(B)(ii), INA §235(b)(1)(B)(ii). 8 CFR §208.30(f).

[14] 8 CFR §1003.1(b)(9).

[15] 22 CFR §§7.1, 50.51 (loss of nationality), and 51.70 (denial of passport). Appeals from the issuance of a certificate of loss of nationality must be made within one year to the Board of Appellate Review.

[16] 8 USC §1481, INA §349. Expatriation is an act that amounts to a relinquishment or renunciation of U.S. citizenship; it is discussed in greater detail in Chapter 7.

[17] *See Afroyim v. Rusk*, 387 U.S. 253 (1967).

[18] 8 USC §1503(a), INA §360(a).

[19] 8 CFR §§1003.1(b)(1) and (2).

Discretionary Relief from Removal. Applications for discretionary relief such as voluntary departure, asylum, CAT, and stays of removal, or other matters that may be sought either outside or as part of a removal proceeding are within the shared jurisdiction of DHS and the IJ, and as such, are governed by different rules. Adverse decisions by an IJ for discretionary relief such as voluntary departure, asylum, or cancellation of removal are reviewable by the BIA.[20] Appeals on adverse decisions on discretionary relief that are sought before DHS, such as for voluntary departure or a stay of removal, are not amenable to administrative review beyond the original decision-maker.[21]

Employment-Based Preference Petitions and Employment-Related Nonimmigrant Visa Classifications. Employment-based immigration preference petitions are submitted to USCIS. A denial may be appealed to the AAO. The beneficiary (the individual) has no right to appeal; the appeal rests with the petitioning employer. The same administrative appeal structure relevant to employment-based preference petitions applies to denials of employment-related nonimmigrant visa applications (*e.g.*, H, L, O, etc.).

Employer Sanctions. Cases involving allegations of violations of the employer sanction provisions of the immigration laws are heard by administrative law judges in the Office of the Chief Administrative Hearing Officer (OCAHO) (part of EOIR); an adverse decision may not be appealed as a matter of right, but the decision may be reviewed *sua sponte* by the Chief Administrative Hearing Officer or by request. Whether the case is reviewed is a matter of discretion.[22]

Extension of Status. A person who is present in the United States on a visa and in status may seek additional time in the United States by filing an application for an extension of status with the local USCIS office.[23]

---

[20] However, an appeal will not lie from a decision by an IJ in removal proceedings where the only ground for appeal is the amount of time granted for voluntary departure. 8 CFR §1003.1(b)(3); 8 CFR §§1003.6 and 1241.6(b) (stay of removal).

[21] 8 USC §1229c(a)(1), INA §240B(a)(1) (pre-hearing voluntary departure); 8 USC §1229c(b), INA §240B(b) (post-hearing voluntary departure); 8 USC §1231(c)(2)(A), INA §241(c)(2)(A); 8 CFR §241.6 (stay of removal).

[22] 28 CFR §68.54(a).

[23] 8 CFR §214.1(c).

There is no appeal from the denial of a request for an extension of status before the agency.[24]

Family-Based Preference Petitions. The initial family-based preference petition is submitted to USCIS. If the application is denied, the petitioner may appeal to the BIA.[25]

Labor Certification. An application for labor certification is submitted to DOL. In cases where the certifying officer issues a denial, the petitioner (employer) may seek review before BALCA.[26]

Naturalization and Revocation. An application for naturalization is submitted to USCIS. In the event that the application is denied, the decision may be appealed to an immigration officer.[27] Naturalization may be revoked by the Secretary of DHS.[28] The statute and regulations authorize an administrative revocation, but these proceedings have been called into question under *Gorbach v. Reno*.[29] According to the regulations, an administrative revocation may be appealed to the AAO.[30]

Nonimmigrant Change of Status. A person present in the United States pursuant to a nonimmigrant visa and is in status may seek a change of his or her nonimmigrant classification by applying to USCIS. A denial of this application is not appealable before the agency.

Nonimmigrant Visa Petitions. As was noted in Chapter 4, some nonimmigrant visa petitions are submitted initially by a U.S. citizen or employer on behalf of a beneficiary who wishes to be admitted. Cases involving a family relationship such as a fiancé/fiancée are initially submitted to the local USCIS office and, if denied, may be appealed administratively to the AAO. Review in cases involving applications submitted by an employer for the issuance of a nonimmigrant visa will depend on

---

[24] 8 CFR §214.1(c)(5).

[25] 8 CFR §1003.1(b)(5).

[26] 20 CFR §656.26. A labor certification application results either in the issuance of a labor certification or a notice of findings (NOF). A NOF is a notice of noncompliance with the labor certification process and, if unrebutted, can result in a denial of the application for labor certification.

[27] 8 USC §1447(a), INA §336(a).

[28] 8 USC §1451(h), INA §340(h).

[29] *Gorbach v. Reno*, 219 F.3d 1087 (9th Cir. 2000). *See* discussion in Chapter 7.

[30] 8 CFR §340.1(e)(1).

whether it involves a certification by DOL, in which case review will be before BALCA. Following the issuance of the certification, the case is filed with USCIS; then, any administrative appeals go to the AAO.[31]

Overseas Visa Petitions. A person overseas applying for an immigrant or nonimmigrant visa before a U.S. consul may ask the consul to seek review of the decision by way of an "advisory opinion" from the DOS Visa Office;[32] such "review" is limited to legal issues and not issues of fact. When a visa application is coupled with a request for a benefit, the denial can be administratively appealed like any other case as if it were submitted in the United States. For example, where a visa applicant is seeking a waiver under 8 USC §§1182(h) or (i), INA §§212(h) or 212(i), the waiver will be adjudicated by the nearest overseas USCIS office and the denial will be reviewable by the AAO. Individuals seeking refugee status through the overseas refugee program have no appeal as a matter of right from a decision denying the petition.

Temporary Protected Status. Applications for TPS are submitted to USCIS and may be reviewed by the AAO.[33]

Waivers. Depending on the circumstances in which a waiver is submitted, it may be reviewed by the BIA or the AAO. Appellate jurisdiction will be determined by whether the request for a waiver was initially submitted to USCIS or to an IJ in a removal hearing. In the former case, review is by the AAO; in the latter, it is by the BIA. Waivers also can be submitted during the consular interview abroad, but, in most cases, they are forwarded to the appropriate USCIS office overseas—therefore, any denial would be reviewed by the AAO.

MOTIONS TO REOPEN OR RECONSIDER

Sometimes additional facts that could provide a basis for a grant of the immigration relief being sought become available after a case has been presented and decided. In these situations, the only way that the new facts can be made part of the record for consideration by the decision-maker is if the case is "reopened." The term "reopen" connotes that the record is being opened again for the consideration of the new evidence. A request to do so is made by way of a "motion to reopen." In contrast

---

[31] *See, e.g.*, 8 CFR §§103.3(a)(3), 1103.3(a)(3).

[32] 22 CFR §§41.121(c) and 42.81(d).

[33] 8 CFR §§244.10 and 1244.10.

to motions to reopen are motions to reconsider. These motions are brought in circumstances not where there are new facts, but where there is a new or restated legal argument.

A motion to reconsider, when made from a decision by DHS, must be filed within 30 days.[34] Reconsideration in cases before IJs, the BIA, the DOS Board of Appellate Review, and DOL also are governed by a 30-day rule and require that the appellant present the facts or law that was improperly understood or applied.[35] While there are no set time periods in requesting reconsideration of a visa refusal or denial, a person's failure to proceed within one year following notification of visa availability will lose his or her priority date, but may have the date reinstated within two years.[36]

The regulations require that a motion to reopen before DHS, the BIA, or an IJ be accompanied by affidavits or other evidentiary materials, and that there be a showing that the new evidence is material and was unavailable at the time of the hearing.[37] A motion to reopen must be filed with DHS within 30 days of the initial decision, but that deadline may be excused where it is shown that the delay was "reasonable and . . . beyond the control of the applicant or petitioner."[38] Motions to reopen to the IJ must be filed within 90 days of the final order and must state whether the case is subject to any judicial or criminal proceeding and whether the person is still in the United States. The motion also must contain the new facts that will be established along with affidavits and other evidentiary material including the completed application for relief.[39] The motion to reopen before the BIA must be filed within 90 days from the date the administrative decision was rendered, and must contain affidavits or other

---

[34] 8 CFR §103.5(a)(1)(i).

[35] *See* 8 CFR §§1003.23(b) and 1003.2(b); 22 CFR §7.10; and 20 CFR §656.26(a)(1)(i). A motion to reconsider an IJ's decision that is on appeal is treated as a motion to remand. A party is only allowed one motion to reconsider in removal cases (8 CFR §1003.2(b)(2)), and these motions are not allowed where the sole basis of the motion is that the case was decided without opinion or by a three-member panel. 8 CFR §1003.2(b)(3). An IJ may reopen or reconsider a case on his or her own motion at any time as long as he or she continues to have jurisdiction over the matter. 8 CFR §1003.23(b)(1). In this regard, the BIA's power to reconsider or reopen is broader as it applies to "any case in which it has rendered a decision." 8 CFR §1003.2(a).

[36] 8 USC §1153(g), INA §203(g).

[37] These regulations are found at 8 CFR §§103.5(a)(2) (DHS), 1003.2(c)(1) (BIA), 1003.23(b)(3) (IJ).

[38] 8 CFR §103.5(a)(1)(i). Forfeiture cases have a shorter, 10-day period for submitting the reconsideration request. *See* 8 CFR §274.19(e).

[39] 8 CFR §1003.23(b)(3). The time restrictions (90 days) may be waived where the motion is submitted jointly by the government. 8 CFR §1003.23(b)(4)(iv).

evidence establishing *prima facie* eligibility for the relief sought and that the evidence could not have been discovered or presented at the former hearing.[40] A party is allowed only one motion to reopen.

Because a motion to reopen is based on new facts that establish eligibility for relief, the motion must demonstrate that the applicant is *prima facie* eligible for the immigration relief being sought.[41] The BIA may deny relief even if there is no opposition presented by DHS, as the decision by the IJ or BIA is given a great deal of deference.[42] Denials may be based on failure to make out a *prima facie* case, failure to reasonably explain why the information was not available earlier, or on grounds where the benefit sought is a discretionary one.[43] Nonetheless, the IJ or BIA must explain its basis for denial and it may not be based on a cursory review of the record.[44]

In cases before EOIR, a motion to reopen is barred if it is filed more than 90 days after a final administrative order is entered, where a previous motion was filed, or where the applicant is no longer in the United States.[45] A final administrative order is either the decision by the BIA or an unappealed decision of the IJ.[46] Notwithstanding any of these provisions, the BIA has broad authority to *sua sponte* reopen the proceedings in exceptional circumstances, and reopening also may be possible where the parties agree to reopening.[47]

APPEALS TO THE BIA

In 1999, the Attorney General promulgated regulations (further amended in 2002) that established "streamlining" or expedited procedures

---

[40] 8 CFR §1003.2(c)(1).

[41] *INS v. Abudu*, 485 U.S. 94, 104 (1988); 8 CFR §1003.2.

[42] *See Abudu*, 485 U.S. 94; *Limsico v. INS*, 951 F.2d 210 (9th Cir. 1991).

[43] *INS v. Rios-Pineda*, 471 U.S. 444 (1985); *Abudu*, 485 U.S. 94.

[44] *Zhao v. DOJ*, 265 F.3d 83, 95–97 (2d Cir. 2001).

[45] 8 CFR §§1003.2(c)(2), 1003.2(d). These time limitations are inapplicable in cases involving asylum, withholding of removal, or Convention Against Torture relief. *See* 8 USC §1229a(c)(7)(C)(ii), INA §240(c)(7)(C)(ii) ("There is no time limit on the filing of a motion to reopen if the basis of the motion is to apply for relief under sections 208 or 241(b)(3) and is based on changed country conditions arising in the country of nationality or the country to which removal has been ordered, if such evidence is material and was not available and would not have been discovered or presented at the previous proceeding.").

[46] *Matter of Goolcharan*, 23 I&N Dec. 5 (BIA 2001).

[47] 8 CFR §§1003.2(a) and (c)(3)(iii).

designed to accelerate the administrative review of cases.[48] Streamlining allows a single BIA member to affirm an IJ's decision without issuing an opinion. Pursuant to the regulations, a single BIA member may summarily affirm any IJ decision if the result was correct, any errors were "harmless or immaterial," and either the issues in the case are controlled by precedent or the factual or legal issues raised are so insubstantial to not warrant a three-member review.[49] Streamlining has led to a sky-rocketing federal court docket as cases move rapidly through administrative review. It also has resulted in an increased willingness on the part of federal courts to remand cases to the BIA.[50]

In the context of discussing appeals, it is important to underscore that cases on appeal are decided solely on the basis of the "record" in the case. For this reason, it is critical to understand what constitutes the record. Only those materials offered by the parties and admitted by the administrative agency or administrative court system make up the record. Thus, conversations and other matters that do not appear in a written form and have not been submitted as part of the original application will not be considered on appeal. All requests for relief should be prepared as thoroughly as possible, as one cannot assume that there will be an opportunity to submit additional evidence. In fact, it is extremely rare that an applicant will have an opportunity to present new evidence in cases where he or she failed to do so initially.

REVIEW BY THE ATTORNEY GENERAL OR SECRETARY OF HOMELAND SECURITY

Authority delegated to functionaries within DOJ and DHS flow from the cabinet-level officers. In the case of DOJ, that person is the Attorney General, and he or she may review a case by assuming jurisdiction over the case through a process called "certification." Certification may occur *sua sponte* by the Attorney General[51] or DHS Secretary.[52] A case may be certified to the Attorney General upon request from the BIA or DHS Secretary.[53] Similarly, those matters that are within the jurisdiction of

---

[48] *See* 8 CFR §§1003.1 and 1003.2; 67 Fed. Reg. 54878 (2002); 64 Fed. Reg. 56135 (1999).

[49] 8 CFR §1003.1(e)(4)(i).

[50] *See, e.g., Haoud v. Ashcroft,* 350 F.3d 201 (1st Cir. 2003); *Denko v. INS,* 351 F.3d 717, 731–32 (6th Cir. 2003).

[51] 8 CFR §1003.1(h)(1)(i).

[52] 8 CFR §2.1.

[53] 8 CFR §§1003.1(h)(1)(ii) and (iii).

DHS may be reviewed by the DHS Secretary.[54] Review by either the Attorney General or DHS Secretary is *de novo*. In 2002, prior to the creation of DHS, the then-Attorney General took a number of cases upon his own certification, a matter that until then had not been done frequently, in deference to the delegated authority to the BIA.[55]

JUDICIAL REVIEW

The 1952 Immigration and Nationality Act[56] had no specific provision for federal court review. Judicial oversight was by way of a habeas corpus action filed in federal district court, with further review in the federal appellate court.[57] In 1961, Congress amended the relevant laws in an effort to expedite the review process, placing exclusive jurisdiction of "final orders of deportation" in the courts of appeal by way of a petition for review.[58] The filing of the petition for review also acted as an automatic stay of the deportation order pending the court's determination.[59] Because not all decisions constituted "final orders of deportation," some matters still had to be reviewed in the federal district courts by habeas[60] or alternative federal remedies such as mandamus, declaratory, or injunctive relief.

In 1996 and 2005, Congress enacted three statutes that significantly impacted the judicial review scheme of the immigration laws. In an effort to severely limit judicial review, Congress, in 1996, enacted AEDPA and IIRAIRA, which removed the federal courts' direct appellate jurisdiction over final orders of deportation (thus, eliminating the direct petition for review established in 1961).[61] Together, AEDPA and IIRAIRA

---

[54] 8 CFR §2.1.

[55] *See Matter of Y–L–, A–G–, R–S–R–*, 23 I&N Dec. 270 (A.G. 2002); *Matter of Jean*, 23 I&N Dec. 373 (A.G. 2002); *Matter of D–J–*, 23 I&N Dec. 572 (A.G. 2002).

[56] Immigration and Nationality Act of 1952 (INA), Pub. L. No. 82-414, 66 Stat. 163 (codified as amended at 8 USC §§1101–1524 (INA).

[57] *See, e.g., Heikkila v. Barber*, 345 U.S. 229 (1953*); Chin Yow v. United States*, 208 U.S. 8 (1908).

[58] *See* Act of Sept. 26, 1961, Pub. L. No. 87-301, §5, 75 Stat. 650, 651.

[59] *Id.*

[60] The 1961 Amendment specifically provided that final orders involving persons seeking admission were limited to review via writs of habeas corpus. *Id.* at 653.

[61] The two amendments were contained in provisions of the Antiterrorism and Effective Death Penalty Act of 1996, Pub. L. No. 104-132, 110 Stat. 1214 (1996) (AEDPA) (eliminated judicial review for persons found deportable for most crimes under the INA), and the Illegal Immigration Reform and Immigrant Responsibility Act of 1996, Pub. L. No. 104-208, 110 Stat. 3009 (1996) (IIRAIRA) (eliminated judicial review for class-based relief and for most discretionary forms of relief, except asylum).

also composed a long list of matters that were no longer amenable to judicial review (enumerated, *infra*).[62] As a result of these 1996 enactments, judicial review was no longer available for many types of cases, and aggrieved parties sought the only remaining available relief—habeas corpus under 28 USC §§1361, 1651, and 2241.[63] The 1996 laws created a situation where the federal district courts were inundated with much habeas litigation over those final orders of deportation that otherwise would have been petitioned to the federal courts of appeal. Nearly a decade later, in 2005, Congress, in an effort to further restrict court review, amended the statute via the REAL ID Act to reinstate petitions for review (though over only a narrow set of issues) to the federal appeals courts and prohibited the district courts from deciding habeas petitions for review of final deportation orders.[64]

In order to better understand the full effect of the legislation enacted in both 1996 and 2005, it is useful to emphasize four principles that have been articulated in court decisions interpreting this legislation.[65] First, notwithstanding congressional authority over the area of judicial review, the federal courts traditionally have looked carefully (and skeptically) at laws curtailing habeas corpus jurisdiction.[66] To preclude review under either both immigration and habeas corpus statutes would give rise to a constitutional question that courts studiously attempt to

---

[62] *See* 8 USC §§1252(a) and (b), INA §§242(a) and (b). Orders under expedited removal are not part of this review. *See* 8 USC §1252(a)(2)(A)(i), INA §242(a)(2)(A)(i). Expedited removal may be reviewed under the 28 USC §2241 (habeas statute), but the statute does not permit the invocation of declaratory, injunctive, or equitable relief. *See* 8 USC §1252(e), INA §242(e).

[63] *See* AEDPA §423, 110 Stat. 1214, 1272.

[64] The provision, codified at 8 USC §1252(a)(2)(C), INA §242(a)(2)(C), provides that: "Notwithstanding any other provision of law (statutory or nonstatutory), including section 2241 of title 28, United States Code, or any other habeas corpus provision, and sections 1361 and 1651 of such title, no court shall have jurisdiction . . . ." *See* Emergency Supplemental Appropriations Act for Defense, the Global War on Terror and Tsunami Relief, Pub. 109-13, §2, Division B, §106(a) (2005). The provision at 8 USC §1252(a)(2)(D), INA §242(a)(2)(D), also amended by REAL ID, in turn limits the jurisdictional bar of subclause (C). The REAL ID legislation also called for the immediate transfer of pending removal-based habeas cases from the district courts to the federal appellate courts. For more regarding the transfer of these pending habeas cases, see the REAL ID Resources page on AILF's website, at *www.ailf.org/lac/lac_realidresources.shtml*.

[65] *See* INS v. St. Cyr, 533 U.S. 289 (2001); *Calcano-Martinez v. INS*, 533 U.S. 348 (2001). *See also* Demore v. Kim, 530 U.S. 510 (2003).

[66] *See, e.g., Harris v. Nelson*, 394 U.S. 286, 290–91 (1969) ("writ of habeas corpus is the fundamental instrument for safeguarding individual freedom against arbitrary and lawless state action").

avoid.[67] Second, the very language of REAL ID permits federal appellate courts to review *constitutional claims* or *questions of law* in removal orders as well as in cases involving relief for persons with criminal convictions.[68] Third, REAL ID does not address habeas review involving detention; presumably this review remains.[69] Fourth, cases not involving final orders of removal or matters prohibited from review still may be amenable to declaratory relief under the Administrative Procedure Act (APA).[70]

As a result of AEDPA, IIRAIRA, and REAL ID, the legal remedies that remain are: (1) direct petitions for review to the appellate courts of all final orders of removal; (2) habeas corpus in district court where the matter being challenged involves constitutional claims or questions of law;[71] and (3) certain mandamus and declaratory actions brought in an appropriate federal district court.

The nature and extent of review may depend on a number of factors, including the date of the decision for which review is sought, as well as its subject matter.[72] Since REAL ID reinstated the petition for

---

[67] A full elimination of habeas relief could implicate *U.S. Const.*, art. I, §9, and art. III. *See* D. Cole, "Jurisprudence and Liberty: Habeas Corpus and Due Process as Limits on Congress' Control of Federal Jurisdiction," 86 *Geo. L.J.* 2481 (1998). Article I, §9 is otherwise referred to as the "Suspension Clause." *Id.* at 2984. For examples of how the court has dealt with these questions, see *St. Cyr*, 533 U.S. 289, and *Calcano-Martinez*, 533 U.S. 348.

[68] Congress specifically did not preclude constitutional claims as 8 USC §1252(a)(2)(D), INA §242(a)(2)(D) provides that "[n]othing in subparagraph (B) or (C), or any other provision of this Act (other than this section) which limits or eliminates judicial review, shall be construed as precluding review of *constitutional claims or questions of law* raised upon a petition for review. . . ." (Emphasis supplied.) One could argue that the REAL ID amendments reinstated federal court review through the petition for review, and expanded the appellate courts' review beyond where it had been prior to the limits created by AEDPA and IIRAIRA. *See Enwonwu v. Gonzales*, 438 F.3d 22, 33 (1st Cir. 2006) (finding jurisdiction to review "colorable" constitutional claims but not matters involving factual or discretionary determinations); *Fernandez-Ruiz v. Gonzales*, 410 F.3d 585 (9th Cir. 2005).

[69] *See* AILF Practice Advisory; "Judicial Review Provisions of the REAL ID Act," 2 (May 12, 2005), available at *www.ailf.org/lac/lac_pa_realid_051205_final.pdf.*

[70] *See, e.g., Zheng v. Pogash*, 416 F. Supp. 2d 550, 555–57 (S.D. Tex. 2006). The APA is codified at 5 USC §701 *et seq.*

[71] *Id.* The statute as amended by REAL ID purports to remove habeas corpus review, and this could be interpreted either as not including habeas corpus involving constitutional claims or as a violation of the Suspension Clause. Article III, §3 of the Constitution specifically provides that "[t]he Privilege of the Writ of Habeas Corpus shall not be suspended, unless when in cases of Rebellion or Invasion the public Safety may require it." REAL ID does not preclude district court habeas review over challenges to detention that are independent of challenges to removal orders. *See* H.R. Conf. Rep. No. 109-72, at 175.

[72] According to AEDPA and IIRAIRA, if the decision for which review is sought was entered on or before October 30, 1996, the governing statute will be former 8 USC §1105a, and if the *continued*

review and required the transfer of pending habeas claims in the district courts involving the review of removal orders, it seems that all cases are governed by some aspect of the new statute.[73]

Petitions for Review of Final Orders of Removal

Under REAL ID, the federal appellate courts have exclusive jurisdiction by way of a petition for review of removal orders with the exception of expedited removal cases.[74] REAL ID broadens the courts' jurisdiction, as the law also includes review involving applicants for admission.[75] In addition to placing jurisdiction over removal cases in the federal appellate courts, the courts may review claims involving constitutional matters, questions of law, or cases under the Convention Against Torture, notwithstanding the general prohibition from judicial review of discretionary determinations.

It is not yet clear how the REAL ID amendments ultimately will be interpreted. There is similar language between REAL ID and the pre–AEDPA/IIRAIRA judicial review statutes. Therefore, it is possible that the extensive case law development of the predecessor statute (pre–AEDPA/IIRAIRA INA) may provide instruction in understanding the proper subject of review under the current statute.[76]

---

decision was subsequent to October 30, 1996, but the case was initiated prior to that date, review would be governed by certain transition rules. These transition rules require that the decision must be appealed within 30 days and the petitioner must separately obtain a stay of the deportation order. According to AEDPA and IIRAIRA, cases that did not fall within either of these time frames were to be governed by their amendments to the INA (those that had eliminated the petition review and relegated all review to habeas petitions). *See* 8 USC §1252(a) (1996), INA §242(a).

[73] Indeed, since the 2005 amendments were enacted, the district courts have been transferring cases to the appellate courts. *See, e.g., Kanivets v. Gonzales*, 424 F.3d 330, 333 (3d Cir. 2005) (cases pending at enactment of REAL ID were converted to petitions for review).

[74] *See* 8 USC §§1252(a)(2)(A)(i) and 1252(a)(2)(D), INA §§242(a)(2)(A)(i) and 242(a)(2)(D).

[75] As was noted previously, Congress consolidated cases involving inadmissibility and deportability into one removal procedure; REAL ID's petitions cover the removal procedure; thus, covering both inadmissibility and deportability cases.

[76] The predecessor (pre–AEDPA/IIRAIRA INA) statute provided for exclusive review of "final orders of deportation" in the federal appellate courts. Review of cases involving persons seeking *admission* was limited to habeas relief. *See Foti v. INS*, 375 U.S. 217, 227 (1963); *Cheng Fan Kwok v. INS*, 392 U.S. 206, 217 (1968). However, some scholars question whether the comparisons between the post–REAL-ID statutory language and earlier statutes are appropriate. *See* G. Neuman, "The REAL ID Act and the Suspension Clause," 9 *Bender's Immigr. Bull.* 1555 (2005).

Under established administrative law doctrine, the petitioner must have "exhausted" all available administrative remedies (discussed, *supra*). Thus, parties may not raise arguments before the federal court that were not made in the course of removal proceedings before the IJ and reviewed by the BIA. Additionally, the current statute requires that the petition be filed within 30 days of the final administrative appeals decision by the BIA, and that it may be only filed in the appeals court in the district where the IJ's decision was rendered.[77] The petitioner must obtain a separate stay of removal order from the court in which the primary action is brought, as the filing of the petition does not act as an automatic stay.[78]

In enacting REAL ID, Congress sought to insulate certain immigration decisions from reversal. The statute now provides that the administrative findings of fact may be disturbed only if a "reasonable adjudicator would be compelled to conclude" otherwise; that a decision finding a person ineligible for admission is conclusive unless manifestly contrary to law; and that discretionary determinations (with respect to asylum determinations) must be upheld unless contrary to the law or an abuse of discretion.[79] At the same time, the statute specifically provides that constitutional claims and those involving questions of law are amenable to review.[80]

Review in Non-Removal Matters

Many of the decisions of the government agencies charged with implementing the immigration laws do not involve adjudications that are part of a removal order. The types of factual situations are too numerous to mention, and range from visa petitions, determination of benefits including permanent residency, to detention issues, waivers, and naturalization.

---

[77] 8 USC §§1252(b)(1) and (2), INA §§242(b)(1) and (2).

[78] 8 USC §1252(b)(3)(B), INA §242(b)(3)(B).

[79] 8 USC §1252(b)(4), INA §242(b)(4). These provisions are, in fact, consistent with established case law. For example, even before REAL ID, factual findings were not to be overturned unless a reasonable fact-finder would be compelled to find otherwise. *Chen v. INS*, 344 F.3d 272, 275 (2d Cir. 2003). Similarly, discretionary determinations in asylum cases have been only overturned where there has been an abuse of discretion. *Marroquin-Manriquez v. INS*, 699 F.2d 129, 133 (3d Cir. 1983) ("We will not disturb the Board's exercise of discretion unless we find 'it is arbitrary, irrational or contrary to law.'") (citing *So Chun Chung v. INS*, 602 F.2d 608, 612 (3d Cir. 1979)).

[80] In *Freeman v. Gonzales*, 444 F.3d 1031 (9th Cir. 2006), the court granted a petition for review involving the beneficiary of an immediate relative petition whose spouse had died, thereby rendering the petition, according to DHS as automatically revoked. The court held that it had jurisdiction, as the matter under review was a purely legal question not involving a discretionary exercise. *Id.* at 1037.

Each type of case has its own procedure for adjudication, administrative appeal, and possible judicial review. Congress sought to place restrictions on the available avenues for judicial review by prohibiting the review of these sorts of discretionary determinations through REAL ID. The types of cases that may be amenable to judicial review and the type of available review depend on the precise application/petition at issue. This discussion will not try to answer all of the questions involving judicial review, but is an attempt to provide a general overview of the types of non-removal matters amenable to judicial review and to what extent such review is available.

Cases not involving the review of removal determinations fall into two broad categories: detention and non-detention matters. Where a person is detained (or has his or her liberty restricted), he or she may seek habeas review in federal district court only where the challenge is not from a removal order.[81] Despite the bar against judicial review for detained aliens at 8 USC §1226(e), INA §236(e), the district court has jurisdiction under habeas corpus, but the review will be limited to constitutional and legal claims and will not involve the broad category of non-reviewable matters enumerated below.

Where a case does not involve a person in detention or whose liberty is not restricted, a declaratory or mandamus action may be the appropriate remedy.[82] The declaratory action is a claim that the agency, in denying a particular application, violated a statute, regulation, or a plaintiff's constitutional right. A mandamus action lies where the government has failed to adjudicate an application where there is a clear duty to do so.[83]

Under the Administrative Procedure Act (APA), federal courts have jurisdiction to review immigration agency action or inaction.[84] Coupled with the Declaratory Judgment Act, federal courts also may render a de-

---

[81] As previously noted, exclusive jurisdiction of removal cases is vested in the federal appeals courts by way of a petition for review. *See* 8 USC §1252(b), INA §242(b).

[82] *See, e.g., Santillan v. Gonzales*, 388 F. Supp. 2d 1065 (N.D. Calif. 2005) (court recognized jurisdiction and certified class in case involving LPRs seeking temporary documentation of status), 2005 WL 3542661 (N.D. Cal. Dec. 22, 2005) (permanent injunction issued).

[83] 28 USC §1361.

[84] 5 USC §702. There also is a line of cases that hold that where the preclusion of judicial review would raise serious constitutional concerns, there may be jurisdiction under the federal question statute. 28 USC §1331. *Sabhari v. Reno*, 197 F.3d 938, 941 (8th Cir. 1999); *Ortiz v. Meissner*, 179 F.2d 718 (9th Cir. 1999).

claratory judgment, grant injunctive relief, or issue a writ of mandamus.[85] Furthermore, an aggrieved party also could challenge an agency's violation of the notice and rulemaking requirements, or the denial of some form of immigration benefit, under the APA.[86] Generally, in non-removal matters, so long as a decision has been made by an administrative officer, courts will decline to review any discretionary decision, absent a constitutional claim.[87] However, where the claim involves inaction, courts are not without jurisdiction.[88] Therefore, applicants who are denied immigration benefits may seek mandamus or declaratory relief where they are challenging inaction or misapplication of the statute.[89]

Matters Not Reviewable

The subject matter of the decision is relevant because certain matters are not reviewable in the federal courts:

- decisions by an IJ or DHS on summary removal except in very limited circumstances (collateral attacks on removal also are precluded);[90]

- decisions on whether to grant certain waivers of grounds of inadmissibility, voluntary departure, adjustment of status, and cancellation of removal;[91]

- removal decisions based on medical certifications;[92]

- "any other decision or action [except asylum] . . . the authority for which is specified . . . [as being within] the discretion of the Attorney General";[93]

---

[85] The Declaratory Judgment Act is codified at 28 USC §2201.

[86] The APA provides that an action may lie to remedy a legal wrong or if the party has been adversely affected or aggrieved by the actions.

[87] *McBrearty v. Perryman*, 212 F.3d 985 (7th Cir. 2000).

[88] *Iddir v. INS*, 166 F. Supp. 2d 903, 905 (N.D. Ill. 2001).

[89] *Dillingham v. INS*, 267 F.3d 996 (9th Cir. 2001) (denial of adjustment of status was based on an improper statutory basis, not exercise of discretion); *Beltran-Tirado v. INS*, 213 F.3d 1179, 1182 (9th Cir. 2000) (applicant denied registry).

[90] 8 USC §§1225(b)(1)(D), 1252(a)(2)(A), and 1252(e), INA §§235(b)(1)(D), 242(a)(2)(A), and 242(e).

[91] 8 USC §1252(a)(2)(B)(i), INA §242(a)(2)(B)(i). This includes waivers under 8 USC §§1182(h) and (i), INA §§212(h) and (i), or to waive inadmissibility for unlawful presence. *See* 8 USC §1182(a)(9)(B)(v), INA §212(a)(9)(B)(v).

[92] 8 USC § 1252(a)(3), INA §242(a)(3).

[93] 8 USC §1252(a)(2)(B)(ii), INA §242(a)(2)(B)(ii).

- where injunctive relief is sought (except direct petitions in the U.S. Supreme Court) to enjoin the operation of removal proceedings (except if it is in an individual case); removal only can be enjoined if there is a showing by clear and convincing evidence that the entry or execution of such order is prohibited as a matter of law;[94]

- DHS's decision or action "to commence proceedings, adjudicate cases, or execute removal orders against any alien under this Act";[95]

- decisions denying the right to seek asylum based on any of the following: protection could have been sought in a safe third country; a prior denial of asylum; failure to file within one year[96] (where the government determines that there were no circumstances justifying an exception to the one-year rule), or the asylum-seeker is considered to be a terrorist;[97]

- decisions involving reinstatement of removal orders;[98]

- discretionary decisions involving release from custody, the grant, denial, or revocation of bond or parole;[99] and

- decisions regarding voluntary departure.[100]

Review in Non-Reviewable Matters

Even though Congress has curtailed and, at times even prohibited, judicial review, the courts have preserved review through other means to avoid a constitutional conflict. The Supreme Court's decisions in *Calcano-Martinez v. INS*,[101] and *INS v. St. Cyr*,[102] illustrate the Court's refusal to allow the denial of all access to the federal courts. In *Calcano-Martinez* (pre–REAL ID), the petitioners were LPRs convicted of aggravated felonies who faced deportation. They filed petitions for review in the

---

[94] 8 USC §1252(f), INA §242(f). Class-based injunctive relief is specifically prohibited. *See id.*

[95] 8 USC §1252(g). INA §242(g).

[96] 8 USC §1158(a)(3), INA §208(a)(3). Following the enactment of the REAL ID Act, some have argued that appeals from where the applicant failed to satisfy the one year filing deadline may be reviewed in federal court.

[97] 8 USC §1158(b)(2)(D), INA §208(b)(2)(D).

[98] 8 USC §1231(a)(5), INA §241(a)(5).

[99] 8 USC §1226(e), INA §236(e).

[100] 8 USC §§1229c(e) and (f), INA §§240B(e) and (f).

[101] 533 U.S. 348 (2001).

[102] 533 U.S. 289, 297–31 (2001).

courts of appeal and habeas petitions in federal district court. In a 5–4 opinion, Justice Stevens wrote that to deny the petitioners any form of judicial review would raise serious constitutional questions and even though there was no jurisdiction in the appeals court on a petition for review (after AEDPA/IIRAIRA but before REAL ID), a habeas claim could lie in district court under 28 USC §2241. Presumably with the REAL ID amendments, the Court could hold now that while there was no jurisdiction over final orders of removal in the district court, 8 USC §1252, INA §242 provides for review in the federal appeals court.

In *St. Cyr*, which was decided the same day as *Calcano-Martinez*, the Court again held that restrictions on review could not bar all access to the federal courts. *St. Cyr* involved a petitioner who had pleaded guilty to a crime that at the time of his plea would have allowed him to pursue a waiver of inadmissibility and deportability (former §212(c) waiver). However, the enactment of IIRAIRA, which eliminated §212(c) relief, if interpreted as being retroactive, would have prevented him from seeking the waiver. The Court, in a 5–4 decision written by Justice Stevens, held that it had jurisdiction, and that while Congress has the power to enact retroactive statutes, there is a strong presumption against retroactivity in the absence of clear congressional intent. In this case, that presumption had not been overcome in the absence of an explicit retroactive application. In both *Calcano-Martinez* and *St. Cyr*, the Court was mindful of the constitutional questions raised and the presumptions in favor of retaining review.[103] While the Court did not decide whether the waiver should be granted, it determined that it had jurisdiction and that the applicant could seek the waiver notwithstanding the government's retroactivity argument.

St. Cyr and *Calcano-Martinez* were decided before the REAL ID's court jurisdiction-stripping provisions were enacted. These decisions reaffirm the view that while Congress has the authority to limit federal appellate court jurisdiction in immigration decisions, courts will make every effort to protect their jurisdiction under habeas corpus. Therefore, it remains to be seen to what extent these most recent efforts at limiting judicial review in immigration cases will survive their own judicial review.

---

[103] The Court noted that "[f]or the INS to prevail, it must overcome both the strong presumption in favor of judicial review of administrative action and the longstanding rule requiring a clear statement of congressional intent to repeal habeas jurisdiction . . . . A construction of the amendments at issue that would entirely preclude review of a pure question of law by any court would give rise to substantial constitutional questions." *Id.* at 298.

CHAPTER 7
U.S. Citizenship

Full participation in government and society has been a basic right of the country symbolizing the full citizenship and equal protection of all.
—Charles Rangel

OVERVIEW

The preceding chapters have focused on the application of the immigration laws to foreign nationals. In this chapter, U.S. citizenship—its acquisition either at birth or through a process called naturalization—will be explored. Once naturalized, a person is no longer subject to the grounds of inadmissibility and deportability, and is protected from the application of the immigration laws.

CITIZENSHIP VS. PERMANENT RESIDENCY

Under U.S. law, there are significant differences in rights and protections between U.S. citizens and lawful permanent residents (LPRs). While an LPR is not required to obtain a visa each time he or she attempts to return from a trip abroad, that person nonetheless is subject to all of the grounds of inadmissibility and deportability, and could be placed in removal proceedings if any of the grounds apply. Furthermore, and critically important, there is no statute of limitation on the grounds of inadmissibility and deportability, and no constitutional prohibition from *ex post facto* laws. Thus, LPRs, like all other noncitizens, remain vulnerable to changing immigration statutes.[1]

---

[1] *See Landgraf v. USI Film Products*, 511 U.S. 244, 266 (1994). Several court decisions have raised the possibility that there may be some arguments for challenging this long-standing position. *See Eastern Enterprises v. Apfel*, 524 U.S. 498 (1998) (concurring opinion of Justice Thomas) (expressing willingness to reconsider whether retroactive civil laws are unconstitutional under the *ex post*
continued

Traditionally, LPRs have been regarded as having greater constitutional protections—like due process rights—than nonimmigrants.[2] However, the constitutional rights historically enjoyed by LPRs are eroding as the government takes positions questioning those rights through its application of the 1996 laws[3] and, perhaps, future legislation.[4]

ACQUIRING CITIZENSHIP

U.S. citizenship can be acquired in a variety of ways: (1) by being born in the United States and subject to the jurisdiction of the United States (commonly referred to as "constitutional citizenship"); (2) from acquisition by birth overseas to one or more U.S. citizen parents; and (3) by naturalization following the lawful acquisition of permanent resident status in the United States.

There also are a number of ways in which citizenship may be terminated. A person may be divested of citizenship through "denaturalization," or he or she may voluntarily relinquish it. In order for relinquishment to be valid, it must be done overseas before a U.S. consul.[5]

In this climate of heightened suspicion of noncitizens as potential terrorists, the U.S. government has increasingly limited the procedural and substantive rights of noncitizens. Thus, possession of U.S. citizenship is now even more important because citizens enjoy greater protection from arbitrary arrest and detention than noncitizens. For this reason, whenever possible, naturalization should be considered.

---

facto clause); *Scheidemann v. INS*, 83 F.3d 1517, 1527 (3d Cir. 1996) (Sarokin, J., concurring) ("If deportation under such circumstances is not punishment, it is difficult to envision what is."); *see also* R. Pauw, "A New Look at Deportation as Punishment: Why at Least Some of the Constitution's Criminal Procedure Protections Must Apply," 52 *Adm. L.R.* 305 (Winter 2000).

[2] For example, returning LPRs are not always regarded as seeking a new admission and are not subject to removal without a hearing. *See Landon v. Plasencia*, 459 U.S. 21, 30–32 (1982) (citing *Kwong Hai Chew v. Colding*, 344 U.S. 590 (1953); *Rafeedie v. INS*, 880 F.2d 506, 524–26 (D.C. Cir. 1989) (returning LPR could not be subjected to §235(c) summary proceedings).

[3] Antiterrorism and Effective Death Penalty Act of 1996, Pub. L. No. 104-132, 110 Stat. 1214 (AEDPA), and Illegal Immigration Reform and Immigrant Responsibility Act of 1996, Division C of the Omnibus Appropriations Act of 1996 (H.R. 3610), Pub. L. No. 104-208, 110 Stat. 3009 (IIRAIRA).

[4] *Ramirez v. U.S.*, 81 F. Supp. 2d 532 (D. N.J. 2000) (Fourth Amendment prohibits unreasonable detention of permanent residents); *but see Tineo v. Ashcroft*, 350 F.3d 382 (3d Cir. 2003) (Congress has the authority to limit the *Fleuti* Doctrine in enacting amendments in 1996). For more on the *Fleuti* Doctrine, AEDPA, IIRAIRA, and effects of retroactivity, see Chapter 2.

[5] For more on loss of citizenship, see "Loss of Citizenship," *infra*.

Citizenship at Birth

According to the 14th Amendment, "all persons born in and subject to the jurisdiction" of the United States are citizens.[6] The principle that birth in the territory of a country may confer citizenship is grounded in ancient Roman law and is referred to as *jus soli* (literally "right of the territory"), a concept recognized in international law.[7] The clause in the 14th Amendment "and subject to the jurisdiction" excludes from citizenship the children of diplomats born in the United States; however, under interpretations of the statute, these children are considered LPRs.[8] A child born overseas to one or both parents who are U.S. citizens may be a citizen depending on the applicable citizenship acquisition statute in effect at the time of the child's birth.[9]

The Supreme Court has held that while the statutes governing the citizenship of persons born outside the United States are within Congress's plenary power, those governing the citizenship of persons born in the United States are controlled by the Constitution.[10] It is for these reasons that citizenship by birth within the United States is referred to as "constitutional" citizenship, while citizenship acquired through other procedures is referred to as "statutory" citizenship. Constitutional citizenship also may be claimed by persons born in U.S. territories that are under the control of the United States.[11]

Whether a person is a U.S. citizen as a result of birth in the United States is a factual question and is not controlled by the documentation that the person may possess.[12] Upon establishing the fact of birth in the United States, the person will be deemed a U.S. citizen. An individual's possession of a valid U.S. passport is *prima facie* proof of U.S. citizenship.[13] Controlling statutes also provide that a child of unknown parentage who

---

[6] Prior to the enactment of the 14th Amendment following the Civil War, birth in the United States was not determinative of citizenship status. *See Dred Scott v. Sandford*, 60 U.S. 393 (1857).

[7] R. Boswell, *Immigration and Nationality Law: Cases and Materials* 711 (3d ed. 2000).

[8] *See U.S. v. Wong Kim Ark*, 169 U.S. 649, 682 (1898); INS Interpretations 320.1(f).

[9] The provisions generally include a requirement that the U.S. citizen parent have resided in the United States for a specified period prior to the child's birth. *See* C. Gordon, S. Mailman & S. Yale-Loehr, *Immigration Law and Procedure* §1.03(8)(d) (2005).

[10] *Rogers v. Bellei*, 401 U.S. 815, 832–35 (1971).

[11] Constitutional citizenship also is supported by statutes. *See, e.g.*, 8 USC §§1401(a) and (b), INA §§301(a) and (b) (defining the term "nationals and citizens of the U.S.").

[12] *See U.S. v. Breyer*, 871 F. Supp. 679 (E.D. Pa. 1993).

[13] *Matter of Villanueva*, 19 I&N Dec. 101 (BIA 1984).

is under the age of five and is found in the United States is deemed a U.S. citizen unless it is established otherwise before the child reaches his or her 21st birthday.[14]

Whether an individual acquired citizenship at birth abroad where one or both parents are U.S. citizens is a complex question controlled by statute. This form of citizenship derives from the Roman law principle *jus sanguinis* (literally "right of blood"). As noted earlier, because this form of citizenship does not derive from the Constitution, Congress has plenary power to enact rules, and may permit distinctions that otherwise would not be permissible.[15] For example, a child born out of wedlock will acquire citizenship differently depending on whether the U.S. citizen parent is the mother or the father.[16]

The rules applicable to acquisition of citizenship by birth abroad depend on the date of the person's birth and the law in force at the time of birth.[17] As a general rule, in order for a U.S. citizen parent to transmit citizenship to a child born overseas, the parent must have resided in the United States for a set period of time.[18] In addition, depending on when the person was born, "citizenship retention" rules could have applied.[19] Under these retention rules, and prior to 1994, the INA[20] provided that a child born outside of the United States to U.S. citizen parents had to reside in the United States for a certain time period in order to keep his or her U.S. citizenship.

---

[14] 8 USC §1401(f), INA §301(f).

[15] 8 USC §§1401(c), (e), (g), and (h), INA §§301(c), (e), (g), and (h).

[16] 8 USC §1409, INA §309. The Supreme Court found these rules as not violative of the Equal Protection Clause in *Nguyen v. INS*, 533 U.S. 53 (2001). The rules on citizenship acquisition at birth overseas to a U.S. citizen differ depending on whether the child is born in or out of wedlock or otherwise meets the definition of child under 8 USC §1101(b), INA §101(b).

[17] For a more thorough description, see I. Kurzban, *Kurzban's Immigration Law Sourcebook*, 10th Ed., Appendix B (AILF 2006). In addition, there are rules on transmission and retention of citizenship that depend on when the person was born. *Id.*

[18] *Savorgnan v. United States*, 338 U.S. 491 (1950), *reh'g denied*, 339 U.S. 916 (1950). *See also* 8 USC §1401, INA §301.

[19] *See* Immigration and Nationality Technical Corrections Act of 1994, Pub. L. 103-416, §103, 108 Stat. 4305, 4307–08 (1994). (Persons born overseas after Oct. 10, 1952, no longer have to reside in the United States for two years in order to keep their citizenship.)

[20] Immigration and Nationality Act of 1952, Pub. L. No. 82-414, 66 Stat. 163 (codified as amended at 8 USC §§1101 *et seq.*) (INA).

Citizenship through Naturalization

The U.S. Constitution vests Congress with the power to establish rules for naturalization in Art. I, §8, Cl. 4. The courts have interpreted the Constitution as placing broad powers in the legislature, and they have accorded it great deference in the realm of naturalization.[21]

To qualify for naturalization, a person must be an LPR; exceptions are provided for persons who serve honorably in the U.S. military for at least one year or who serve in a time of war or declared hostilities.[22] An applicant for naturalization must be at least 18 years old[23] and have resided continuously in the United States for five years following receipt of permanent residency;[24] the residency requirement is reduced to three years for persons who obtained their status based on marriage to a U.S. citizen.[25] A spouse or child who obtained permanent residency under the Violence Against Women Act,[26] as a result of battery or extreme cruelty, also may apply for naturalization within the three-year period.[27]

---

[21] *Reyes v. INS*, 910 F.2d 611 (9th Cir. 1990) (striking down a presidential executive order permitting service members serving in Grenada to benefit from this provision on the grounds that the President does not have the authority to make area restrictions under the statute, only time restrictions); Exec. Order No. 12582, 52 Fed. Reg. 3395 (1987); 3 CFR §201 (1987); 8 USC §1440 and 1440-1, INA §§329 and 329a (permitting the grant of posthumous citizenship to service members who serve honorably in an active duty status during a designated period of hostility, and die as a result of injury or disease incurred in or aggravated by that service).

[22] Those serving in time of military hostilities who continue to be in the military, or who have been honorably discharged, have no residency or physical presence requirements. 8 USC §1440, INA §329. Those who have served honorably for one year (irrespective of whether engaged in any hostilities) and who apply while in the service, or within six months of separation, also are exempt from any residency or physical presence requirements. 8 USC §1439, INA §328. The President declared that military hostilities following September 11, 2001, qualify under these expedited naturalization provisions.

[23] 8 USC §1445(b), INA §334. The age requirement may be waived for persons naturalizing as members of the armed services. 8 USC §1440(a), INA §329(a). Notwithstanding the general age requirement, a child whose parents naturalize also becomes a U.S. citizen. 8 USC §1431, INA §320.

[24] Absences of a continuous period of less than six months are permitted and absences of greater than six months but less than one year create a rebuttable presumption of a break in continuity of residence. 8 USC §1427(b), INA 316(b). An absence greater than one year creates a conclusive break unless the applicant is working for the U.S. government, a recognized U.S. research institution, corporation or a public international organization of which the United States is a member. *Id.*

[25] The applicant must be in "marital union" immediately preceding the date of the application. 8 USC §1430(a), INA §319(a).

[26] Violence Against Women Act of 1994, Pub. L. No. 103-322, 108 Stat. 1902–55 (codified as 8 USC §§1151, 1154, 1186a note, 1254, 2245).

[27] *Id. See also* 8 USC §1430(a), INA §319(a).

An individual applying for naturalization must reside for at least three months immediately preceding the date of filing in the state in which the petition is filed.[28] He or she also must be physically present in the United States for at least half of the applicable continuous residency period, and must have maintained such continuous residency since filing the naturalization application.[29] An absence of more than one year during the residency period is not permitted (as it breaks the continuous residency), and an absence greater than six months raises a rebuttable presumption that the naturalization application has been abandoned.[30]

Last, in order to qualify for naturalization, an applicant must be a person of good moral character for the requisite five years (three years in cases of a spouse of a U.S. citizen or VAWA applicants; one year if a person is in the military under §1440(b), INA §329(b)).[31] The definition of good moral character is provided in the statute that sets forth disqualifying acts (though a finding of lack of good moral character can be based on acts other than those enumerated—it is a discretionary finding).[32] Finally, the applicant must have a minimal level of ability to read, write, and understand English, and must understand the fundamental history and principles of the government of the United States.[33]

Other Naturalization Programs

In addition to the naturalization paths described above, Congress has created special programs for limited groups of people. A special naturalization provision was created for members of the Hmong tribe (including their widows) in Laos who served with U.S. forces during the period of the Vietnam War. In order to qualify, the veterans or their widows

---

[28] 8 USC §§1427(a)(1), INA §316(a)(1).

[29] 8 USC §§1427(a) and 1427(a)(2), INA §§316(a) and (a)(2). This continuity requirement may be waived where the U.S. citizen spouse is employed abroad either by the U.S. government or with a public international organization; is engaged in missionary work; or works for an American firm engaged in developing U.S. trade and commerce. 8 USC §1427(b), INA §316(b); *see also* 8 CFR §316.20.

[30] 8 USC §1427(b), INA §316(b) and 8 CFR §§316.5(c)(1)(i) and (ii). Absences are exempted for person who served in the military abroad, for certain employees working abroad who obtained prior permission from DHS, and for spouses, children, and parents of U.S. citizens who died in combat or spouses of persons granted posthumous citizenship.

[31] 8 USC §1427(a)(3), INA §316(a)(3).

[32] 8 USC §1101(f), INA §101(f).

[33] 8 USC §§1423(a)(1) and (2), INA §§312(a)(1) and (2). Persons who are over 50 and have been LPRs for 20 years, and those who are over 55 years and have been permanent residents for 15 years, are exempt from the English language requirement. 8 USC §1423(b)(2), INA §312(b)(2).

would have had to apply by November 1, 2003.[34] The INA also provides that in special cases, as determined by the CIA Director, the Attorney General, and the Department of Homeland Security (DHS) Secretary, a person who has made an extraordinary contribution to the national security of the United States may be naturalized as a U.S. citizen without regard to the normal residency and physical presence requirements, except that he or she must have resided in the United States for one year prior to naturalization.[35]

Naturalization Decisions and Oath Administration

Prior to 1990, the naturalization process was within the exclusive jurisdiction of the federal courts; immigration officials made a "recommendation" on behalf of an applicant. The Immigration Act of 1990[36] created a system whereby legacy Immigration and Naturalization Service (INS)/U.S. Citizenship and Immigration Services (USCIS) performs not just the interview and investigatory role, but also the administration of the oaths of naturalization.[37] Federal district courts and certain state courts also may administer oaths of allegiance to persons residing within those jurisdictions.[38]

Where USCIS fails to decide a case within 120 days of examining the applicant, the person may seek relief in federal district court.[39] In the event that the naturalization application is denied, the applicant may seek administrative review by filing an appeal within 30 days.[40] The administrative review must be completed within 180 days.[41] If the administrative appeal is denied, the applicant may seek *de novo* review in federal district court.[42]

---

[34] Hmong Veterans' Naturalization Act. Pub. L. No. 106-207, 114 Stat. 316 (May 26, 2000).

[35] Only five persons per year may be naturalized under this program; persons who are aggravated felons, who have persecuted others, or have committed serious nonpolitical crimes are ineligible. *See* 8 USC §1427(f), INA §316(f).

[36] Pub. L. No. 101-649, 104 Stat. 4978 (1990) (IMMACT90).

[37] 8 USC §§1421(a), (b), and (d) INA §§310(a), (b), and (d).

[38] 8 USC §§1421(b)(1) and 1435(c), INA §§310(b)(1) and 324(c).

[39] 8 USC §1447(b), INA §336(b). *See U.S. v. Hovsepian*, 359 F.3d 1144, 1159–64 (9th Cir. 2004) (en banc).

[40] 8 CFR §336.2(a).

[41] 8 CFR §336.2(b).

[42] 8 USC §§1421(c) INA §310(c).

Derivative Citizenship

Under the Child Citizenship Act of 2000,[43] a person may acquire citizenship derivatively through his or her parents' naturalization.[44] The child must be under 18, be an LPR, and reside in the United States in the legal and physical custody of the citizen parent. The Child Citizenship Act allows children to acquire citizenship through the naturalization of either parent without the need to prove that the parents were legally separated or divorced, and that the child was in the custody of naturalized parent *when* that parent naturalized.[45] The INA also provides that an orphan who was adopted abroad prior to being issued an immigrant visa is immediately eligible for U.S. citizenship.[46]

LOSS OF CITIZENSHIP

A native-born citizen can lose his or her citizenship by voluntary relinquishment only through an act of expatriation.[47] A naturalized citizen may lose citizenship either by voluntary relinquishment or by "denaturalization" (sometimes referred to as "revocation" of naturalization). Denaturalization is the process whereby the government—through a legal proceeding—takes away U.S. citizenship previously conferred by naturalization.[48]

Voluntary Relinquishment

The most significant changes in the law on voluntary relinquishment have come about not through statutory enactments, but via case law. The statutory provisions are contained at 8 USC §1481, INA §349,

---

[43] Pub. L. No. 106-395 §101, 114 Stat. 1631 (2000).

[44] 8 USC §§1431 INA §320.

[45] Under the law that existed prior to the Child Citizenship Act, a child could only receive citizenship derivatively if one parent became naturalized while the child was under 18 and the child was residing in the United States as an LPR in the custody of that parent. Under that law, if the parents were separated, the applicant was required to show that the parents were previously married and that they were subsequently legally separated or divorced, and that the child was in the naturalized citizen parent's lawful custody. Former 8 USC §1431(a); *Moussa v. INS*, 302 F.3d 823, 826–27 (8th Cir. 2002).

[46] *See* 8 USC §§1101(b)(1)(F) and 1433(a), INA §101(b)(1)(F) and 322(a); Interim Rule: Children Born Outside the United States; Applications for Certificate of Citizenship, 66 Fed. Reg. 32138–66 (2001).

[47] *See Afroyim v. Rusk*, 387 U.S. 253 (1967).

[48] 8 USC §1451, INA §340. The term "revocation" appears in the statute; the term "denaturalization appears in the cases. *See, e.g., Fedorenko v. U.S.*, 449 U.S. 490, 493 (1981).

which sets forth six ways for a person to lose U.S. citizenship: (1) obtaining naturalization in a foreign state; (2) making an oath, affirmation, or other formal declaration to a foreign state or its political subdivisions; (3) entering or serving in the armed forces of a foreign state engaged in hostilities against the United States, or serving as a commissioned or noncommissioned officer in the armed forces of a foreign state; (4) accepting employment with a foreign government if one has the nationality of that foreign state, or if a declaration of allegiance is required in accepting the position; (5) formally renouncing U.S. citizenship before a U.S. consular officer outside the United States in the form prescribed, or formally renouncing U.S. citizenship within the United States before an officer designated by the Attorney General (but only "in time of war");[49] or (6) conviction for an act of treason or attempt or conspiracy to overthrow the government.

Supreme Court precedent suggests that there may be constitutional issues with expatriation based on all but the last action listed in INA §349 (treason and overthrow). The Supreme Court, in 1967, held that pursuant to the 14th Amendment, Congress lacked the power to deprive a person of citizenship without that person's consent.[50] An opinion by the Attorney General issued two years later, as well as a second Supreme Court decision, established that in order to perfect a loss of citizenship, the government would have to prove that the relinquishment was done knowingly, voluntarily, and with full knowledge of the consequences of relinquishment.[51] In addition, there is a principle of international law that attempts to deter statelessness, such that a relinquishment would not be valid if the consequence would be to render a person without citizenship in any country.[52]

The following acts of expatriation, which are provided for at 8 USC §1481, INA §349, have been rejected by courts where voluntary

---

[49] *See* 8 USC §§1481(a)(5) and (6), INA §§349(a)(5) and (6). For a more comprehensive discussion, see L. Grossman & L. Wildes, "Expatriation: Overview and Special Renunciation Problems," *Immigration & Nationality Law Handbook* (AILA 1999–2000 Ed.).

[50] *Afroyim*, 387 U.S. 253.

[51] Expatriation of U.S. Citizens: Attorney General's Statement of Interpretation, 34 Fed. Reg. 1079 (1969). In *Vance v. Terrazas*, 444 U.S. 252, *reh'g denied*, 455 U.S. 920 (1980), the Supreme Court held that the government was required to show that when engaging in the act of expatriation, the person did so with the intent of relinquishing citizenship. *Id.* at 270.

[52] It is for this reason that relinquishment is carried out before a U.S. consul overseas, and one of the questions included on the form is whether the person is acquiring immigration status in another county.

relinquishment was not otherwise established: (1) naturalization in another country, including a pledge of allegiance;[53] (2) assuming a position in the legislature of another country;[54] (3) military service in a foreign army;[55] and (4) voting in an election in another country.[56]

Denaturalization

Loss of citizenship also may occur through denaturalization, otherwise referred to as revocation of naturalization. The revocation procedure is described at 8 USC §1451(a), INA §340(a). A person may be denaturalized if his or her U.S. naturalization was procured illegally or by concealment of a material fact or willful misrepresentation,[57] or if his or her permanent residence status was obtained improperly or through misrepresentation.[58]

Denaturalization may result as a consequence of a criminal conviction for knowingly committing fraud in the naturalization process (28 USC §1425) whereby the sentencing judge in the criminal proceeding may strip the person of his or her citizenship. In other cases, denaturalization begins by an action in a court (state or federal) competent to hear naturalization matters under the INA.

The action is initiated by a DHS or assistant U.S. attorney; given the nature of the right being revoked—citizenship—the government bears a very heavy burden. The government must prove its case by "clear, unequivocal, and convincing" evidence that does not leave "the issue in doubt."[59]

In 1996, Congress amended the INA to provide for revocation of naturalization via administrative immigration proceedings. The procedure permits the immigration authorities "to correct, reopen, alter, modify, or vacate an order naturalizing [a] person."[60] The implementing regulations required the government to prove its case by "clear, convincing, and un-

---

[53] *Afroyim*, 387 U.S. at 257.

[54] *Kahane v. Shultz*, 653 F. Supp. 1486 (E.D.N.Y. 1987).

[55] *Breyer v. Ashcroft*, 350 F.3d 327 (3d Cir. 2003); *but see U.S. v. Schiffer*, 831 F. Supp. 1166, 1186–96 (E.D. Pa. 1993).

[56] *Afroyim v. Rusk*, 387 U.S. 253 (1967).

[57] 8 USC §1451(a), INA §340(a).

[58] *See U.S. v. Szehinskyj*, 277 F.3d 331 (3d Cir. 2002); *U.S. v. Tittjung*, 235 F.3d 330, 340–42 (7th Cir. 2000).

[59] *Fedorenko v. U.S.*, 449 U.S. 490, 505 (1981).

[60] 8 USC §1451(h), INA §340(h).

equivocal evidence."[61] Upon a federal court challenge, the regulations implementing administrative denaturalization were invalidated as *ultra vires*, and the court found that the statute does not give the Attorney General the power to revoke naturalization; that power remains expressly and exclusively with the federal courts.[62] A national permanent injunction was issued, and, to date, no new regulations have been promulgated.[63]

CITIZENSHIP PROCEDURE

Citizenship questions can arise in a number of different settings, and, thus, thorough understanding of these rules is imperative. In some cases, a person facing removal may actually (unbeknownst to the person) be a U.S. citizen; only through careful analysis of the facts surrounding his or her birth and family can citizenship be established. For instance, where a person was born in the United States and became a citizen of another country at a young age, or where the person's parents were naturalized while the person was under the age of 21, he or she may unwittingly be a U.S. citizen. Indeed, a case involving a person facing proceedings due to an aggravated felony conviction—and, thus, ineligible for any form of relief—may be favorably resolved if the person is, in fact, found to be a citizen. In a situation where an individual is facing removal proceedings, and counsel learns that he or she is a U.S. citizen, an appropriate motion would be a motion to terminate proceedings based on the fact that U.S. citizenship renders the immigration court without jurisdiction.

Where the government alleges that a person returning to the United States has committed an act of renunciation, the person will be placed in removal proceedings as inadmissible. An effective representation will require a clear comprehension of the laws of expatriation and the applicable constitutional limits. In an expatriation case, the government would be required to initiate proceedings and would bear the burden of proving the renunciation. If the government meets this initial burden, the respondent could come forward with rebuttal evidence showing that the act was not intended to be a voluntary relinquishment of U.S. citizenship.

Clear knowledge of U.S. citizenship laws is required in assisting a person who is applying for a U.S. passport—either from abroad or

---

[61] 8 CFR §340.1(b)(6).

[62] *Gorbach v. Reno*, 219 F.3d 1087 (9th Cir. 2000).

[63] *Gorbach v. Reno*, Case No. C-98-0278R (W.D. Wash. Feb. 14, 2001), *discussed at* 78 *Interpreter Releases* 442–43 (Mar. 5, 2001).

within the United States. In cases where the DOS Passport Office refuses to issue a passport, the case may be appealed administratively to DOS and then to a federal district court for declaratory relief.[64] In order to obtain relief for a person who is outside the United States and is denied a passport, one must request a certificate of identity from a consular officer so that the person can travel to the United States to seek readmission, at which time proceedings are instituted and a decision is made by an immigration judge.[65]

The documentation of citizenship by birth abroad to one or more U.S. citizen parents is facilitated by either of the parents' registration of the child's birth with the nearest U.S. consul.[66] Note, however, that a failure to register a child's birth does not determine citizenship, since in such a situation, citizenship is a purely factual question, and is not dependent on procedures.[67]

Citizenship by naturalization requires the applicant to properly present the application, and submit to background and other checks that are prerequisites to obtaining it. While the application for naturalization subjects the applicant to greater scrutiny and possible institution of removal proceedings, the newly acquired citizenship insulates the person from being subject to immigration laws that would force a person's removal or prevent his or her admission. Therefore, even though a person may remain indefinitely in the United States as an LPR without ever obtaining citizenship, and can be removed only upon the commission of an act that triggers inadmissibility or deportability under the statute, that person remains subject to the increasingly restrictive provisions of U.S. immigration laws.

---

[64] 8 USC §1503(a), INA §360(a).

[65] 8 USC §1503(b), INA §360(b). Persons with a claim to U.S. citizenship are not subject to expedited removal.

[66] 22 CFR §§50.5, 50.7–.8.

[67] *See U.S. v. Breyer*, 841 F. Supp. 679, 684 (E.D. Pa. 1994). While it is a factual question, there is a procedure for settling the matter of citizenship by obtaining a certificate of citizenship. *See* 8 USC §1452(a), INA §341; 8 CFR Part 341.

APPENDIX 1
Key Definitions and Concepts

ADJUSTMENT OF STATUS. The process of obtaining LAWFUL PERMANENT RESIDENT STATUS in the United States without having to leave the United States to do so. Adjustment of status should be distinguished from "change of status," which generally applies to NONIMMIGRANTS moving from one nonimmigrant status to another. The adjustment of status option is unavailable to many (but not all) persons who entered the United States without INSPECTION, or who violated status while in the United States, or on whose behalf an application for labor certification or a preference petition was not filed on or before April 30, 2001. *See* 8 USC §1255, INA §245.

ADMISSION. The process of allowing someone to physically and legally be permitted to be in the United States. Admission is part of the INSPECTION process. A person may be inspected and admitted or PAROLED into the United States or, instead of being admitted, placed in REMOVAL proceedings or removed through EXPEDITED REMOVAL. Once a person is admitted, a number of legal rights and protections attach.

AFFIDAVIT OF SUPPORT. An affidavit given by a U.S. citizen or LAWFUL PERMANENT RESIDENT who resides in the United States and who will provide financial support to an alien who is seeking to enter the United States or adjust status.

AGGRAVATED FELONY. Any one of a number of crimes specifically defined in 8 USC §1101(a)(43), INA §101(a)(43), that may make a person deportable. Aggravated felon status creates numerous substantive and procedural disabilities with respect to, *e.g.*, ASYLUM, INADMISSIBILITY, REMOVAL, and judicial review, set forth in 8 USC §§1158, 1182, 1127–1252, INA §§208, 212, 237–42. An aggravated felon is ineligible for most forms of immigration relief from removal, and following completion of his or her criminal sentence, will likely be placed in an expeditious process for removal.

ALIEN. Any person who is not a citizen or a national of the United States. Only "aliens" are subject to the immigration laws. Even a person who is a lawful permanent resident is considered an "alien" until he or she becomes a U.S. citizen, and as such, is still subject to the immigration laws—including all of the grounds for removal.

ASYLUM. A discretionary benefit accorded to certain persons inside the United States who are able to demonstrate that they are unable or unwilling to return to their country on account of persecution or a well-founded fear of persecution based on race, religion, nationality, membership in a particular social group, or political opinion. 8 USC §§1101(a)(42), 1158; INA §§101(a)(42), §208. One year after the receipt of asylum status, the asylee may apply for lawful permanent residence. *See also* REFUGEE.

The new recently passed REAL ID Act, Pub. L. No. 109-13 (May 11, 2005), altered the standards and evidentiary burdens governing asylum applications, applications for WITHHOLDING OF REMOVAL, and other discretionary grants of relief from removal. It requires asylum applicants to demonstrate that one of the enumerated grounds was or will be "at least one central reason" for their persecution, and allows immigration judges to require credible asylum and withholding applicants to obtain corroborating evidence "unless the applicant does not have the evidence and cannot reasonably obtain the evidence."

BORDER CROSSING CARD (BCC). An identity card issued to an alien who is lawfully admitted for permanent residence, or to an alien who is a resident in Mexico or Canada, by a consular officer or an immigration officer for the purpose of crossing the border from Canada or Mexico. 8 USC §1101(a)(6), INA §101(a)(6). The new biometric BCC is a laminated, credit-card-style document with many security features and has a validity period of 10 years. Called a "laser visa," the card is both a BCC and a B1/B2 visitor's visa. Mexican visitors to the United States, whether traveling to the border region or beyond, receive a laser visa.

CANCELLATION OF REMOVAL. A discretionary remedy for a LAWFUL PERMANENT RESIDENT who has been a permanent resident for at least five years and has resided continuously in the United States for at least seven years after having been admitted in any status and has not been convicted of an AGGRAVATED FELONY, *or* anyone physically present in the United States for a continuous period of not less than 10 years immediately preceding the date of such application or the date of a Notice to Appear (NTA), who has been a person of good moral character during such period, has not been convicted of certain offenses, and who establishes that removal would result in exceptional and extremely unusual hardship to the applicant's U.S. citizen or permanent resident spouse, parent, or child. 8 USC §1229b, INA §240A. Applicant can be absent from the United States for up to 180 days during the 10 years.

CONSULAR PROCESSING. The process of applying for an IMMIGRANT VISA at a U.S. consular post outside the United States for prospective IMMIGRANTS who are not in the United States or who are ineligible to ADJUST STATUS in the United States. *See* 22 CFR Parts 40 and 42.

CRIME OF MORAL TURPITUDE (CMT). A particularly depraved offense that rises to the level of serving as a ground for inadmissibility or removal under 8 USC §1182(a)(2)(A)(i)(I), INA §212(a)(2)(A)(i)(I). Defined in the Department of State's *Foreign Affairs Manual* (9 FAM 40.21(a) N2.2) as the following: "Statutory definitions of crimes in the United States consist of various elements, which must be met before a conviction can be supported. Some of these elements have been determined in judicial or administrative decisions to involve moral turpitude. A conviction for a statutory offense will involve moral turpitude if one or more of the elements of that offense have been determined to involve moral turpitude. The most common elements involving moral turpitude are: (1) Fraud; (2) Larceny; and (3) Intent to harm persons or thing."

DEPARTMENT OF HOMELAND SECURITY (DHS). The agency into which INS was folded effective March 1, 2003. The benefits functions of the former INS transferred to the U.S. Citizenship and Immigration Services (USCIS), while the enforcement functions transferred to Customs and Border Protection (CBP) and Immigration and Customs Enforcement (ICE).

DEPORTABILITY. Acts that, when proven by the government, make a person subject to deportation. The specific grounds of deportability appear in the immigration statute at 8 USC §1227(a), INA §237(a).

DEPORTATION. The removal, ejectment, or transfer of a person from a country because his or her presence is deemed inconsistent with the public welfare. Prior to 1996, the term "deportation" was used to describe the ejectment of a person who had managed to gain "entry" to the United States either legally or illegally. IIRAIRA replaced the term "deportation" with "REMOVAL." Deportation is not considered to be a form of punishment. Grounds for deportation are set out at 8 USC §1251, INA §241. LAWFUL PERMANENT RESIDENTS are subject to removal if any of the grounds of deportability apply to them.

DERIVATIVE CITIZENSHIP. Citizenship conveyed to children through the naturalization of parents or, under certain circumstances, to foreign-born children adopted by U.S. citizen parents, provided certain conditions are met. 8 USC §1431, INA §320; 8 CFR §320.

DIVERSITY LOTTERY. The generic name given to the immigrant visa lottery program established by the Immigration Act of 1990 (IMMACT90), Pub. L. No. 101-649, that makes available up to 55,000 immigrant visas per federal fiscal year to persons from low-admission states and low-admission regions. 8 USC §1153, INA §203(c). The Diversity Immigrant Visa Lottery (DV) program is administered by the Department of State, which establishes the rules for the lottery and tracks the available visa numbers.

DUAL NATIONALITY. The simultaneous possession of two citizenships. It results from the fact that there is no uniform rule of international law relating to the acquisition of nationality. Dual nationality can occur by birth in one country to citizens of another country, by marriage to a foreign national, and by foreign naturalization. Though dual nationality is not favored under U.S. law, and U.S. naturalization law requires renunciation of allegiance to all other sovereigns, U.S. law does not require that the country whose allegiance a naturalization applicant is renouncing act in any way to withdraw or revoke citizenship upon its renunciation by the naturalization applicant when taking the Oath of Allegiance to the United States in naturalization proceedings. Certain countries do not accept dual citizenship, and require relinquishment of former citizenship upon naturalization to U.S. citizenship.

EMPLOYMENT AUTHORIZATION DOCUMENT (EAD). A USCIS document, Form I-688B, evidencing the right of certain aliens to accept employment while in the United States. *See* WORK PERMIT.

EXCHANGE VISITOR. An foreign national coming temporarily to the United States as a participant in a program approved by the Secretary of State for the purpose of teaching, instructing or lecturing, studying, observing, conducting research, consulting, demonstrating special skills, or receiving training.

EXCLUSION. The procedure existing prior to IIRAIRA for the ejectment of persons seeking admission to the United States. The term "exclusion" under current immigration law refers to the various bases under which a person could be found to be inadmissible to the United States. The grounds for exclusion (now inadmissibility) are set out at 8 USC §1182, INA §212.

EXPEDITED REMOVAL. A procedure, established by the Illegal Immigration Reform and Immigrant Responsibility Act of 1996 (IIRAIRA), Pub. L. No. 104-208, that authorizes ICE to quickly remove certain inadmissible aliens from the United States. The authority covers aliens who are inadmissible because they have no entry documents or because they have used counterfeit, altered, or otherwise fraudulent or improper documents. The authority covers aliens who arrive in, attempt to enter, or have entered the United States without having been admitted or paroled by an immigration officer at a port of entry. ICE has the authority to order the removal, and the alien is not referred to an immigration judge except under certain circumstances after an alien makes a claim to legal status in the United States or demonstrates a credible fear of persecution if returned to his or her home country. 8 USC §1225, INA §235; 8 CFR §235.3(b).

GREEN CARD. An expression that refers to the document carried by a LAWFUL PERMANENT RESIDENT, which provides proof of his or her status. The document is officially referred to as an "I-551" (Alien Registration Receipt Card or Permanent Resident Card). The card is no longer green.

IMMIGRANT. A LAWFUL PERMANENT RESIDENT of the United States. Defined, in the negative, as "every alien except an alien who is within one of the . . . classes of NONIMMIGRANT aliens" under the INA. 8 USC §1101(a)(15), INA §101(a)(15). This characterization of immigrants shifts the burden to the person seeking admission to establish his or her clear eligibility. Accordingly, all aliens are, with some exceptions, generally presumed to be immigrants until they establish that they are entitled to nonimmigrant status. 8 USC §1184(b), INA §214(b).

IMMIGRANT VISA. Permission obtained from a U.S. consul (abroad) to seek admission to the United States. A visa is issued subsequent to establishing eligibility for admission on a permanent basis under the Immigration and Nationality Act, as amended. An immigrant visa permits an alien to be admitted to the United States for permanent residence. It has a six-month validity and the intending immigrant must apply for ADMISSION during this period. *See also* PREFERENCE CATEGORIES, LABOR CERTIFICATION, and VISA.

IMMIGRATION JUDGE. Sometimes referred to in the U.S. Code/INA and Code of Federal Regulations as "Special Inquiry Officer," the person responsible for presiding over removal hearings. 8 USC §§1101(b)(4), 1229a; INA §§101(b)(4), 240. Immigration judges are employed by the Executive Office for Immigration Review (EOIR), a division of the Department of Justice.

INADMISSIBILITY. Any one of numerous grounds listed in 8 USC §1182(a), INA §212(a), that make a person ineligible for lawful admission into the United States.

INSPECTION. The process that all persons must go through when they arrive at the border. A person is questioned and asked to present proof of his or her right to enter the country. At the end of the process of inspection, a person is either ADMITTED, REMOVED, or PAROLED into the country.

LABOR CERTIFICATION. Certification by the Department of Labor (DOL) that there exists an insufficient number of U.S. workers who are able, willing, qualified, and available at the place of proposed employment, and that employment of the alien for whom certification is sought will not adversely affect the wages and working conditions of U.S. workers similarly employed (the employer must therefore be offering the job at the "prevailing wage" in the particular market). 8 USC §1182(a)(5), INA §212(a)(5). An employer's obtaining a labor certification does not entitle the person to admission if there is an annual QUOTA on the numbers of foreign workers who may be admitted to the United States. In December 2004, DOL issued its long-awaited PERM regulations, which, effective March 28, 2005, established a new system for filing labor certifications. 69 Fed. Reg. 77325 (Dec. 27, 2004).

LABOR CONDITION APPLICATION (LCA). An attestation by an employer seeking to hire an H-1B nonimmigrant to four conditions of employment: (1) that the employer is paying the H-1B nonimmigrant at least the higher of the actual wage paid by the employer to others in the same occupation with similar experience and qualifications or the prevailing wage for the occupation in the geographical area of the work site; (2) that the employment of the H-1B nonimmigrant will not adversely affect the working conditions of similarly employed workers; (3) that there is not a strike, lockout, or work stoppage in the occupation for which the H-1B nonimmigrant is being hired; and (4) that notice of the hiring of the H-1B nonimmigrant has been provided.

LASER VISA. See BORDER CROSSING CARD.

LAWFUL PERMANENT RESIDENT (LPR). A person accorded the benefit of being able to reside in the United States on a permanent basis. Such a person may engage in employment but may not vote in U.S. elections. LPR status is the status gained by a person who is admitted to the United States with an IMMIGRANT VISA or has had his or her status adjusted to permanent residence after having first been admitted as a NONIMMIGRANT. Lawful permanent residence also may be obtained after a person has been granted ASYLUM or was admitted to the United States as a REFUGEE. In addition, a person who has been in the United States for more than 10 years and is able to establish the requisite degree of hardship may be granted permanent residency following the "cancellation" of his or her removal proceeding. LPR status may be taken away for the commission of certain acts that can result in deportability or inadmissibility or lost through "abandonment." Also called legal permanent resident or GREEN CARD holder.

LEGACY INS—A reference to the Immigration and Naturalization Service (*e.g.*, "a legacy INS memo") that acknowledges its status as the predecessor to the DEPARTMENT OF HOMELAND SECURITY.

LEGALIZATION. A program established by the Immigration Reform and Control Act of 1986 (IRCA), Pub. L. No. 99-603, that permitted the grant of temporary residence status to certain aliens, who were later entitled to apply for permanent residence. 8 USC §1255a, INA §245A. Also referred to as "temporary resident status" and "amnesty."

NATURALIZATION. "[T]he conferring of nationality of a state upon a person after birth." 8 USC §1101(a)(23), INA §101(a)(23).

NONIMMIGRANT. A person who can establish that he or she has a residence abroad that he or she has no intention of abandoning, who is coming to the United States for a temporary period, and who fits into specifically defined categories under 8 USC §1101(a)(15), INA §101(a)(15). Some of the nonimmigrant categories include students, tourists, treaty investors, and foreign government officials. *See* IMMIGRANT.

NONIMMIGRANT VISA— A document signifying that a consular officer believes that the alien to whom the visa was issued is eligible to apply for ADMISSION in a particular nonimmigrant category. However, a visa does not guarantee admission; an immigration inspector can deny entry if he or she believes that a particular alien is not eligible to be admitted in the category for which the visa was issued. The period of validity of a particular visa establishes the time during which the alien may present him- or herself at a U.S. port of entry. Visas may be valid for as few as 30 days or up to 10 years; visas may be limited to a single entry or may be valid for multiple entries during the period of their validity. The period of validity of a visa is not the same as the authorized period of temporary stay in the United States. The authorized period of temporary stay, which is indicated on a small white card—Form I-94, Arrival-Departure Record—stapled into the passport, may be less than the period of validity of the visa, or may be much longer than the period during which the visa itself is valid (typically when single-entry visas are valid only for a limited period of time). It is important to understand that it is always the I-94, and not the visa in the passport, that determines a nonimmigrant alien's status and its validity as to time and purpose. An alien is not out of status if he or she was properly admitted pursuant to a valid visa and the visa has expired, provided the person is still within the authorized period of stay indicated on Form I-94.

PAROLE. Permission granted by DHS allowing a person to physically enter the United States yet still be considered to have not legally entered the country. Parole is a legal fiction. A person paroled into the United States is treated in a legal sense as if he or she were still at the border's edge seeking permission to enter. *See* 8 USC §1182(d)(5), INA §212(d)(5). While parolees are not afforded any legal rights or benefits greater than those seeking admission, they are provided with legal documents that permit their presence in the United States. Examples include parole for humanitarian or family unification purposes, and parole to proceed with the process of adjustment of status that would otherwise be considered to have been abandoned.

PERM. A new system, effective March 28, 2005, for filing LABOR CERTIFICATIONS. PERM (for Program Electronic Review Management System) uses automated computer systems to scan attestation forms filed by employers regarding their compliance with all regulatory requirements. 20 CFR Parts 655 and 656.

PREFERENCE CATEGORIES. Immigrant visas are allocated on the basis of an annual QUOTA. In order to qualify for admission, the intending immigrant must show that: (1) he or she is married to a LAWFUL PERMANENT RESIDENT or is the unmarried son or daughter of a lawful permanent resident; or (2) he or she is the son, daughter, or sibling of a

U.S. citizen (irrespective of marital status); or (3) his or her employer has obtained a LABOR CERTIFICATION for eventual employment in the United States. Whether the person meets the quota restriction will depend on his or her relationship as described above with a U.S. citizen or lawful permanent resident, or whether the employment is of a skilled or unskilled nature.

PREINSPECTION. Complete immigration inspection of airport passengers before departure from a foreign country. No further immigration inspection is required upon arrival in the United States other than submission of Form I-94 for nonimmigrant aliens. *See* 8 USC §1225a, INA §235A.

PRIORITY DATE. The date on which a person submitted documentation establishing prima facie eligibility for an immigrant visa. For family-based immigrants, a person's priority date is the date on which he or she filed the family-based preference petition. 8 CFR §204.1(c). If the alien relative has a priority date on or before the date listed in the Visa Bulletin, then he or she is currently eligible for an immigrant visa. For employment-based cases, it is the date of the filing of the LABOR CERTIFICATION application, or if no labor certification is required, the date the immigrant visa petition is filed. 8 CFR §204.5(d).

QUOTAS. There are annual numerical restrictions on many forms of immigration status. Certain nonimmigrant visa categories are restricted to a set number of persons who may be admitted in any given fiscal year. Similarly, the number of persons who may be granted permanent residency is also restricted each fiscal year and allocated between family and employment immigrant categories under a quota system. In allocating the quota system, strict attention is paid to the immigrant category, as well as making sure that persons are issued visas in the order in which they applied and that no more than 25,620 (7 percent of the total) are issued to nationals of any one country in a given fiscal year. *See* PREFERENCE CATEGORIES.

REDUCTION IN RECRUITMENT (RIR). An alternative method of LABOR CERTIFICATION under the system in place before March 28, 2005. Since that time, RIR and conventional labor certification were completely revamped by the Department of Labor's PERM rules.

REFUGEE. A person outside of the United States who is unable or unwilling to return to his or her country because of persecution or a well-founded fear of persecution on account of race, religion, nationality, membership in a particular social group, or political opinion. 8 USC

§1101(a)(42), INA §101(a)(42). Refugee admission to the United States is based on annual allocations as established between the executive and legislative branches. A refugee, once admitted, may apply in one year for permanent resident status. See also ASYLUM.

REMOVAL. The procedure used to eject persons who are seeking admission as well as those who have been admitted to the United States. Prior to enactment of IIRAIRA in 1996, the terms "DEPORTATION" and "EXCLUSION" were used.

SERVICE CENTERS. Five offices established to handle the filing, data entry, and adjudication of certain applications for immigration services and benefits. The applications are mailed to USCIS service centers; service centers are not staffed to receive walk-in applications or questions.

SEVIS (Student and Exchange Visitor Information System). An Internet-based software application to track and monitor nonimmigrant students and exchange visitors and their dependents.

TEMPORARY PROTECTED STATUS (TPS). A status allowing residence and employment authorization to nationals of foreign states for a period of not less than six months or no more than 18 months, when such states have been appropriately designated by the government because of extraordinary and temporary political or physical conditions in such state(s). See 8 USC §1254a, INA §244; 8 CFR §§244.2, 1244.2.

UNLAWFUL PRESENCE. Presence in the United States after the expiration of the authorized period of stay, or presence in the United States without having been admitted or paroled. The period of authorized stay, which is usually noted on Form I-94, or Form I-94W, must end on a date certain. Thus, Canadians admitted without being issued an I-94, and F, J, and M students and exchange visitors admitted for "duration of status" (D/S) who overstay, do not accrue unlawful presence until and unless an immigration judge or DHS official finds such person to be out of status. Violation of status (*e.g.*, the F-1 student who works without authorization) does not constitute unlawful presence. Depending on the period of unlawful presence, a person may be barred from re-admission for a period of three or 10 years. See 8 USC §1182(a)(9)(B), INA §212(a)(9)(B).

US-VISIT (U.S. Visitor and Immigrant Status Indicator Technology program). A program designed by the Department of Homeland Security to collect and share information on foreign nationals traveling to the United States. This system allows the U.S. government to record the entry and exit of non–U.S. citizens and verify the identity of travelers coming in and out of the United States.

VISA. An official endorsement, obtained from a U.S. consul (abroad), certifying that the bearer has been examined and is permitted to proceed for purposes of seeking admission to the United States at a designated port of entry. There are both immigrant visas and nonimmigrant visas. A visa does not grant the bearer the right to enter the United States; it merely allows one to attempt to seek admission at a port of entry.

VISA WAIVER PROGRAM (VWP). A program under which nationals of countries with which the United States has certain agreements can enter the United States for up to 90 days as visitors for business or pleasure without first obtaining a visa from a U.S. embassy or consulate. No extension or change of status is permitted. It was a pilot program (Visa Waiver Pilot Program or VWPP) until October 30, 2000, when it became a permanent program.

VOLUNTARY DEPARTURE. A procedure granting permission for a removable alien to leave the United States voluntarily. There is a limit of 120 days for pre-hearing voluntary departure or 60 days for post-hearing voluntary departure.

WAIVERS. Certain grounds of inadmissibility, as well as the two-year home-country physical presence requirement for an exchange visitor, can be waived under certain circumstances. These waivers remove an impediment to obtaining a visa or status. Also, USCIS can grant a waiver of labor certification and job offer to professionals with advanced degrees and aliens of exceptional ability if in the national interest.

WITHHOLDING OF REMOVAL. A remedy available to persons able to establish that their lives or freedom would be threatened if deported to their home country on account of race, religion, nationality, membership in a particular social group, or political opinion. 8 USC §1231(b)(3), INA §241(b)(3). Withholding of removal does not confer on persons a right to stay in the United States, as they may be removed to any country willing to accept them. Also known as "restriction on removal."

WORK PERMIT—There is no single document in U.S. immigration law that is a "work permit." Citizens, nationals, and LAWFUL PERMANENT RESIDENTS of the United States are automatically authorized to be employed in the United States. Certain NONIMMIGRANT VISA categories include, as an incident of their status, employment authorization in the

United States either with or without limitation to a particular employer or after application and approval from USCIS for authorization to be employed. Virtually all employment authorization for nonimmigrants or undocumented aliens (where authorized) is limited as to time, and most such authorization is limited as to nature of employer and employment. Other aliens physically present in the United States may have the right to apply for an EMPLOYMENT AUTHORIZATION DOCUMENT (EAD).

APPENDIX 2
Abbreviations and Acronyms

AAO—Administrative Appeals Office (formerly the Administrative Appeals Unit (AAU))

AC—Associate Commissioner (of INS)

AC21—American Competitiveness in the 21st Century Act of 2000

ACE—Accelerated Citizen Examination

ACPA—Assistant Chief Patrol Agent

ACWIA—American Competitiveness and Workforce Improvement Act of 1998

ADD—Assistant District Director. Also, ADDE (Examinations); ADDI (Investigations); ADDM (Management)

ADIT—Alien Documentation, Identification and Telecommunications system

AEDPA—Antiterrorism and Effective Death Penalty Act of 1996

AFACS—A-Files Accountability and Control System

AG—Attorney General of the United States

AILA—American Immigration Lawyers Association

AILF—American Immigration Law Foundation

ALC—Alien Labor Certification

ALJ—Administrative Law Judge

AMIS—Asset Management Information System

AO—(1) Administrative Officer; (2) Asylum Officer

AOC—Asylum Officer Corps

AOIC—Assistant Officer-in-Charge

AOS—(1) Adjustment of Status (as used by USCIS and most immigration lawyers); (2) Affidavit of Support (as used by the Dep't of State)

ARC—Alien Registration Card (also called Permanent Resident Card or Green Card)

A/S—Adjustment of Status

ASC—Application Support Center

ASVI—Alien Status Verification Index

AVLOS—Automated Visa Lookout System

AWO—Affirmance Without Opinion

BALCA—Board of Alien Labor Certification Appeals

BAR—Board of Appellate Review

BCA—Bureau of Consular Affairs

BCC—I-186 or I-586 Nonresident Alien Border Crossing Card

BIA—Board of Immigration Appeals

BIT—Bilateral Investment Treaty

BOP—Bureau of Prisons; also, Burden of Proof

BP—Border Patrol

CAT—United Nations Convention Against Torture and Other Cruel, Inhuman or Degrading Treatment or Punishment

CBP—U.S. Customs and Border Protection

CCA—Child Citizenship Act

CFR—Code of Federal Regulations

CGFNS—Commission on Graduates of Foreign Nursing Schools

CIJ—Chief Immigration Judge

CIS—(1) Central Index System; (2) (now, more commonly, USCIS) U.S. Citizenship and Immigration Services. (The use of CIS may possibly be confused with Center for Immigration Studies (CIS))

CLAIMS—Computer Linked Application Information Management System

CLN—Certificate of Loss of Nationality

CMT—Crime of Moral Turpitude (also known as Crimes Involving Moral Turpitude (CIMT))

CO—Certifying Officer (of DOL)

ConOff—Consular Officer

CORAP—Central Office of Refugee, Asylum and Parole

COS—Change of Status

CPT—Curricular Practical Training

CR—Conditional Resident

C/S—Change of Status

CSC—California Service Center

CSPA—Child Status Protection Act

CUSA—Citizenship U.S.A.

D&D—Detention and Deportation

DAO—(1) District Adjudication Officer; (2) Deputy Adjudications Officer

DCPA—Deputy Chief Patrol Agent

DD—District Director

DDD—Deputy District Director

DED—Deferred Enforced Departure

DFS—Designated Fingerprint Service

DHS—Department of Homeland Security

DO—(1) District Office; (2) Deportation Officer

DOE—Date of Entry

DOJ—Department of Justice

DOL—Department of Labor

DOS—Department of State

DOT—Dictionary of Occupational Titles

D/S—Duration of Status

DSO—Designated School Official

DV—Diversity Visa Lottery Program

EAC—Eastern Adjudication Center (now Vermont Service Center)

EAD—I-688B Employment Authorization Document

EAJA—Equal Access to Justice Act

ENFORCE—Enforcement Case Tracking System

EOIR—Executive Office for Immigration Review

EOS—Extension of Stay

ER—Expedited Removal

E/S—Extension of Status or Stay

ETA—Employment and Training Administration

EVD—Extended Voluntary Departure

EWI—Entry Without Inspection

EWIC—Essential Worker Immigration Coalition

FAM—Foreign Affairs Manual

FARES—Fees and Applications Receipt and Entry System

FCCPT—Foreign Credentialing Commission on Physical Therapy

FCN—Treaty of Friendship, Commerce, and Navigation

Fed. Reg.—Federal Register

FGM—Female Genital Mutilation

FMG—Foreign Medical Graduate

FOIA—Freedom of Information Act

FR—Federal Register

FSN—Foreign Service National

FSO—Foreign Service Officer

FTA—Free Trade Agreement

FTO—Free Trade Officer

GAL—General Administration Letter of DOL

GEMS—General Counsel Management System

GPO—Government Printing Office

HB—House Bill

HR —House Report

HRIFA—Haitian Refugee Immigration Fairness Act

IA—Immigration Agent

IBIS—Interagency Border Inspection System

ICE—U.S. Immigration and Customs Enforcement

ICMS—Investigations Case Management System

IDENT—Automated Fingerprint Identification System

IE—Immigration Examiner

IFM—Inspector's Field Manual

IG—Inspector General

II—Immigration Inspector

IIO—Immigration Information Officer

IIRAIRA—Illegal Immigration Reform and Immigrant Responsibility Act of 1996 (also IIRIRA)

IJ—Immigration Judge

ILT—AILA's *Immigration Law Today*

IMFA—Immigration Marriage Fraud Amendments Act

IMMACT90—Immigration Act of 1990

INA—Immigration and Nationality Act

INS—Immigration and Naturalization Service

INSPASS—INS Passenger Accelerated Service System

INTCA—Immigration and Nationality Technical Corrections Act of 1994

INV—Investigations

IO—Immigration Officer

IRCA—Immigration Reform and Control Act of 1986

IR—*Interpreter Releases* (Thomson West)

ISD—Immigrant Services Division (now Service Center Operations)

IV—Immigrant Visa

LAPR—Lawfully Admitted for Permanent Residence

LAU—Legalization Appeals Unit

LAW—Lawfully Authorized or Admitted Worker

LCA—Labor Condition Application

LC—Labor Certification

LIFE—Legal Immigration and Family Equity Act of 2000

LIN—Northern Service Center (now Nebraska Service Center)

LPR—Lawful Permanent Resident

MRD—Machine Readable Document

MSC—Missouri Service Center

MS&D—Maintenance of Status and Departure bond

MTINA—Miscellaneous and Technical Immigration and Nationality Act Amendments of 1991

NACARA—Nicaraguan Adjustment and Central American Relief Act

NACS—Naturalization Automated Casework System

NAFTA—North American Free Trade Agreement

NAILS—National Automated Immigration Lookout System

Natz—Naturalization

NBCOTA—Noncitizen Benefit Clarification and Other Technical Amendments Act of 1998

NBCOT—National Board for Certification of Occupational Therapists

NOIF—Notice of Intent to Fine

NIV—Nonimmigrant Visa

NIW—National Interest Waiver

NOF—Notice of Findings

NRC—National Record Center

NSC—Nebraska Service Center

NSEERS—National Security Entry Exit Registration System

NTA—Notice to Appear

NVC—National Visa Center

OARS—Outlying Area Reporting Station

OCAHO—Office of the Chief Administrative Hearing Officer

ODP—Orderly Departure Program

OES—Occupational Employment Statistics

OIC—Officer-in-Charge

OIL—Office of Immigration Litigation of DOJ's Civil Division

OI—Operations Instructions

OMB—Office of Management and Budget

O*NET—Occupational Information Network

ONO—Office of Naturalization Operations (now ISD)

OOH—Occupational Outlook Handbook (DOL)

OPT—Optional Practical Training

O/S—Out of Status, or overstay

OSC—Order to Show Cause; also, Office of Special Counsel

OTM—Other than Mexican

PA—(Border) Patrol Agent

PERM—Program Electronic Review Management System

PLC—Permanent Labor Certification

POE—Port of Entry

PRC—Permanent Resident Card (also called an Alien Registration Card or Green Card)

PT—Practical Training

QDE—Qualified Designated Entity

RAW—Replenishment Agricultural Worker

RC—Regional Commissioner of USCIS

RD—Regional Director of USCIS

RFE—Request for Evidence

RIR—Reduction in Recruitment Labor Certification Procedure

RN—Registered Nurse

RO—Responsible Officer of J-1 Exchange Visitor Program

RSC—Regional Service Center

RTD—Refugee Travel Document

RVIS—Remote Video Inspection System

SAO—Security Advisory Opinion

SAO—Supervisory Adjudication Officer

SA—Special Agent

SAW—Special Agricultural Worker

SB—Senate Bill

SC—Service Center

SDAO—Supervisory District Adjudications Officer

SENTRI—Secure Electronic Network for Travelers Rapid Inspection

SEVIS—Student and Exchange Visitor Information System

SIE—Supervisory Immigration Examiner

SII—Supervisory Immigration Inspector

SIO—(1) Supervisory Immigration Officer; (2) Special Inquiry Officer (former title for Immigration Judges)

SK—Specialized Knowledge for L Visa

SRC—Southern Regional Center (now Texas Service Center)

SR—Senate Report

SVP—Specific Vocational Preparation

SWA—State Workforce Agency

TA—Trial Attorney

TAG—Technical Assistance Guide No. 656—Labor Certifications (1981)

TCN—Third Country National

TPCR—Transition Period Custody Rules

TPS—Temporary Protected Status

TN—Trade NAFTA

TSA—Transportation Security Administration

TSC—Texas Service Center

TWOV—Transit Without Visa

UNHCR—United Nations High Commissioner for Refugees

UPL—Unauthorized Practice of Law

US-VISIT—United States Visitor and Immigrant Status Indicator Technology Program

USA PATRIOT Act—Uniting and Strengthening America by Providing Appropriate Tools Required to Intercept and Obstruct Terrorism Act of 2001

USC—(1) U.S. Code; (2) U.S. Citizen

USCIS—U.S. Citizenship and Immigration Services

USCS—U.S. Customs Service

VAWA—Violence Against Women Act

VD—Voluntary Departure

VO—Visa Office

VOLAG—Volunteer Agency

VSC—Vermont Service Center

VTC—Video Teleconferencing

VWPP—Visa Waiver Pilot Program

VWP—Visa Waiver Program

WAC—Western Adjudication Center (now California Service Center)

APPENDIX 3
Immigrant Classifications and Visas

Immigrant Classifications and Visas	Government Information
Immigrant Visas	• Lawful Permanent Residency • Dept. of State: Tips for U.S. Visas: Immigrants • Green Card Renewal
Family-Based Immigration	• Immigration Through A Family Member • Dept. of State: Tips for U.S. • Visas: Family-Based Immigrants • How Do I Get My Spouse or Children Derivative Asylum Status in the United States?
Immediate Relatives (Spouses of US citizens (USCs), unmarried children under 21 years of age of USCs, and parents of USCs Note: A USC must be over the age of 21 to petition for his/her parent	*Spouse* • Petitioning Procedures: Bringing A Spouse to Live in the United States • How Do I Bring My Spouse to Live in the United States? • How Do I Remove the Conditions on Permanent Residence Based on Marriage? *Child* • Petitioning Procedures: Bringing a Child, Son or Daughter to Live in the United States • How Do I Bring My Child, Son or Daughter to Live in the United States? • How Do I Prevent My Child From Losing Benefits at Age 21 ("Aging Out") *Parent* • Petitioning Procedures: Bringing a Parent to Live in the United States • How Do I Bring My Parents to Live in the United States *INA Section 201; 8 CFR 204 and 205*

Immigrant Classifications and Visas	Government Information
First Preference (Unmarried sons or daughters over 21 years of age of USC)	• Petitioning Procedures: Bringing a Child, Son or Daughter to Live in the United States • How Do I Bring My Child, Son or Daughter to Live in the United States? *INA Sections 201 and 204: 8 CFR 204, 205*
Second Preference (Spouses and children of Legal Permanent Resident, or LPR)	*Spouse* • Petitioning Procedures: Bringing a Spouse (Husband or Wife) to Live in the United States • How Do I Bring My Spouse (Husband or Wife) to Live in the United States? *INA Sections 202, 203(a)(2)(A) and 204; 8 CFR 204, 205* *Child* • Petitioning Procedures: Bringing a Child, Son or Daughter to Live in the United States • How Do I Bring My Child, Son or Daughter to Live in the United States? *INA Sections 202, 203(a)(2)(B) and 204; 8 CFR 204, 205*
Spouses and children	*INA Sections 202, 203(a)(2)(A), and 204; 8 CFR 204, 205*
Unmarried sons or daughters over 21 years of age of LPR	*INA Sections 202, 203(a)(2)(B), and 204; 8 CFR 204, 205*
Third Preference (Married children of USC)	• Petitioning Procedures: Bringing a Child, Son or Daughter to Live in the United States • How Do I Bring My Child, Son or Daughter to Live in the United States? *INA Sections 202, 203(a)(2)(B), and 204; 8 CFR 204, 205*
Fourth Preference (Siblings of adult USC)	• Petitioning Procedures: Bringing a Sibling to Live in the United States • How Do I Bring a Sibling to Live in the United States? *INA Sections 202, 203(a)(4), and 204; 8 CFR 204, 205*

Immigrant Classifications and Visas	Government Information
Employment-Based Immigration	• Immigration Through Employment • How Do I Apply for Immigrant Status Based on Employment Information on Visas for Employers • Dept. of State: Tips for U.S. Visas: Employment-Based Visas
EB-1 *First Preference:* Priority Workers	• EB-1 Eligibility and Filing *INA Section 203(b)(1)(A); 8 CFR 204.5*
EB-2 *Second Preference:* Professionals with advanced degrees, and persons with exceptional ability	• EB-2 Eligibility and Filing *INA Section 203(b)(1)(B); 8 CFR 204.5*
EB-3 *Third Preference:* Skilled workers, professional and other workers	• EB-3 Eligibility and Filing *INA Section 203(b)(1)(C); 8 CFR 204.5*
EB-4 *Fourth Preference:* Certain special immigrants	• EB-4 Eligibility and Filing *INA Section 203(b)(1)(D); 8 CFR 204.5*
SK-1 Certain Retired International Organization Employees	*INA Section 101a(27)(I)(iii)*
SK-2 Spouse of SK-1	*INA Section 101(a)(27)(I)(iv)*
SK-3 Certain Unmarried Sons or Daughters of an International Organization Employee	*INA Section 101(a)(27)(I)(i)*
SK-4 Certain Spouses of a deceased International Organization Employee	*INA Section 101(a)(27)(I)(ii)*
INV *Fifth Preference*: Employment EB-5 creation (investors)	• Immigration Through Investment *INA Section 203(b)(1)(E); 8 CFR 204.5*

APPENDIX 4
Nonimmigrant Visa Classifications

Nonimmigrant Classifications and Visas	General Information on Nonimmigrant Benefits
Foreign Government Officials	
A-1 Ambassador, public minister, career, diplomatic or consular officer, and members of immediate family.	INA Section 101(a)(15)(A)(i) 8 CFR 214.2(a)
A-2 Other foreign government official or employee, and members of immediate family.	INA Section 101(a)(15)(A)(ii) 8 CFR 214.2(a)
A-3 Attendant, servant, or personal employee of A-1 and A-2, and members of immediate family.	INA Section 101(a)(15)(A)(iii) 8 CFR 214.2(a)
Visitors	Business or Pleasure Visitors Tips for U.S. Visas - Business or Pleasure Visitors
B-1 Temporary visitor for business	INA Section 101(a)(15)(B) 8 CFR 214.2(b)
B-2 Temporary visitor for pleasure	INA Section 101(a)(15)(B) 8 CFR 214.2(b)
Visa Waiver Program	• Visa Waiver Program • Immigration.gov • Visa Waiver Program (Dept. of State)
Aliens in Transit	
C-1 Alien in transit directly through U.S.	INA Section 101(a)(15)(C) 8 CFR 214.2(c)
C-1D Combined transit and crewman visa	INA Section 101(a)(15)(C) & (D) 8 CFR 214.2(c)
C-2 Alien in transit to UN headquarters district under Section 11.(3), (4), or (5) of the Headquarters Agreement	INA Section 101(a)(15)(C) 8 CFR 214.2(c)
C-3 Foreign government official, members of immediate family, attendant, servant, or personal employee, in transit	INA Section 212(d)(8) 8 CFR 214.2(c)

Nonimmigrant Classifications and Visas	General Information on Nonimmigrant Benefits
Aliens in Transit, continued	
C-4 Transit without Visa, see TWOV	INA Sections 212(d)(3), and 212(d)(5) 8 CFR 212.1(f)
Crewmen	
D-1 Crewmember departing on same vessel of arrival	INA section 101(a)(15)(D) 8 CFR 214.2(d)
D-2 Crewmember departing by means other than vessel of arrival	INA section 101(a)(15)(D) 8 CFR 214.2(d)
Treaty Traders and Treaty Investors	Instructions for Form I-129: Petition for a Nonimmigrant Worker
E-1 Treaty Trader, spouse and children	INA Section 101(a)(15)(E)(i) 8 CFR 214.2(e)(1)
E-2 Treaty Investor, spouse and children	INA Section 101(a)(15)(E)(ii) 8 CFR 214.2(e)(2)
E-3 Add in E-3 for Australians	INA Section 101(a)(15)(E)(iii)
Academic Students	• Dept. of State: Implementation of ISEAS • Information on Student Visas • How Do I Become an Academic Student in the United States? • Dept. of State: Tips for U.S. Visas: Foreign Students • Dept. of State: Information on Student Visas • Dept. of State: What Consuls Look For • Dept. of State: New Legal Requirements for F-1 Foreign Students in Public Schools • How Do I Apply to Qualify My School for Foreign Student Assistance?
F-1 Academic Student	INA Section 101(a)(15)(F)(i) 8 CFR 214.2(f)
F-2 Spouse or child of F-1	INA Section 101(a)(15)(F)(ii) 8 CFR 214.2(f)

For Foreign Medical Graduates (see individual categories H-1B, J-1, O-1, TN, E-2)

Nonimmigrant Classifications and Visas	General Information on Nonimmigrant Benefits

Foreign Government Officials to International Organizations

G-1	Principal resident representative of recognized foreign member government to international organization, and members of immediate family.	INA Section 101(a)(15)(G)(i) 8 CFR 214.2(g)
G-2	Other representative of recognized foreign member government to international organization, and members of immediate family.	INA Section 101(a)(15)(G)(ii) 8 CFR 214.2(e)(1)
G-3	Representative of non-recognized or nonmember government to international organization, and members of immediate family	INA Section 101(a)(15)(G)(iii) 8 CFR 214.2(g)
G-4	International organization officer or employee, and members of immediate family	INA Section 101(a)(15)(G)(iv) 8 CFR 214.2(g)
G-5	Attendant, servant, or personal employee of G-1, G-2, G-3, G-4, or members of immediate family	INA Section 101(a)(15)(G)(v) 8 CFR 214.2(g)

Temporary Workers	• Immigration.gov Information on Temporary Workers • Dept. of State: Tips for U.S. Visas: Temporary Workers • Instructions for Form I-129: Petition for a Nonimmigrant Worker • How Do I Apply for Health Care Worker Certification?
H-1B	Specialty Occupations, DOD workers, fashion models	INA Section 101(a)(15)(H)(i)(b) 8 CFR 214.2(h)(4)
H-1C	Nurses going to work for up to three years in health professional shortage areas	INA Section 101(a)(15)(H)(i)(c) 8 CFR 214.2(h)(3)
H-2A	Temporary Agricultural Worker	INA Section 101(a)(15)(H)(ii)(a) 8 CFR 214.2(h)(5)
H-2B	Temporary worker: skilled and unskilled	INA Section 101(a)(15)(H)(ii)(b) 8 CFR 214.2(h)(6)
H-3	Trainee	INA Section 101(a)(15)(H)(iii) 8 CFR 214.2(h)(7)
H-4	Spouse or child of H-1, H-2, H-3	INA Section 101(a)(15)(H)(iv) 8 CFR 214.2(h)(9)(iv)

Nonimmigrant Classifications and Visas	General Information on Nonimmigrant Benefits
Foreign Media Representatives	Dept. of State: Revalidation of "I" Journalist Visas
I Visas for foreign media representatives	INA Section 101(a)(15)(I) 8 CFR 214.2(i)
Exchange Visitors	• Dept. of State: Implementation of ISEAS
	• Immigration.gov Information on Exchange Visitors
	• How Do I Get a Waiver of the Foreign Residence Requirement if I am an Exchange Visitor
	• Dept. of State: Tips for U.S. Visas: Exchange Visitors
	• How Do I Apply for Health Care Worker Certification?
J-1 Visas for exchange visitors	INA Section 101(a)(15)(J)(i) 8 CFR 214.2(j)
J-2 Spouse or child of J-1	INA Section 101(a)(15)(J)(ii) 8 CFR 214.2(j)
Fiancé (e) of US Citizen	
K-1 Fiancé (e)	• How Do I Bring My Fiance(e) to the United States?
	• Dept. of State: Tips for U.S. Visas: Fiance(e)s
	• How Do I Change My Fiance(e)'s Status to Lawful Permanent Resident?
	INA Section 101(a)(15)(K) 8 CFR 214.2(k)
K-2 Minor child of K-1	INA Section 101(a)(15)(K) 8 CFR 214.2(k)
K-3 Spouse of a U.S. Citizen (LIFE Act)	• How Do I Become a K-Nonimmigrant as the Spouse or Child of a U.S. Citizen?
	• Dept. of State: The New K and V
	INA Section 101(a)(15)(K)(ii) 8 CFR 214.2(k)
K-4 Child of K-3 (LIFE Act)	INA Section 101(a)(15)(K)(iii) 8 CFR 214.2(k)

Nonimmigrant Classifications and Visas	General Information on Nonimmigrant Benefits
Intracompany Transferee	• Immigration.gov Information on Temporary Workers • Dept. of State: Tips for U.S. Visas: Temporary Workers • Instructions for Form I-129: Petition for a Nonimmigrant Worker
L-1A Executive, managerial	INA Section 101(a)(15)(L) 8 CFR 214.2(l)
L-1B Specialized knowledge	INA Section 101(a)(15)(L) 8 CFR 214.2(l)
L-2 Spouse or child of L-1	INA Section 101(a)(15)(L) 8 CFR 214.2(l)
Vocational and Language Students	• Immigration.gov Information on Student Visas • How Do I Become a Vocational Student in the United States? • Dept. of State: Implementation of ISEAS • Dept. of State: Tips for U.S. Visas: Foreign Student Visas • Dept. of State: Applying for a foreign Student Visa • Dept. of State: What Consuls Look For - Student Visas • Dept. of State: New Legal Requirements for F-1 Foreign Students in U.S. Public Schools • How Do I Apply to Qualify My School for Foreign Student Attendance
M-1 Vocational student or other nonacademic student	INA Section 101(a)(15)(M)(i) 8 CFR 214.2(m)
M-2 Spouse or child of M-1	INA Section 101(a)(15)(M)(ii) 8 CFR 214.2(m)
N-8 Parent of alien classified SK-3 "Special Immigrant"	INA Section 101(a)(15)(N)(i)
N-9 Child of N-8, SK-1, SK-2, or SK-4 "Special Immmigrant"	INA Section 101(a)(15)(N)(ii) through (iv)
NAFTA North American Free Trade Agreement (NAFTA) (see TN, below)	

Nonimmigrant Classifications and Visas	General Information on Nonimmigrant Benefits
North Atlantic Treaty Organization	
NATO-1 Principal Permanent Representative of Member State to NATO and resident members of official staff or immediate family	Not included in the INA Article 12, 5 US Treaties 1094 Article 20, 5 US Treaties 1098 8 CFR 214.2(s)
NATO-2 Other representatives of member State; Dependents of Member of a Force entering in accordance with the provisions of NATO Status-of-Forces agreement; Members of such a Force if issued visas	Article 13, 5 US Treaties 1094 Article 1, 4 US Treaties 1794 Article 3, 4 US Treaties 1796 8 CFR 214.2(s)
NATO-3 Official clerical staff accompanying Representative of Member State to NATO or immediate family	Article 14, 5 US Treaties 1096 8 CFR 214.2(s)
NATO-4 Official of NATO other than those qualified as NATO-1 and immediate family	Article 18, 5 US Treaties 1096 8 CFR 214.2(s)
NATO-5 Expert other than NATO officials qualified under NATO-4, employed on behalf of NATO and immediate family	Article 21, 5 US Treaties 1100 8 CFR 214.2(s)
NATO-6 Member of civilian component who is either accompanying a Force entering in accordance with the provisions of the NATO Status-of-Forces agreement; attached to an Allied headquarters under the protocol on the Status of International Military headquarters set up pursuant to the North Atlantic Treaty; and their dependents	Article 1, 4 US Treaties 1794 Article 3, 5 US Treaties 877 8 CFR 214.2(s)
NATO-7 Servant or personal employee of NATO-1, NATO-2, NATO-3, NATO-4, NATO-5, NATO-6, or immediate family	Articles 12-20, 5 US Treaties 1094 – 1098 8 CFR 214.2(s)
Workers with Extraordinary Abilities	• Immigration.gov Information on Temporary Workers
	• Dept. of State: Tips for U.S. Visas: Temporary Workers
	• Instructions for Form I-129: Petition for a Nonimmigrant Worker
	• How Do I Apply for Health Care Worker Certification?
O-1 Extraordinary ability in Sciences, Arts, Education, Business, or Athletics	INA Section 101(a)(15)(O)(i) 8 CFR 214.2(o)(1), 8 CFR 214.2(o)(2), 8 CFR 214.2(o)(3)

Nonimmigrant Classifications and Visas	General Information on Nonimmigrant Benefits
Workers with Extraordinary Abilities, continued	
O-2 Alien's (support) accompanying O-1	INA Section 101(a)(15)(O)(ii) 8 CFR 214.2(o)(4)
O-3 Spouse or child of O-1 or O-2	INA Section 101(a)(15)(O)(iii) 8 CFR 214.2(o)(5)
Athletes and Entertainers	• Immigration.gov Information on Temporary Workers • Dept. of State: Tips for U.S. Visas: Temporary Workers • Instructions for Form I-129: Petition for a Nonimmigrant Worker
P-1 Individual or team athletes	INA Section 101(a)(15)(P)(i) 8 CFR 214.2(p)(4)
P-1 Entertainment groups	INA Section 101(a)(15)(P)(i) 8 CFR 214.2(p)(4)
P-2 Artists and entertainers in reciprocal Exchange programs	INA Section 101(a)(15)(P)(ii) 8 CFR 214.2(p)(5)
P-3 Artists and entertainers in culturally unique programs	INA Section 101(a)(15)(P)(iii) 8 CFR 214.2(p)(6)
P-4 Spouse or child of P-1, 2, or 3	INA Section 101(a)(15)(P)(iv) 8 CFR 214.2(p)(8)(iii)(D)
International Cultural Exchange Visitors	
Q-1 International cultural exchange visitors	• Immigration.gov Information on Exchange Visitors • Dept. of State: Tips for U.S. Visas: Exchange Visitors • Instructions for Form I-129: Petition for a Nonimmigrant Worker INA Section 101(a)(15)(Q)(i) 8 CFR 214.2(q)
Q-2 Irish Peace Process Cultural and Training Program (Walsh Visas)	Walsh Visa Program INA Section 101(a)(15)(Q)(ii)(I) 8 CFR 214.2(q)(15)
Q-3 Spouse or child of Q-2	INA Section 101(a)(15)(Q)(ii)(II) 8 CFR 214.2(q)(15)
Religious Workers	• Immigration.gov Information on Temporary Workers • Dept. of State: Tips for U.S. Visas: Temporary Religious Workers • Instructions for Form I-129: Petition for a Nonimmigrant Worker

Nonimmigrant Classifications and Visas	General Information on Nonimmigrant Benefits
Religious Workers, continued	
R-1 Religious workers	INA Section 101(a)(15)(R) 8 CFR 214.2(r)
R-2 Spouse or child of R-1	INA Section 101(a)(15)(R) 8 CFR 214.2(r)
Witness or Informant	
S-5 Informant of criminal organization information	INA Section 101(a)(15)(S)(i)
S-6 Informant of terrorism information	INA Section 101(a)(15)(S)(ii)
T Victims of a Severe Form of Trafficking in Persons	• Victims of Trafficking and Violence Protection Act of 2000 • Fact Sheet on T Application Process • Dept. of State: Trafficking in Persons Report • Dept. of State: Foreign Affairs Manual, Section 41.84
T-1 Victim of a severe form of trafficking in persons	INA Section 101(a)(15)(T)(i) 8 CFR 214.11
T-2 Spouse of a victim of a severe form of trafficking in persons	INA Section 101(a)(15)(T)(ii) 8 CFR 214.11(o)
T-3 Child of victim of a severe form of trafficking in persons	INA Section 101(a)(15)(T)(ii) 8 CFR 214.11(o)
T-4 Parent of victim of a severe form of trafficking in persons (if T-1 victim is under 21 years of age)	INA Section 101(a)(15)(T)(ii) 8 CFR 214.11(o)
North American Free Trade Agreement (NAFTA)	• Dept. of State: Professionals Under NAFTA • Changes to NAFTA and new 2004 Trade Agreements
TN Trade visas for Canadians and Mexicans	INA Section 214(e)(2) 8 CFR 214.6 Canadians: 8 CFR 214.6(d) Mexicans: 8 CFR 214.6(e)
North American Free Trade Agreement (NAFTA), continued	
TD Spouse or child accompanying TN-	INA Section 214(e)(2) 8 CFR 214.6(j)
Transit Without Visa	
TWOV Passenger	INA Sections 212(d)(3) and 212(d)(5) 8 CFR 212.1(f)

Nonimmigrant Classifications and Visas	General Information on Nonimmigrant Benefits
Transit Without Visa, continued	
TWOV Crew	INA Sections 212(d)(3) and 212(d)(5) 8 CFR 212.1(f)
U Victims of Certain Crimes	
U-1 Victim of Certain Criminal Activity	INA Section 101(a)(15)(U)
U-2 Spouse of U-1	INA Section 101(a)(15)(U)
U-3 Child of U-1	INA Section 101(a)(15)(U)
U-4 Parent of U-1, if U-1 is under 21 years of age	INA Section 101(a)(15)(U)
Certain Second Preference Beneficiaries	• How Do I Become a V-Nonimmigrant as the Spouse or Child of a U.S. Permanent Resident? • Dept. of State: The New K and V Visas
V-1 Spouse of an LPR who is the principal beneficiary of a family-based petition (Form I-130) which was filed prior to December 21, 2000, and has been pending for at least three years	INA Section 101(a)(15)(V) 8 CFR 214.15
V-2 Child of an LPR who is the principal beneficiary of a family-based visa petition (Form I-130) that was filed prior to December 21, 2000, and has been pending for at least three years.	INA Section 101(a)(15)(V) 8 CFR 214.15
V-3 The derivative child of a V-1 or V-2	INA Section 101(a)(15)(V) 8 CFR 214.15
Humanitarian Parole	Immigration.gov Information on Humanitarian Parole
Temporary Protected Status (TPS)	• Immigration.gov Information on Temporary Protected Status • How Do I Apply for Temporary Protected Status?
TPS Temporary Protected Status	INA Section 244 8 CFR 244

APPENDIX 5
Conversion Table: 8 USC to INA

8 USC	INA	8 USC	INA	8 USC	INA
1101	101	1204	224	1284	254
1102	102	1221	231	1285	255
1103	103	1222	232	1286	256
1104	104	1223	233	1287	257
1105	105	1224	234	1288	258
1105a	106	1225	235	1301	261
1151	201	1225a	235A	1302	262
1152	202	1226	236	1303	263
1153	203	1227	237	1304	264
1154	204	1228	238	1305	265
1155	205	1229	239	1306	266
1156	206	1229a	240	1321	271
1157	207	1229b	240A	1322	272
1158	208	1229c	240B	1323	273
1159	209	1230	240C	1324	274
1160	210	1231	241	1324a	274A
1161	210A	1252	242	1324b	274B
1181	211	1252a	242A	1324c	274C
1182	212	1252b	242B	1324d	274D
1183	213	1253	243	1325	275
1183a	213A	1254	244	1326	276
1184	214	1255	245	1327	277
1185	215	1255a	245A	1328	278
1186a	216	1256	246	1329	279
1186b	216A	1257	247	1330	280
1187	217	1258	248	1351	281
1188	218	1259	249	1352	282
1189	219	1260	250	1353	283
1201	221	1281	251	1354	284
1202	222	1282	252	1355	285
1203	223	1283	253	1356	286

8 USC	INA	8 USC	INA	8 USC	INA
1357	287	1430	319	1457	346
1358	288	1431	320	1458	347
1359	289	1432	321	1481	349
1360	290	1433	322	1482	350
1361	291	1435	324	1483	351
1362	292	1436	325	1484	352
1363	293	1437	326	1485	353
1363a	294	1438	327	1486	354
1363b	295	1439	328	1487	355
1401	301	1440	329	1488	356
1402	302	1440-1	329A	1489	357
1403	303	1441	330	1501	358
1404	304	1442	331	1502	359
1405	305	1443	332	1503	360
1406	306	1444	333	1504	361
1407	307	1445	334	1521	411
1408	308	1446	335	1522	412
1409	309	1447	336	1523	413
1421	310	1448	337	1524	414
1422	311	1449	338	1531	501
1423	312	1450	339	1532	502
1424	313	1451	340	1533	503
1425	314	1452	341	1534	504
1426	315	1453	342	1535	505
1427	316	1454	343	1536	506
1428	317	1455	344	1537	507
1429	318	1455	345		

APPENDIX 6
Selected Bibliography and
Electronic Resources

PART I—PRINT RESOURCES

Publisher Contact Information

AILA Publications
PO Box 753
Waldorf, MD 20604-0753
1-800-982-2839
Fax: (301) 843-0159

Amnesty International
322 8th Avenue
New York, NY 10001
(212) 807-8400

Aspen Publishers
1185 Avenue of the Americas
New York, NY 10036
1-800-317-3113

Carolina Academic Press
700 Kent Street
Durham, NC 27701
(919) 489-7486
Fax: (919) 493-5668

Carswell Thomson Professional
Publishing
One Corporate Plaza
2075 Kennedy Road
Toronto, Ontario M1T 3V5
(416) 609-8000
Fax: (416) 298-5094

Center for Migration Studies
209 Flagg Place
Staten Island, NY 10304
(718) 351-8800

Immigrant Legal Resource Center
1663 Mission St., #602
San Francisco, CA 94103
(415) 255-9499
Fax: (415) 255-9792

Juris Publishing
71 New Street
Huntington, NY 11743
1-800-887-4064
Fax: (631) 351-5712

Matthew Bender & Company, Inc.
P.O. Box 22030
Albany, NY 12201-2030
1-800-223-1940
Fax: (212) 448-2570

NAFSA: Association of International Educators
1307 New York Avenue, NW,
8th Floor
Washington, DC 20005
(202) 737-3699

Oxford University Press
Journals Subscription Department
2001 Evans Road
Cary, NC 27513
1-800-852-7323 or (919) 677-0977
Fax: (919) 677-1714

Practising Law Institute
810 Seventh Avenue
New York, NY 10019
1-800-260-4PLI
Fax: 1-800-321-0093

Refugee Law Center
705 Centre Street
Boston, MA 02130
(617) 522-2100
Fax: (617) 522-9359

Shepard's
P.O. Box 22030
Albany, NY 12201-2030
1-800-899-6000 or 1-800-223-1940
Fax: (719) 481-7391

Stanford University Press
Stanford, CA 94305-2235
(650) 723-9434
Fax: (650) 725-9457

U.S. Government Printing Office
Superintendent of Documents
Washington, DC 20402
(202) 512-1800 or 1-866-512-1800

The William S. Hein & Co., Inc.
1285 Main Street
Buffalo, NY 14209
1-800-828-7571 or (716) 882-2600
Fax: (716) 883-8100

West Group
610 Opperman Drive
Eagan, MN 55123
1-800-762-5272
Fax: (800) 854-1597

Primary Source Materials

Statutes

Immigration and Nationality Act, 2006 Ed. [AILA]

Bender's Immigration and Nationality Act Pamphlet, 2006 Ed.

Federal Immigration Laws and Regulations, 2006 Ed. [West]

Regulations

Immigration Regulations, 2006 Ed. (CFR Titles 6, 8, 20, 22, 28, and 42) [AILA] (two vols.)

Bender's Immigration Regulations Service

Code of Federal Regulations Annotated Title 8, Aliens and Nationality, 2006 Ed. [West]

CFR from the Government Printing Office (GPO)
- Title 8
- Title 20, Pts. 400–499 and 500–end (2 vols.)
- Title 22 (2 vols.)
- Title 28 (2 vols.)
- Title 42, Pts. 1–399

Legislative History

INA Legislative History and Related Documents (Microfiche) (1958–1977), Oscar M. Trelles & James F. Bailey, Eds. 15 Vols. [Wm. Hein]

Immigration and Nationality Acts Legislative History and Related Documents (1977–1986, 1997 Supplement Set), James F. Bailey, Ed., 32 Vols. [Wm. Hein]

Legislative History of the Immigration and Nationality Act of 1990, Pub. L. 101-649 (1997), Second Series, Kavass, Igor I., Reams, Bernard D. Jr., Eds. 23 Vols. (set) [Wm. Hein]

Citators and Reporter Services

Shepard's Immigration and Naturalization Citations (all inclusive subscription), One Vol., includes one year of updates [Shepard's]

Administrative Decisions Under Immigration and Nationality Laws of the U.S. Department of Justice, Reprint, Precedent decisions of the INS and BIA, 22 Vols. (1940–2000) [Wm. Hein]

Hein Interim Decision Service to Administrative Decisions Under Immigration and Nationality Laws (1995); 1998–2002 Service w/2 binders; 2003 Service (6/1/02–5/31/03) [Wm. Hein]; [GPO]

General Immigration Law Treatises, Casebooks, and Other Resource Services

Kurzban's Immigration Law Sourcebook, 10th Edition (2006), Ira J. Kurzban [AILA]

Essentials of Immigration Law (2006), Richard A. Boswell [AILA]

Essentials of Removal and Relief: Representing Individuals in Immigration Proceedings (2006), Joseph A. Vail [AILA]

Immigration Law and Procedure, Charles Gordon, Stanley Mailman, and Stephen Yale-Loehr, loose-leaf, updated with supplements and revisions. 20 Vols. [Bender]

Immigration Law Service, 2d., loose-leaf, updated with supplements and revisions, 11 Vols. [West]

Immigration Practice, 2005–06 Ed., Robert C. Divine, One Vol. [Juris]

Steel on Immigration Law, 2d (2005), Richard D. Steel, loose-leaf, updated annually, One Vol. [West]

Immigration Law and Procedure: Desk Edition, Stanley Mailman, One Vol. [Bender]

Bender's Immigration Bulletin [Bender]

Immigration Case Reporter, loose-leaf, updated with new cases monthly, 3 Vols. [Bender]

Immigration and Citizenship: Process and Policy, 5th Ed., T. Alexander Aleinikoff, David A. Martin, and Hiroshi Motomura, One Vol. [West]

Immigration and Nationality Law: Cases and Materials, 3rd Ed. (2000, plus supplement), Richard A. Boswell, One Vol.; Statutory Supplement (2001); 2005 Supplement [Carolina Academic Press]

Immigration Fundamentals: A Guide to Law and Practice, 4th Ed. (1996), Austin T. Fragomen and Steven C. Bell (Updated annually), One Vol. [Practising Law Institute]

Handling Immigration Cases (1996), Bill Ong Hing, Two Vols. [Wiley Law Publications]

Weissbrodt's and Danielson's Immigration Law and Procedure in a Nutshell, 5th Ed., David Weissbrodt and Laura Danielson, One Vol. [West]

Immigration Law and Defense, 3rd Edition (1999), National Immigration Project of the National Lawyers Guild, loose-leaf, updated with supplements, Two Vols. [West]

Immigration and Naturalization Service, Annual Report (1957–1979), 11 Vols. (set) [Wm. Hein]

Periodicals

AILA's Immigration Law Today, Tatia L. Gordon-Troy, Managing Editor, annual subscription bar magazine (bi-monthly, 6 issues) [AILA]

Interpreter Releases, Annual Subscription (weekly) [West]; two 3-ring binders included

Immigration Briefings, annual subscription (12 issues) [West}

Immigration Business News & Comment, Austin T. Fragomen, Jr. and Steven C. Bell, annual subscription (semimonthly) [West]

Georgetown Immigration Law Journal, Vols. 1–16 (1985–2002) [Wm. Hein]; Vols. 1–16 (microfiche)

Immigration and Nationality Law Review [Wm. Hein] Vols. 1–22 (1976–2001) (set); Vols. 1–7 (1976–84), (1986–90); Vols. 13–14 (1991–92); Vols. 15–16 (1993–94, 94–95); Vol. 17 (1994–95); Vol. 18–20 (1997–99); Vol. 21–22 (2000–01). Order No. 103280

Government Publications/Directories

Occupational Outlook Handbook (2006–07), U.S. Department of Labor, Bureau of Labor Statistics, Soft Cover Paper Ed., One Vol. [GPO]

Dictionary of Occupational Titles, 4th Ed. (1991), U.S. Department of Labor, Employment and Training Administration, Two Vols. [GPO]

Foreign Consular Offices in the United States (2006 Fall/Winter), Department of State, single issue, *www.state.gov/s/cpr/rls/fco*

Board of Immigration Appeals Practice Manual (2004) and Questions and Answers Handbook [AILA reprint] (available at *www.usdoj.gov/eoir/bia/qapracmanual/apptmtn4.htm*)

Immigration Judge Benchbook, 4th Ed. (Oct. 2001), One Vol. [AILA reprint]; CD-ROM

INS Inspector's NAFTA Handbook, One Vol. [AILA reprint]

Citizenship Laws of the World [AILA reprint]

Practical Guides / "How-To's"

AILA's Immigration Litigation Toolbox, 2nd Ed. (2005), Charles H. Kuck, Editor-in-Chief, One Vol. [AILA]

AILA's Immigration Practice Toolbox, 2nd Ed. (2006), Editors-in-Chief: James D. Acoba and Andrew R. Lerner, One Vol. [AILA]

AILA's Labor Department Directory for Immigration Lawyers, 2003 Ed., Eds.: Jane W. Goldblum and Ester Greenfield, One Vol. [AILA]

Coming to America: Entry Issues in the Current Immigration Landscape (2002), Eds.: Michael Turansick and Kathleen Campbell Walker, One Vol. [AILA]

Immigration Procedures Handbook (2006), Austin T. Fragomen, Jr., Alfred J. Del Rey, Jr., and Steven C. Bell, Two Vols. [West]

Immigration Legislation Handbook (2005), Steven C. Bell, Austin T. Fragomen, Jr., and Thomas E. Mosley, One Vol. [West]

H-1B Handbook (2006), Steven C. Bell and Austin T. Fragomen, Jr., One Vol. [West]

Specific Area Publications

NACARA

Winning NACARA Suspension Cases (2005), Mark Silverman and Linton Joaquin, with Charles Wheeler and Dan Kesselbrenner (on CD-ROM only) [ILRC]

Business and Employment-Based Immigration

U.S. Tax Guides for Foreign Persons and Those Who Pay Them: U.S. Taxation of H-1B Specialty Workers (2006), Paula N. Singer [Windstar Publishing; distributed by AILA]

U.S. Tax Guides for Foreign Persons and Those Who Pay Them: L-1 Intracompany Transferees on U.S. Assignment (2006), Paula N. Singer [Windstar Publishing; distributed by AILA]

U.S. Tax Guides for Foreign Persons and Those Who Pay Them: J-1 Nonstudent Exchange Visitors Performing U.S. Services (2006), Paula N. Singer [Windstar Publishing; distributed by AILA]

Immigration Options for Investors and Entrepreneurs (2006), Editor-in-Chief: Lincoln Stone [AILA]

Immigration Options for Physicians (2004), Editor-in-Chief: Margaret A. Catillaz [AILA]

Immigration Options for Nurses and Allied Health Care Professionals (2004), Editor-in-Chief: James D. Acoba [AILA]

Immigration Options for Academics and Researchers (2005), Editors-in-Chief: Scott M. Borene and Dan H. Berger [AILA]

Immigration Options for Religious Workers (2005), Editor-in-Chief: Rodney M. Barker [AILA]

Immigration Practice Under NAFTA and Other Free Trade Agreements (2006), Editors-in-Chief: Janet H. Cheetham and William Z. Reich, One Vol. [AILA]

The David Stanton Manual on Labor Certification (2005), Editors-in-Chief: Josie Gonzalez and Ester Greenfield [AILA]

Labor Certification Handbook (2006), Steven C. Bell and Austin T. Fragomen, Jr., One Vol. [West]

PERM Guidebook for Foreign Labor Certification (2005), Ed: Stephen Yale-Loehr [Matthew Bender]

Immigration Procedures Handbook (2006), Alfred J. Del Rey, Jr., Austin T. Fragomen, Jr., and Steven C. Bell, Two Vols. [West]

The PERM Book (2005), Ed: Joel Stewart [ILW]

Immigration Employment Compliance Handbook (2006), Austin T. Fragomen and Steven C. Bell, One Vol. [West]

Canada-U.S. Relocation Manual: Immigration, Customs, Employment and Taxation, Jacqueline R. Bart and Austin T. Fragomen, Jr., One Vol. loose-leaf, filed to date, with two months' free service [Carswell Thomson] (includes binder and supplements)

Canada-U.S. Work Permits: Issues for Human Resources Professionals, Tony G. Schweitzer, One Vol. loose-leaf, filed to date, with two months' free service [Carswell Thomson] (includes binder and supplements)

Professionals: A Matter of Degree, Fourth Ed., Martin J. Lawler, Two-Vol. set [AILA]

AILA's Global Immigration Guide: A Country-by-Country Survey (2005), Editor-in-Chief: Scott M. Borene [AILA]

Immigration Law and Business, Austin T. Fragomen, Jr., Alfred J. Del Rey, Jr., and Sam Bernsen, 3 Vols. (Loose-leaf with updates) [West]

Family Immigration

Immigration Law and the Family, Sarah B. Ignatius, Elisabeth S. Stickney, and Mary A. Kenney, One Vol. (loose-leaf, updated annually) [West]

Citizenship and Naturalization

U.S. Citizenship and Naturalization Handbook (2006), Daniel Levy and National Immigration Project of the National Lawyers Guild, One Vol. [West]

Removal and Criminal Defense

Essentials of Removal and Relief: Representing Individuals in Immigration Proceedings (2006), Joseph A. Vail [AILA]

Immigration Consequences of Criminal Activity: A Guide to Representing Foreign-Born Defendants (2d Ed. 2005), Mary E. Kramer [AILA]

Immigration Law and Crimes (2006*), Dan Kesselbrenner and Lory D. Rosenberg, Loose-leaf, *updated semiannually, One Vol. [West]

In Defense of the Alien [Center for Migration Studies]

Consular Processing

The Visa Processing Guide and Consular Posts Handbook: Process and Procedures at U.S. Consulates and Embassies (2006–07), Senior Editors: Charles M. Miller, Jan M. Pederson, and Douglas S. Weigle, One Vol. [AILA]

Refugees and Asylum

AILA's Asylum Primer: A Practical Guide to U.S. Asylum Law and Procedure (4th Ed. 2005), Regina Germain, One Vol. [AILA]

Winning Asylum Cases (2004), Robert Jobe, Mark Silverman, and Larry Katzman, One Vol. [ILRC]

Law of Asylum in the United States, 3rd Ed., Deborah E. Anker, One Vol. [RLC]

U.S. Law and Procedures 2002 Supplement (69 pp.) [RLC]

Asylum Case Law Sourcebook: Master Index and Case Abstracts for Federal Court Decisions, 5th Ed. (2005), David A. Martin, One Vol. [West]

Amnesty International Report, 2006 [AI; *www.amnesty.org*]

Country Reports on Human Rights Practices for 2005 (released 2006), Department of State, Two Vols. [GPO; *www.state.gov/g/drl/hr/c1470.htm*]

International Journal of Refugee Law (2006), Editor-in-Chief: Geoff Gilbert [Oxford University Press] annual subscription (4 issues)

Foreign Students and Scholars

NAFSA *Advisor's Manual* Subscription Service (yearly subscription service, *Advisor's Manual* text, supplemented with news and updates) [NAFSA]

General/Miscellaneous Reading

Essentials of Immigration Law (2006), Richard A. Boswell [AILA]

Immigration & Nationality Law Handbook (2006–07) [AILA]

AILA's Immigration Case Summaries, Vol. 2, 2004–05, selected and written by Trina A. Realmuto and Regina Germain; Vol. 1, 2003–04, selected and written by Trina A. Realmuto [AILA]

Immigration Law in the Ninth Circuit (Selected Topic) (2005) [AILA reprint]

Immigration Classifications and Legal Employment of Foreign Nationals in the United States Wall Chart (2005) [NAFSA]

Immigration Law and Health, Sana Loue, One Vol. [West]

Dahl's Law Dictionary, 3rd Ed., English-Spanish/Spanish-English, One Vol. [Wm. Hein]

39th Annual Immigration & Naturalization Institute (2006), One Vol. [Practising Law Institute]

Identities in North America: The Search for Community (1995), Robert L. Earle and John D. Wirth, Eds., One Vol. [Stanford]

Controlling Immigration: A Global Perspective, Wayne A. Cornelius *et al.*, Eds., One Vol. [Stanford]

Immigration Commission Reports, U.S. Immigration Commission, 41 Vols. (in 38 books) [GPO reprint] [Wm. Hein reprint]

AILA's Client Brochures, H-1B, Labor Certification (English & Spanish), E Visas, L Visas, O & P Visas, F-1 Students, Family Immigration (English & Spanish), and I-9 Preparation [AILA]

Immigration Law for Paralegals (2005), Maria I. Casablanca and Gloria Roa Bodin (for AILA members only) [Carolina Academic Press; distributed by AILA]

Ethics in a Brave New World (2004), Editor-in-Chief: John L. Pinnix [AILA]

Homeland Security, Business Insecurity (2003), Editors: Nancy-Jo Merritt, Charles M. Miller, and Laura Foote Reiff. One Vol. [AILA]

Agency Interpretations of Immigration Policy: Cables, Memos, and Liaison Minutes, Jan.– Dec. 2005 (2006), One Vol. [AILA]

PART II—TECHNOLOGY RESOURCES FOR THE IMMIGRATION PRACTITIONER

General Guide

AILA's Guide to Technology and Legal Research for the Immigration Lawyer, Third Edition
American Immigration Lawyers Association
918 F Street NW
Washington, DC 20004
1-800-982-2839
Fax: (301) 843-0159

Case Management/Forms Programs

EILA
Cerenade
EILA offers several different software options, including a desktop version, per use version, and monthly license to meet your needs and budget. All versions provide case management and forms software providing database integration of client data for form completion; however, the different versions use different databases, and only the more robust versions allow certain levels of client access. EILA also allows you to generate detailed reports.
www.cerenade.com

EmpPet
Cityon Systems, Inc.
EmpPet is a database-driven software providing step-by-step instructions and guidance for H-1B petitions. The software validates entered information to avoid

human mistakes, and maintains all the addresses needed to file a petition. It also provides Prevailing Wage Rate data and includes automated reminders. EmpPet Enterprise provides detailed information on clients and employers. Features include reports; database backup, restore and repair; templates; LCA tracking; and a calendar.

magnesium.secure-website.net/emppet/index.asp

ILW Website

Although ILW is primarily a website dedicated to providing articles and news on immigration, additional features such as immigration forms, form filling, and case tracking are available. ILW case management tools feature sections for attorneys, employers, and aliens.

www.ilw.com

ImmForms Plus

West Group

After West Group stopped bundling Immigrant Pro with its Law Desk research software, it developed a similar product called ImmForms Plus. ImmForms Plus provides instant electronic access to more than 85 immigration forms that can be filled out, edited, saved, or printed and includes line-by-line instructions and procedural guidance.

west.thompson.com

Immigrant Pro

Immigrant Pro is a forms processor, case tracking, and management tool known to most immigration practitioners. In addition to basic forms completion, it provides a "To-do" calendaring module and a report builder.

www.immigrantsoftware.com

Immigrant Forms Gold

Immigrant Forms Gold is the upgrade to Immigrant Pro. It supports several different database formats such as Microsoft 2000 Data Engine and SQL Server, and allows association of beneficiaries, petitioners, and forms. The Gold version includes reports and automatic tracking of important dates with reminders, and now integrates with a Web component, Immigrant Online. Immigrant Online allows clients to input and edit their own data.

www.immigrantsoftware.com

ImmigrationTracker

ImmigrationTracker was designed by AILA member Julie Pearl to serve her firm's corporate clients. The software consists of a Microsoft Access database with forms integration and Web tracking. It also creates reports on caseload, pending cases, expiration dates, billing, etc.

www.immigrationtracker.com

INSzoom

INSzoom is an Internet immigration application, where users log-on using a secure id and password. It allows users to create frequently updated records required for the immigration process, and allows clients to monitor case status using the Internet. INSzoom also provides messaging service for clients and attorneys.

www.inszoom.com

ImmigrationWorks

Teleneos

ImmigrationWorks is a comprehensive immigration case management system, providing access to all case management features and functions from one user-friendly Web-based platform. It features self-service module allowing clients, petitioners, and beneficiaries to check case status and verify information directly. ImmigrationWorks also generates invoices and reports. Users have the option running the software from the ImmigrationWorks website or in-house if they have their own server.

www.immigrationworks.com

Aria®

Walther Solutions, Inc.

The ARIA® Client Service System integrates case management, assembly, and communication tools to enhance efficiency in immigration practice. Users are enabled to predefine packages of forms and documents that auto generate at designated points in a project. Additionally, ARIA®'s reporting and e-mail features simplify communication with clients.

www.ariaportals.com/WSI/index.html

Immigration Research Services

AILALink

American Immigration Lawyers Association

A powerfully searchable CD-ROM collection of immigration resources. Includes both primary and secondary sources, including *Kurzban's Immigration Law Sourcebook,* Vail's *Essentials of Removal and Relief,* and Germain's *Asylum Primer.* Also includes more than 160 immigration forms.

www.ailapubs.org

AILA InfoNet

American Immigration Lawyers Association

Electronic bulletin board containing the latest news and information in the immigration law field. Items posted daily.

www.aila.org

LexisNexis® Matthew Bender®

Provides authoritative, comprehensive, and accurate legal information in print and CD-ROM formats, and via the Internet, on immigration authored by leading experts in the legal community.

bender.lexisnexis.com

Immigration Law Library

Matthew Bender & Company, Inc.

CD-ROMs containing authoritative, comprehensive, and accurate legal information on immigration authored by the leading experts in the legal community.

www.bender.com

Geographic Assessor® software

ERI Economic Research Institute

Provides the Geographic Assessor® software. Allows practitioners to determine prevailing wages for immigration, and wage and salary geographic differentials covering 10,000 U.S. and Canadian cities.

www.erieri.com

ILW Website

Although ILW is primarily a website dedicated to providing articles and news on immigration, additional features such as immigration forms, form filling, and case tracking are available. ILW case management tools feature sections for attorneys, employers, and aliens.

www.ilw.com

Immigration Research Information Service (IRIS)

West Group

IRIS from West. Allows instant electronic access to comprehensive, authoritative analysis for all aspects of immigration law. Provides full text of judicial cases and administrative decisions and all primary source materials.

west.thomson.com

Immigration-Related Websites

American Immigration Lawyers Association
www.aila.org
www.ailapubs.org

Asylum Resources
www.asylumlaw.org

Board of Immigration Appeals
www.usdoj.gov/eoir

U.S. Citizenship and Immigration Services
www.uscis.gov

CAPWEB—Internet Guide to the U.S. Congress
www.capweb.net

Code of Federal Regulations
www.gpoaccess.gov/cfr/retrieve.html

Congressional Reports on Immigration (Congressional Research Service (CRS), The Library of Congress)
www.loc.gov/index.html

U.S. Customs and Border Protection
www.cbp.gov

Department of Homeland Security
www.dhs.gov

Department of Justice
www.usdoj.gov

Department of Labor
www.dol.gov

DOL Prevailing Wages
www.flcdatacenter.com

Department of State
www.state.gov
www.travel.state.gov

DOS's *Foreign Affairs Manual*
www.foia.state.gov/REGS/Search.asp

DOS's Visas Main Page
www.travel.state.gov/visa/visa_1750.html

Dictionary of Occupational Titles
www.oalj.dol.gov/libdot.htm

Executive Office for Immigration Review
www.usdoj.gov/eoir

Federal Register
www.gpoaccess.gov/fr/index.html

Government Printing Office
www.access.gpo.gov

U.S. Immigration and Customs Enforcement
www.ice.gov

Immigrant Software Corporation
www.immigrantsoftware.com

Information Technology Assoc. of America
www.itaa.org

J Exchange Visitor Program, Educational and Cultural Affairs, DOS
www.travel.state.gov/visa/temp/types/types_1267.html

Latour and Lleras, P.A.
www.Usvisanews.com

Lexis-Nexis
www.lexisnexis.com/practiceareas/immigration

Murthy Law Firm
www.murthy.com

NAICS—North American Industry Classification System
www.census.gov/epcd/www/naics.html

NAFSA—Association of International Educators
www.nafsa.org

National Visa Center
travel.state.gov/visa/immigrants/types/types_1309.html

O*NET OnLine—Occupational Information Network
online.onetcenter.org

OOH—Occupational Outlook Handbook
www.bls.gov/oco

OES—Occupational Employment Statistics
www.bls.gov/oes

Office of the Law Revision Counsel (publisher of the U.S. Code)
uscode.house.gov

Public Laws
www.access.gpo.gov

Law Offices of Carl Shusterman
www.shusterman.com

Siskind, Susser
www.Visalaw.com

Thomas (Library of Congress)
thomas.loc.gov

U.S. Code
www.gpoaccess.gov/uscode/index.html

U.S. Legislative Branch Resources via GPO Access
www.gpoaccess.gov/legislative.html

U.S. House of Representatives
www.house.gov

U.S. Senate
www.senate.gov

Visa Bulletin
www.travel.state.gov/visa/frvi/bulletin/bulletin_1360.html

Visa Reciprocity Tables
www.travel.state.gov/visa/reciprocity/index.htm

West Group
west.thompson.com

PART III—OTHER SOURCES OF INFORMATION

Call AILA for more information on the following additional information sources:

Immigration Law Conference Materials

There are a number of annual immigration law conferences conducted by AILA chapters, universities, and other organizations that produce excellent conference proceedings.

- Immigration Law Conference Cassette Tapes

  Conference sessions of the AILA Annual Conferences are recorded, and tapes are made available. Other conferences may also record their sessions and offer tapes after the program.

- AILA Chapter Newsletters

  A number of AILA chapters produce extensive, monthly newsletters. While much of the information has a local and/or regional orientation, many newsletters contain important decisions, memoranda, and other materials of national significance.

Other Materials

- GAO Reports and Other Government Reports

  The Government Accountability Office (GAO), as well as other government agencies, produces a number of investigative reports on immigration matters. In addition, USCIS publishes a number of booklets on immigration laws and benefits. Contact the GPO to obtain a free subscription to the relevant catalogues. These reports are free for the first copy.

- Bender's Immigration Cases Reporter (Matthew Bender and Co., 1993–) (contains selected court cases and administrative agency decisions; formerly Immigration Law and Procedure Reporter).
- BIA Index Decisions Reporter (Washington, DC: AILA, 1986–1995) (4 issues/year; annual from 1986–89).
- Federal Immigration Law Reporter (Washington Service Bureau, 1983–1990) (contains selected court cases and administrative agency decisions).
- Thomas Alexander Aleinikoff *et al.*, *Immigration Process and Policy* (5th ed., West Group, 2003).
- *Basic Immigration Law* (Practising Law Institute, 1989–, annual).
- *A Guide to Naturalization* (Form M-476, USCIS).
  www.uscis.gov/graphics/services/natz/English.pdf
- David Carliner, *The Rights of Aliens and Refugees: The Basic ACLU Guide to Alien and Refugee Rights* (2d ed., Southern Illinois University Press, 1990).
- *The Immigration Act of 1990 Today* (2005–06), Stuart I. Folinsky and Helen A. Sklar [Clark, Boardman, Callaghan] (annual with cumulative supplement).
- *A Legal Guide for INS Detainees: Petitioning for Release from Indefinite Detention* (ABA, 2002).
- Stephen H. Legomsky, *Immigration Law and Policy* (4th ed., Foundation Press, Inc., 2005).
- Richard B. Lillich, *The Human Rights of Aliens in Contemporary International Law* (Wm Hein & Co, 1985).
- Pravinchandra J. Patel, *Patel's Citations of Administrative Decisions Under Immigration and Nationality Laws*, 2005–06 Ed. (ILW).
- Pravinchandra J. Patel, *Patel's Immigration Law Digest: Decisions from 1940* (Lawyers Co-operative Pub. Co., 1982–98) (2 vols. Loose-leaf).

- Gregory H. Siskind *et al.*, *J Visa Guidebook*, 2005 Ed. (Matthew Bender and Co., 2005) (2 vols.).

- United Nations High Commissioner for Refugees, *Conclusions on the International Protection of Refugees*, HCR/IP/2/Eng/Rev.1994 (1994) (a new volume is issued every so often).

- United Nations High Commissioner for Refugees, *Handbook on Procedures and Criteria for Determining Refugee Status*, U.N. Doc. HCR/IP/4/Eng/Rev.1, Re-edited Geneva, Jan. 1992, UNHCR 1979 (The Handbook is available in English, French, and Spanish at *www.unhcr.org*, search under "Publications").

- United Nations High Commissioner for Refugees, *Refugee Protection in International Law*, Eds: Erika Feller, Volker Türk, and Frances Nicholson (available at *www.unhcr.org*, search under "Publications").

- U.S. Department of Labor, *Dictionary of Occupational Titles* (4th ed. Rev., GPO, 1991) (available at *www.oalj.dol.gov/libdot.htm*).

- *U.S. Citizenship and Naturalization Handbook*, 2006, Daniel Levy and the National Immigration Project of the National Lawyers Guild [West] (annual softcover volume).

- IRIS (Immigration Resource and Information Service) CD-ROM (West Group, quarterly updates) (full-text immigration library including statutes, BIA decisions, and secondary sources).

- LEXIS IMMIG Library (federal immigration statutes, court cases, administrative decisions, regulations, and treatises).

- LEXIS LEGIS Library (federal bills, bill tracking, Congressional Record, legislative histories, and other information related to the legislature).

- REFWORLD on CD-ROM (UNHCR). REFWORLD on CD-ROM is a collection of databases developed by the UNHCR Centre for Documentation and Research (CDR).

  REFWORLD contains authoritative information on refugees including current country reports, legal and policy-related documents and literature references. For more information on the CD-ROM, see *www.unhcr.org/refworld*.

- WESTLAW (federal immigration statutes, court cases, administrative decisions, regulations, and other materials).

- American Civil Liberties Union, Immigrants' Rights

  www.aclu.org/ImmigrantsRights/ImmigrantsRightsMain.cfm

  ACLU immigration materials and information on immigration and civil liberties information.

- Legal Information Institute, U.S. Code

  www4.law.cornell.edu/uscode

  Contains the text of U.S. Code, along with finding aids (keyword searching).

- Thomas Legislative Information

  thomas.loc.gov/home/thomas.html

  Provides very timely access to pending legislation, status of bills, and recent enactments; prepared by the Library of Congress.

- U.S. Citizenship and Immigration Services (USCIS) (within the Department of Homeland Security (DHS)).

  www.uscis.gov

  USCIS processes all immigrant and nonimmigrant benefits provided to visitors to the United States, including family-based petitions, employment-based petitions, asylum and refugee processing, naturalization, and document issuance and renewal.

- U.S. Department of Homeland Security (DHS)

  www.dhs.gov

  Legacy Immigration and Naturalization Service (INS) has transitioned to U.S. Citizenship and Immigration Services (USCIS), Immigration and Customs Enforcement (ICE), and Customs and Border Protection (CBP), all of which are within DHS.

- U.S. Department of Labor, Office of Administrative Law Judges Law Library, Immigration Collection

  www.oalj.dol.gov/libina.htm

  Contains the full-text of recent BALCA en banc decisions, full-text of immigration decisions, the *Judges' Benchbook: Alien Labor Certification* (2d ed. with supplements), and selected labor-related immigration statutes and regulations.

- U.S. Supreme Court (Cornell)

  www.law.cornell.edu/supct/index.html

  This site provides access to Supreme Court decisions (Keyword searching).

SUBJECT MATTER INDEX

Alphabetization is word-by-word (e.g., "R visas" precedes "REAL ID Act")